AMERICAN JURY TRIAL FOUNDATION

TRIAL

by

JURY

By J. Kendall Few

VOLUME 2

Trial by jury is a privilege of the highest and most beneficial nature and our most important guardian both of public and private liberty. Our liberties cannot but subsist so long as this palladium remains sacred and inviolate, not only from all open attacks, but also from all secret machinations which may sap and undermine it.

—**Justice William Blackstone (1768-69)**

Justice William Blackstone (1769)

Q. TRIAL BY JURY AS A WEAPON IN THE ARSENAL OF DEMOCRACY*

The concept of the jury system is as close as any society has ever come to true democracy.[550]

On the battlefield at Gettysburg on November 19, 1863, Abraham Lincoln declared that "the great task remaining before us" was to "highly resolve" that *"government of the people, by the people, for the people, shall not perish from the earth."*

One principal function of government is the administration of justice and trial by jury is justice *"by the people"* in its truest sense. It has been called "courthouse democracy,"[551] "democracy unalloyed,"[552] "the most democratical of juridicial institutions,"[553] "the unadulterated voice of the people,"[554] and "a vital artery in the bloodstream of the democratic process."[555]

Today, there is a grave danger that this vital artery may become occluded and the last vestige of justice by the people may indeed perish from the earth. For, as Charles Fletcher Dole (1845-1927) wrote in *The Spirit of Democracy,* "democracy is on trial in the world, on a more colossal scale than ever before."[556] Likewise, William James said in 1897:

The deadliest enemies of nations are not their foreign foes; they always dwell within their borders. And from these internal enemies civilization is always in need of being saved.... Democracy is still upon its trial. The civic genius of our people is its only bulwark.[557]

---

[550]Di Perna, *Juries on Trial: Faces of American Justice,* p. 1 (1984).

[551]Lambert, "In Defense of the Civil Jury," 29 *NACCA L.J.* 27 (1963).

[552]Santayana, *Dominions and Powers,* p. 413 (1951).

[553]Plucknett, *Taswell-Langmead's English Constitutional History,* p. 101 (11th ed. 1960).

[554]Hallam, *The Constitutional History of England,* Vol. 1, p. 233 (1827).

[555]Meagher, "Trial by Jury Deserves a Fair Trial," 36 *N.Y.S.B.J.* 309 (August, 1964).

[556]*Bartlett's Familiar Quotations,* p. 809a (14th ed. 1968).

[557]*Bartlett's, supra,* p. 795b.

*Some of the quotations in this volume have been condensed due to space limitations.

If William James is correct and democracy is truly on trial by its deadliest enemies who dwell within our borders, how can the civic genius of our people save it from destruction? When Patrick Henry sounded the battle cry of the American Revolution, he said:

> *I have but one lamp by which my feet are guided and that is the lamp of experience. I know of no way of judging the future but by the past.*[558]

If we shine this lamp of experience back some 2,300 years to that eminent Greek philosopher Aristotle (384-322 B.C.),[559] we will find this ancient wisdom:

> *If liberty and equality, as thought by some, are chiefly to be found in democracy, they will be best attained when all persons alike share in government to the utmost.*[560]

Therefore, the lamp of experience tells us that if liberty and equality are to be achieved through our unique system of American democracy, this worthy goal "will be best attained when *all persons alike* share in the government *to the utmost*." Does that mean that the cause of liberty and equality will be advanced by the substitution of so-called "blue ribbon panels" of expert arbitrators or wise and learned judicial officials for an impartial American jury of our fellow citizens? Obviously not.

Robert Maynard Hutchins (1899-1977), former Dean of Yale Law School, Chancellor of the University of Chicago and editor of *The Great Books of the Western World*,[561] wrote that:

> *Democracy . . . is the only form of government that is founded on the dignity of man, not the dignity of some men, of rich men, of educated men, or of white men, but of all men. . . . Equality and justice, the two great distinguishing characteristics of democracy, follow inevitably from the conception of men, all men, as rational and spiritual beings.*[562]

---

[558] Wirt, *The Life of Patrick Henry*, pp. 138-139 (1836).

[559] *Guide to American Law Encyclopedia*, Vol. 1, p. 300 (West Publishing Company 1984).

[560] *Bartlett's Familiar Quotations*, supra n.556, p. 98b.

[561] *Guide to American Law*, supra n.559, Vol. 6, p. 109.

[562] *Bartlett's Familiar Quotations*, supra n.556, p. 1045b.

If liberty and equality, as thought by some, are chiefly to be found in democracy, they will be best attained when all persons alike share in government to the utmost.

—**Aristotle (384-322 B.C.)**

One of the primary attacks upon our civil jury system today is the claim that our fellow citizens who serve upon our civil juries are not sufficiently intelligent to comprehend the complicated concepts of complex litigation. But this contention is not new. The authors of a recent article on "Jury Trial, Progress and Democracy," wrote that "from the record it is clear that the competence of the common man and the validity of the jury trial are two basic closely related notions upon which American democracy has *always* rested."[563]

"*We, the people" are the American jury*,[564] and as Judge Henry Clay Caldwell of Arkansas said in 1899, "when you impeach the impartiality and integrity of the jury, you impeach the impartiality and integrity of the whole body of people from whom they are drawn, and of which they are a representative part."[565] An attack upon the intelligence of the American jury is an attack upon American democracy.

In 1916, W. J. Kallbrier of Kentucky wrote of trial by jury that:

> *It has proved a strong security for life, liberty, and property, the three inalienable rights of the English and American people. It is based on the proper principles of representation and is the only method of giving the American people a share in the administration of justice. . . .*
>
> *The jury should consist of twelve honest and intelligent men [and women] from the community. If we say the American citizen is not equal to his task, we belie American manhood, contradict the course of judicial proceedings, and fail in the duty to communities which rely upon us for a legislative machine by which juries are to be secured.*
>
> *Trial by jury is an institution which the people control. To take it away would be depriving the people of their share of the right in the administration of justice.*[566]

---

[563]Kuhlman, Pontikes and Stevens, "Jury Trial, Progress and Democracy," 14 *John Marshall L.R.* 679 (1981).

[564]Ring, "We, the Jury," 6 *Trial Diplomacy J.* 19 (1983).

[565]Caldwell, "Trial by Judge and Jury," 33 *American L.R.* 321, 340 (1899). *See* pp. 357-359 below.

[566]Kallbrier, "Trial by Jury," 4 *Ken. L.J.* 25, 18-29 (1916).

In his *History of Freedom in Antiquity* (1907), John Dahlberg Acton wrote that "the one pervading evil of democracy is the tyranny of the majority."[567] To deprive the people of their share of the right in the administration of justice will deprive the individual American citizen of his best protection against that "inclination to injustice" which makes democracy necessary.

> *Man's capacity for justice makes democracy possible, but man's inclination to injustice makes democracy necessary.*[568]

In a 1909 article in the *Harvard Law Review*, George W. Warvelle of Chicago wrote that the general jury verdict is "not only in consonance with the true principle of the common law, but is peculiarly applicable to a free government where it is advisable that the people should retain in their own hands a large measure of the administration of justice."[569] In 1918, Delphin M. Delmas, "the silver-tongued spellbinder of the Pacific Coast," called trial by jury "the democracy of justice."[570]

In 1956, Clarence R. Runals, vice president of the New York State Bar Association, called trial by jury "a cherished right" which, to the American people, "is and has been a symbol of democracy"[571] and in 1965, Stanley E. Sacks of Norfolk, Virginia, wrote that "the civil jury, one of our most cherished democratic institutions, is being threatened with extinction."

> *Admittedly, the civil jury system is not infallible, but it is truly the best method yet devised by our civilization for the orderly and effective settlement of controversies. Trial by jury has long been recognized as a most effective weapon in "democracy's arsenal to combat tyranny."... Its history teaches that it has earned well a permanent place in democratic forms of government.*[572]

---

[567] *Bartlett's Familiar Quotations*, supra n.556, p. 750a.

[568] Niebuhr, *The Children of Light and the Children of Darkness* (1944). See *Bartlett's*, supra n.556, p. 1024b.

[569] Warvelle, "The Jurors and the Judge," 23 *Harvard L.R.* 123, 128 (1909).

[570] See Delmas, *The Democracy of Justice* on p. 368 below.

[571] "Jury Trial on Trial — A Symposium," 28 *N.Y.S.B.J.* 322, 330 (October, 1956).

[572] Sacks, "Preservation of the Jury System," 22 *Wash. & Lee L.R.* 76 (1965).

In April, 1967, Judge Irving R. Kaufman, of the U.S. Court of Appeals for the Second Circuit and Chairman of the Judicial Conference Committee on the Operation of the Jury System, said that "there can be no universal respect for law unless all Americans feel that it is *their* law — that they have a stake in making it work."

> *... Trial before a jury of one's peers is one of a democratic society's primary techniques for achieving truth. Imperfect though it may be, we have devised no better. When we strengthen that institution we strengthen the framework of our democratic society.*[573]

In a series of lectures on *The Abuse of Power* presented by the Law Society of Upper Canada in 1979, Canadian Justice E. L. Haines said that "trial by jury is our oldest institution against the abuse of power" and that "it represents a deep commitment to the use of laymen in the administration of justice — therein lies its strength against tyranny."[574]

In 1981, English author M.D.A. Freeman wrote that "the jury represents democratic self-government" and that attacks upon it are "the predatory ravages of authoritarianism."[575] And in January, 1987, John V. Singleton, Chief Judge of the U.S. District Court for the Southern District of Texas, referred to trial by jury as an "esteemed institution" which has served "as a cornerstone of our democracy."[576]

In 1924, Marquette University law professor A. C. Umbreit wrote that trial by jury provides "the last opportunity the great mass of the people have of participating in any way in any of the activities of government."[577] Ten years later, Stanley F. Brewster of the New York Bar in his book, *Twelve Men In A Box*, wrote that the jury system was "an integral part of the administration of justice" and "in a democracy, such as ours, constitutes the basis of free government."[578]

---

[573] Kaufman, "A Fair Jury — The Essence of Justice," 51 *Judicature* 88, 91-92 (October, 1967).

[574] *Special Lectures of the Law Society of Upper Canada on the Abuse of Power*, pp. 31, 34 (Toronto 1979).

[575] Freeman, "The Jury on Trial," 34 *Current Legal Problems* 65 (1981).

[576] Singleton, "Jury Trial: History and Preservation," 1988 *Tr. Law. Guide*, p. 273 (Callaghan & Co. 1988).

[577] Umbreit, "Is Trial by Jury: An Ineffective Survival?" 8 *Marquette L.R.* 125, 132-133 (1924).

[578] Brewster, *Twelve Men In A Box*, pp. 3-4 (1934).

Trial by a jury of one's peers is one of a democratic society's primary techniques for achieving truth. When we strengthen that institution we strengthen the framework of our democratic society.
—**Judge Irving R. Kaufman, U.S. Court of Appeals (1967)**

In 1961, Truman B. Rucker of Tulsa, Oklahoma, warned against "driv[ing] another nail into the coffin of democracy," and said that we should "preserve the American system of jurisprudence, of which the civil jury is an integral part."[579] In 1991, Cynthia J. Cohen of Boston wrote that "proponents of the civil jury considered it to be a crucial political system which would empower ordinary citizens, and act as a populist check on the judicial system."[580]

In August, 1964, Jefferson F. Meagher of Binghamton, New York, wrote that "no machinery for the resolution of legal issues is or can be more democratic" than trial by jury.

> *... In a democracy the jury is much closer to the people, their mores, their established attitudes and unquestioned postulates than any judge can hope to be.*
>
> *In a day when greater professions of faith in pure democracy are abroad in the land than ever before, it seems odd that our one great democratic institution, apart from the free ballot, should not only be tampered with, but even marked for destruction in the widest area of its operation without a whimper being heard from the professional champions of the people. . . . New ways for personal involvement in democratic government should be sought in preference to deliberate elimination of existing institutions requiring citizen participation.*
>
> *It should be of profound significance to those considering abolition of jury trial that it provides the sole mechanism for the citizen to act and participate as a rational creature in the administration of justice.*
>
> *To abolish trial by jury is to rupture a vital artery in the bloodstream of the democratic process. Without such an organic link with the people, the continuity of our system is threatened. . . .*[581]

---

[579] Rucker, "Justice and the American Civil Jury,".33 *N.Y.S.B.J.* 133, 140 (June, 1961).

[580] Cohen, "Whatever Happened to the *Seventh Amendment?*" 35 *Boston Bar J.* 17 (November/December 1991).

[581] Meagher, "Trial by Jury Deserves a Fair Trial," 36 *N.Y.S.B.J.* 303 (August, 1964).

In "Jury Trial, Progress, and Democracy" (1981), Richard S. Kuhlman, *et al.*, of Chicago concluded:

> *Early American ... jurisprudence ... recognized the fundamental importance of the individual: "The government of the union is ... truly a government of people. In form and in substance, it emanates from them. Its powers are granted by them, and are to be exercised directly on them, and for their benefit." Moreover, "the very essence of civil liberty ... consists in the right of every individual to claim the protection of the laws whenever he receives an injury. One of the first duties of government is to afford that protection. ..."*
>
> *Similarly, the public legal institutions of the United States were based on the assumed individual capacity of citizens to maintain them through intelligent participation in the political process. People who could vote the lawmakers in or out of power in the ultimate sense "owned" the laws. In addition, government and jurisprudence ... were oriented toward protection of individual interests as the ultimate end to be served.*
>
> *Thus the individual-oriented legal framework of American democracy has always rested, in both the public and private spheres, on notions of citizen competence quite different from the assumptions of non-democratic states where in earliest times, laws were presumed to be inflicted upon the incompetent masses by malevolent deities speaking through the local king or priest. ...*
>
> *To the extent that the individual sees himself no longer as the controlling force in his institutions, alienation results. Government becomes not the creation of its citizens, but their master. Legal process under that government is perceived as imposed upon the individual rather than voluntarily accepted. The proposed curtailment of the right to trial by jury will further remove individual citizens from control of their institutions.*[582]

---

[582]Kuhlman, Pontikes & Stevens, "Jury Trial, Progress, and Democracy," 14 *John Marshall L.R.* 679, 693-696 (1981).

From the outset, trial by jury was based upon the principle of representation. William Stubbs, in his *Constitutional History of England* (1880), wrote that "the institution of the jury was itself based on a representative idea" and was "a step in the growth of a representative system" of government.[583]

In *The American System of Trial by Jury* (1887), D. H. Chamberlain said that if civil liberty "reposes for its ultimate security on the capacity of the people at large to guard their rights and exercise their privileges," then "it is upon such a representative body of the whole community as the jury presents, that we ought to, and must, rely for administering . . . . the machinery of civil society. . . ."

> *No single feature of our civil life presents such freedom from officialism, from professional or class influences, and the influences of routine and artificial life, as the jury as now constituted in this country. No other agency may, therefore, be so safely relied on to enforce and administer those rules of property and conduct, the infraction of which is the occasion and warrant of nearly all our civil laws and jurisprudence.*[584]

This is the question that we must confront today. Will we allow our modern industrial aristocracy and their allies in the insurance industry and the American Medical Association to take the control of the administration of our civil justice system away from the people and give it to a few imminently corruptible political appointees in our state and federal judiciary or to some "blue ribbon panel" of professional arbitrators? If we are going to call ourselves a democracy, *then we should be a democracy* and leave the administration of the affairs of our government in the hands of the people where it belongs. This will require strengthening our civil jury system rather than undermining it, and the removal of those legislative limitations on the discretionary powers of civil juries which are already clogging this "vital artery in the bloodstream of the democratic process."

---

[583]Stubbs, *The Constitutional History of England*, Vol. 1, p. 682 (Clarendon Press 1880).

[584]Chamberlain, *The American System of Trial by Jury*, pp. 17-21 (George E. Crosby Press, Boston 1887).

Nothing among the English was more ancient than the idea and practice of popular justice. The jury system is characterized by its intrinsic fairness and is the most rational mode of determining questions of fact.
—James Bradley Thayer, Harvard Law Professor (1898)

Twelve jurors know more of the common affairs of life than does one man, and they can draw wiser and safer conclusions than a single judge.
—U.S. Supreme Court Justice Ward Hunt (1873)

R. TRIAL BY JURY VS. TRIAL BY JUDGE

The more I see of trial by judge, the more highly I think of trial by jury.
—**Australian King's Counsel B. R. Wise (1948)**[585]

It is a basic obligation of civil government to provide a means for the impartial reconciliation of civil disputes. In *Marbury v. Madison* (1803), Chief Justice John Marshall called this principle "the very essence of civil liberty."

The very essence of civil liberty certainly consists in the right of every individual to claim the protection of the laws whenever he receives an injury. One of the first duties of government is to afford that protection.[586]

It has been argued that this function of our judicial system could safely be entrusted to what Edmund Burke called "the cold neutrality of an impartial judge."[587] For, notwithstanding the cryptic comment of Australian King's Counsel B. R. Wise, quoted above, when all things are considered, America is blessed with a seemingly inexhaustible supply of capable judges. But justice is administered on an individual basis and, as Alfred C. Coxe wrote in the inaugural issue of the *Columbia Law Review* in 1901:

In all lands and in every age there are conspicuous instances of judges who have proved arbitrary, ignorant, bigoted, cruel and corrupt. Even in our own country, we have seen the ermine upon the shoulders of despicable creatures, the complaisant agents of aggregated wealth or the willing tools of political vampires. Fortunately, these instances are few, but they prove the danger of leaving the determination of controversies solely to the bench.[588]

In 1680, British author Henry Care wrote "of the advantages Englishmen enjoy by trial by juries, above any other nation under heaven," from which we quote:

---

[585] Jacobs, "Trial by Jury—Its Origin and Merits," 21 *Aus. Law J.* 462 (April, 1948).
[586] *Marbury v. Madison*, 5 U.S. (1 Cranch) 137, 163 (1803).
[587] *Bartlett's Familiar Quotations, supra* n.556, p. 454b.
[588] Coxe, "The Trials of Jury Trials," 1 *Columbia L.R.* 286, 290 (1901).

Now let any man of sense consider, whether this method be not more proper for bolting out the truth, for finding out the guilty, and preserving the innocent, than if the whole decision were left to the examination of a judge, or two or three, whose interests, passion, haste, or multiplicity of business may easily betray them into error.[589]

The famous British political philosopher Jeremy Bentham (1748-1832) has said that "where conflicting facts are to be discussed or conflicting evidence to be heard, a jury is perhaps the best forum for such a case; *a single judge perhaps the worst.*"[590] Likewise, British author and critic G. K. Chesterton in his essay entitled, "The Twelve Men," wrote that "our civilization has decided, and very justly decided," that "when it wishes anything done which is really serious, it collects twelve of the ordinary men" of an impartial English jury to do the job.[591]

Likewise, in *A Discourse on Trial by Jury,* read before the American Philosophical Society in May of 1863, Eli K. Price said:

And are not jurors an important assistance in the administration of justice? The best judges bear testimony that they are. If justice be done to the wheel by placing in it the most intelligent citizens of all occupations, every traverse jury of twelve men should possess an aggregate of practical information, that should be greater than the judge on the bench, however good his legal information, and as a rule, judges admit this to be their experience as to jury trials....[592]

In support of Eli K. Price's conclusions concerning the superiority of the collective wisdom of a jury, we have collected the views of 15 notable members of the English and American Bench on this subject. We begin with Charles Pratt, Lord Camden, Chief Justice of the Court of Common Pleas (1761-1766) and Chancellor of England (1766-1770):

---

[589]Care, *English Liberties,* pp. 205, 208-209 (1680).

[590]Note: "The Jury System," 12 *Albany Law J.* 292 (1875).

[591]Helfrich, "Chesterton on Juries," 191 *N.Y.L.J.* 2 (February 15, 1984), quoting from Chesterton, "The Twelve Men," in *Tremendous Trifles* (1909).

[592]Price, *Discourse on the Trial by Jury,* p. 9 (Caxton Press, Philadelphia 1863).

Our civilization has very justly decided that when it wishes anything done which is really serious, it collects twelve of the ordinary men of an English jury.

—**G. K. Chesterton (1909)**

ILLUSTRATION BY DAVID LEVINE

The discretion of a judge is the law of tyrants; it is always unknown; it is different in different men; it is casual and depends upon constitution, temper, and passion. In the best it is oftentimes caprice; in the worst it is every crime, folly, and passion to which human nature is liable.[593]

In 1828, Henry Peter Brougham, Lord Chancellor of England from 1830 through 1834, called "the method of juries a most wholesome, wise and almost perfect invention, for the purpose of judicial inquiry."

Lastly, what individual can so well assess the amount of damages which a plaintiff ought to recover for any injury he has received [than] . . . an intelligent jury?[594]

On our side of the Atlantic, U.S. Supreme Court Justice Levi Woodbury (1789-1851), wrote that juries are "peculiarly fitted to decide questions depending upon the veracity of witnesses."[595] And in 1873, U.S. Supreme Court Justice Ward Hunt wrote that a jury of "twelve men know more of the common affairs of life" and "can draw wiser and safer conclusions" than a single judge.[596]

Among state court judges, Justice Edward W. Whelpley of the New Jersey Court of Errors and Appeals, declared that "the more I see of juries and their verdicts, the more I am satisfied that it is the best mode of determining disputed facts ever devised by the wit of man."[597]

Further south, Justice Joseph Henry Lumpkin of the Supreme Court of Georgia wrote in 1849 that "the general diffusion of knowledge and education among the people of this country, much better fits them for weighing and comparing the evidence, than in any other nation or age since the institution of trial by jury."[598]

---

[593] Tongue, "In Defense of Juries as Exclusive Judges of the Facts," 35 *Ore. L.R.* 143, 166 (April, 1956). For more on Lord Camden, *see* p. 316 below.

[594] *See* Henry Peter Brougham (1828) on p. 321 below.

[595] Moore, *A Treatise on Facts or the Weight and Value of Evidence*, Vol. 1, p. 26 (Edward Thompson Co. 1908).

[596] *See* Justice Ward Hunt on the superiority of a civil jury on pp. 344-345 below.

[597] *Black v. Shreve*, 13 N.J.Eq. 455, 469 (1960).

[598] *Potts v. House*, 6 Ga. 324, 345 (1849).

In 1897, U.S. District Judge William H. Brawley of South Carolina wrote that "the judgment of twelve impartial men of the average of the community, applying their separate experiences of life to the solution of such doubts as may arise, is more likely to be wise and safe than the conclusion of any single judge."[599] Meanwhile, Judge Brawley's midwestern counterpart, Judge Henry Clay Caldwell, Judge of the Eighth Circuit Court of Appeals, observed in 1899:

> *. . . The constitutional mode of ascertaining the sense of reasonable men on disputed questions of fact in common law actions is by the verdict of twelve jurymen, and not by the opinions of judges. It was because the people knew the judges were poor judges of the facts that they committed their decisions to a jury, and every day's experience confirms the wisdom of their action.*[600]

That same year, James H. Hazelrigg, Chief Justice of the Kentucky Court of Appeals, asserted that "the jury are taken from the various walks of life, and their combined knowledge and experience afford the very best opportunity for safe and wise conclusions."[601] Six years later, Judge W. H. Holt, who presided over the inaugural U.S. Court of Puerto Rico, published an article on "The Jury System" in the *Albany Law Journal*. In it, he wrote:

> *Our judiciary has as a rule been remarkably free from corruption; but it is in the main created by political favor. It has already been given immense power [and] should not in addition be invested with the jury power, which was born of the sovereignty of the people.*[602]

---

[599] *Traveler's Ins. Co. v. Selden*, 78 Fed. 285, 287 (4th Cir. 1897).

[600] *Myers v. Chicago, St.P., M. & O. Ry. Co.*, 95 Fed. 406, 414 (8th Cir. 1899).

[601] *Hudson v. Adams Adm'r*, 49 S.W. 192 (Ky. 1897).

[602] Holt, "The Jury System," 67 *Albany Law J.* 298, 300 (1905). The "sovereignty of the people" is a precious commodity. In the 13th century the barons took on King John to gain it for the aristocracy. In the 17th century the Parliamentary forces fought a civil war to extend it to the middle class and in the 18th century we endured a Revolution to guarantee it to every American citizen through the preservation of the fundamental individual rights of representative democracy and trial by jury.

In 1929, Judge Frederick E. Crane of the Court of Appeals of New York argued that "there is no better or healthier system . . . . than to have disputed questions of fact, both in civil and criminal cases, passed upon by ordinary citizens of ordinary intelligence." In the same article, he quotes Frederick Edwin Smith, Lord Birkenhead, Chancellor of England (1919-1922), for the "simple principle that what twelve ordinary men think of the facts is on the whole more likely to be right than a very highly instructed legal functionary."[603]

Judge Harold R. Medina, who served on the Second Circuit Court of Appeals for more than 30 years, maintained that "twelve heads are better than one" and that "the joint effect of twelve people going over a case together and trying their level best to do what is right is one of those products of our type of democracy for which we should be everlastingly grateful."[604]

In May of 1958, Lord Goddard, Chief Justice of England, wrote that it is "more satisfactory to have the opinion of twelve people as to what . . . a plaintiff should receive when he has suffered grievous injuries, than that of only one man, however experienced he may be."[605] Six years later, Justice Howard T. Hogan of the Supreme Court of New York expressed the opinion of many American judges when he said:

> *Judges try the same type of action day after day. Our judgment on issues of fact must always be based in part on what we, as individuals, are — the sum total of our experiences, our backgrounds, our prejudices and our limitations. There can be no "averaging out" such as there is when twelve individuals are gathered together, most of them serving as jurors only a few times in their lives. They, or at least some of them, can approach a case with a fresh outlook, without a subconscious predetermination of one sort or another about the type of case or, perhaps, the attorneys or the litigants.*[606]

---

[603]Crane, "Judge and Jury," 15 *ABAJ* 201, 202-203 (1929).

[604]*Judge Medina Speaks,* p. 219 (Matthew Bender & Co. 1954). Judge Medina was honored by the Court on the occasion of his 100th birthday, *see* Proceedings in 859 F.2d (February 16, 1988) and upon the occasion of his death at age 102, 915 F.2d (May 21, 1990).

[605]Hart, *Long Live* the *American Jury,* p. 64 (Case Press 1964) [by Justice Walter R. Hart of New York].

[606]Hogan, "Some Thoughts on Juries in Civil Cases," 50 *ABAJ* 752, 753 (August, 1964).

Twelve heads are better than one, the joint effort of twelve people who are trying their best to do what is right is one product of our democracy for which we should be everlastingly grateful.
—**Judge Harold R. Medina, U.S. Court of Appeals (1954)**

The opinions of these judges are consistent with those of the vast majority of the lawyers who appear before them, criminal or civil, plaintiff or defendant, regardless of age or geography. In 1884, an unnamed lawyer from Lebanon, Pennsylvania, wrote in the *American Law Review* that "trial by judge would greatly endanger public confidence in the courts." Trial by judge, he said, "would not satisfy the unsuccessful suitor, as does trial by persons of his own way of life and habits of thought."[607] Similar sentiments were expressed in the Chicago *Sunday Tribune* on March 10, 1907, by John F. Geeting who declared that "trial by jury must be preserved."

> *Judicial officers . . . are to some degree influenced by party prejudices, ties of friendship, public sentiment, or ambition; but jurors, not self-nominated, assume a humbler but more independent function. Jurors are summoned from the community at large; . . . have no rivals seeking to unseat them; . . . are actuated alone by a desire to accomplish justice; they assemble today; perform their public service; dispense tomorrow and disappear from the public gaze.*[608]

Delphin M. Delmas of California remarked in 1918 that "it needs but to recall that men are but men, even though they be judges" and that elevation to the bench does not endow the human soul "with the attributes of a godlike infallibility."

> *. . . In the discharge of their high office, . . . [a judge] may be swayed by the promptings of ambition or warped by the blight of prejudice. . . . He brings with him upon the bench his own political opinions, his own views upon questions of governmental policies, his own attitude toward sociological problems, his own conception of the proper relations of the different classes of society and of their respective rights. He has and retains his own partisan affiliations, his own social duties, his own family ties, his own religious beliefs.*[609]

---

[607] Correspondence, "The Jury System," 18 *American L.R.* 875-877 (1884).

[608] *See* Geeting, 69 *Albany L.J.* 134 (1907).

[609] Delmas, "The Democracy of Justice — The Jury," 6 *Ken. Law J.* 245, 249-250 (1918). For more on Delphin M. Delmas as the "silver-tongued spell-binder of the Pacific Coast," *see* p. 368 below.

In "The Case for the Jury System," Joseph T. Karcher wrote in 1969 that with an American jury, "the composite intelligence, dedication, comprehension, evidence recall, and the emotional balance and ability to render a just, fair and impartial verdict is at least equal to, if not superior to, that of a single judge."[610] In the *American Bar Association Journal* in 1974, Rudolph Janata of Columbus, Ohio, then serving as president of the Defense Research Institute, wrote that "trial lawyers know that juries afford better justice and are the only protection against an arbitrary judiciary."

> *. . . Having tried many, many cases before both judges and juries, I am satisfied that juries do excellent work — better than could be done by judges in the majority of cases. A jury is able to bring the standards of the community to play in the matter before it — standards which a judge, by the very nature of his position, cannot employ. The cost of the jury system is insignificant. The delay caused by the jury system, if any, is minimal. The value of the jury system is immeasurable.*[611]

In 1983, Peter W. Culley of Maine authored "In Defense of Civil Juries," in which he contended that "one of the more fundamental arguments for use of the jury is that the jury provides a check on the corrupt or biased judge."[612] And in 1988, Sigfredo A. Cabrera, Director of Publications of the California District Attorneys Association, called trial by jury "the best protection against judicial injustice."[613]

But the most uninhibited indictment of the potential perils of trial by judge was delivered by Ned Good of Los Angeles. For he saw, and described in intimate and picturesque detail, the same type of judicial tyranny that many of us who serve in the trenches unfortunately see "more than a fair share of" in the courtrooms of America today.

---

[610]Karcher, "The Case for the Jury System," 45 *Chicago-Kent L.R.* 157, 168 (1969).

[611]Janata, "Federal Jury Trials Should Not Be Abolished," 60 *ABAJ* 934, 936 (August, 1974).

[612]Culley, "In Defense of Civil Juries," 35 *Maine L.R.* 17, 29 (1983).

[613]Cabrera, "Why the Jury System is Important to the Legal System," 101 *L.A. Daily Journal* 4 (January 7, 1988).

> *Federal judicial dictatorship is worse than executive or legislative dictatorship because the executive and legislative branches of government periodically come up for reelection. They are accountable and responsible to the people. However, the federal judiciary is insulated from any accountability or responsibility to the people. They have a lifetime appointment. ... Therein lies the main threat and danger to freedom. A judicial system responsible to no one is a judicial system which has irresponsibility built into itself. ...*
>
> *To take away the right of citizens to participate in jury service, and through their vote decide controversial issues, is a reckless suggestion, regardless of the motives or title of the person making the suggestion. ...*
>
> *There are many outstanding and respected federal judges who are brilliant, kind, polite, humble, witty, and before whom it is a pleasure to appear and entrust important legal rights. But there is also more than a fair share of federal judges who have set up little kingdoms and have a widespread, well-deserved reputation for arrogance, dictatorship, rudeness, unpleasantness, procrastination, and inability to make a decision, and who display a lack of judicial courtesy, patience, and temperament to the litigants and the lawyers whom they were appointed to serve.*[614]

This is our choice. Will we have judicial democracy or judicial dictatorship? Will the people of our country decide the important issues of safety, reliability and civil responsibility, or will those decisions be left to judicial appointees in long black robes, or professional arbitrators in pin-striped suits? The choice is up to us. Patrick Henry, Thomas Jefferson and James Madison have no vote this time around. But armed with the wisdom of their words, can we not say to those who would sever this vital artery in the bloodstream of democracy:

> *We know not what course others may take, but as for us, give us liberty, freedom, equality, justice, government by the people, and trial by an impartial American jury.*

---

[614] Ned Good, "In Praise of Jury Trials," 7 *Litigation* 51-52 (1951).

What individual can so well assess the amount of damages which a plaintiff ought to recover for an injury he has received than an intelligent jury?
—**Henry Peter Brougham, Lord Chancellor of England (1828)**

The right of being tried by his fellow citizens who simply decide according to what they believe to be the truth gives every man a conviction he will be dealt with impartially and inspires him to mete out to others the same measure of equity that is dealt to himself.
—William Forsythe, *History of Trial by Jury* (1852)

S. THE JURY AS AN INSTRUMENT OF JUSTICE

1. The Trials of Alexander Murray and William Owen (1751-1752). As the mantle of authority gradually moved from the House of Stuart to the House of Commons, the supreme arrogance which inevitably accompanies unbridled authority moved with it. As it was with Oliver Cromwell's hand-picked Parliament of Puritan saints who prosecuted Lt.Col. John Lilburne in 1653, it was also with George II's "Honourable House of Commons" which persecuted Alexander Murray and William Owen in 1751 and 1752.

In a closely-contested Parliamentary election in the Borough of Westminster between George Vandeput and Granville Gower, Alexander Murray claimed that Peter Leigh, as High Bailiff of Westminster, had "smuggled the election" for Gower and that Gower and Leigh were "two great villains." On November 20, 1751, the House of Commons adopted a resolution charging Murray with contempt, found him guilty, directed him to be committed to Newgate Prison, and ordered him to appear before the Bar of the House of Commons "to receive his said sentence there upon his knees."

Shortly thereafter, an anonymous pamphlet appeared on the streets of London entitled, *The Case of the Honourable Alexander Murray, Esquire in an Appeal to the People of Great Britain.* Among other things, this pamphlet alleged that these quasi-judicial proceedings before the Bar of the House of Commons were "an open violation of the *Constitution*" which were "manifestly founded in oppression and injustice" and that Murray's conviction was based upon the testimony of two "Janus-headed witnesses," in the persons of a journeyman button trimmer and a tripe merchant.

Calling Murray's trial and conviction by the House of Commons *The British Inquisition*, the pamphlet concluded:

> *What shall distinguish Britons from those who groan under the most arbitrary governments, if subject to the like tyrannical acts of oppression? And what shall defend a free people whenever their representatives shall think fit to constitute themselves their judges, and wantonly inflict the severest pains and penalties by virtue of their mere will and pleasure? ... Though the law of the land has provided that every subject shall be tried by his jury, have we not seen [the House of Commons] uniting the three inconsistent capacities of judge, jury and prosecutor? ...* [615]

---

[615] The Trial of William Owen, 18 *How. St. Tr.* 1203-1230 (1752).

A typical non-jury trial before the **Spanish Inquisition.**

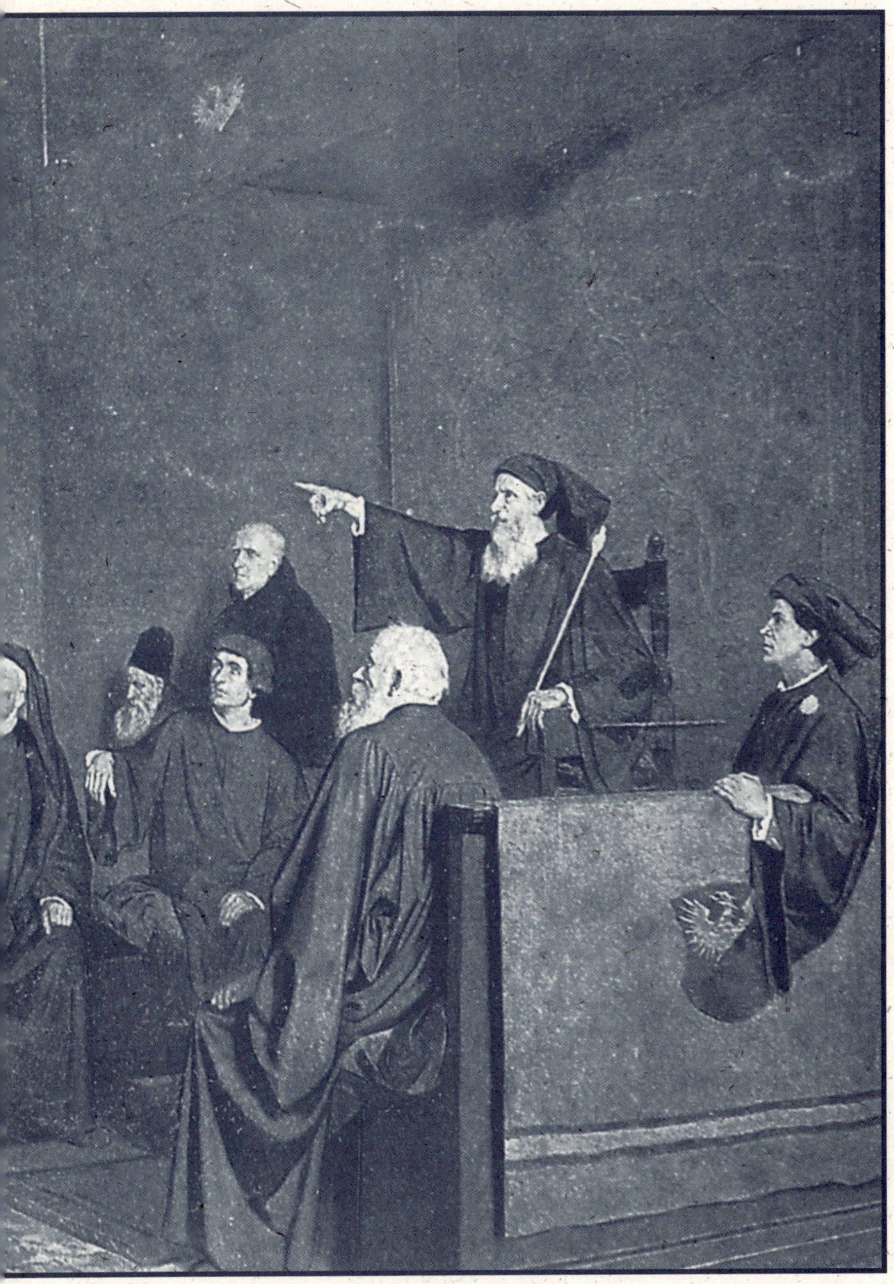

BETTMANN ARCHIVE

A complaint was lodged against this pamphlet and, when it was produced and read before the House of Commons, that august body then resolved:

> *That the said pamphlet is an impudent, malicious, scandalous, and seditious libel, falsely and most injuriously reflecting upon, and aspersing the proceedings of this House, and tending to create misapprehensions of the same in the minds of the people, to the dishonour of this House, and in violation of the privileges thereof.*

Unable to identify the author, the House directed the Attorney General to prosecute "the printer or printers, and the publisher or publishers." Thus, William Owen, book seller, was tried at the Guildhall of London on July 6, 1752, for "acting in open defiance of the authority" of the House of Commons by "wickedly and audaciously representing their proceedings in Parliament as cruel, arbitrary and oppressive."

For the prosecution, Dudley Ryder, Attorney General, argued that the pamphlet was "the most scandalous and astonishing libel that ever appeared in the world." Joining him, the Solicitor General contended that the only question of fact for the jury was whether Owen had published the pamphlet, it having been previously declared libelous by a vote of the House of Commons.

Appearing for the defendant, Serjeant Ford responded:

> *The House of Commons have voted this pamphlet a libel . . . and where is the man who dares to . . . contradict the opinion of the House? I dare not, and bold must be the man who dares; he knows the risk he runs, . . . for what cannot a House of Commons do, whose power is so great? . . .*

However, Mr. Ford asserted that William Owen was merely the printer, and not the author of the pamphlet, and that the prosecution had failed to prove the necessary malicious intent to justify the charge.

Next came "the cold neutrality of an impartial judge." According to the report:

> *The Chief Justice next summed up the evidence; and delivered it as his opinion, that the jury ought to find the defendant guilty; for he thought the fact of publication was fully proved; and if so, they could not avoid bringing in the defendant guilty.*

On July 6, 1752, 537 years and 21 days after King John sealed the *Magna Carta* on the great plain at Runnymede, a London jury consisting of the following:

 Richard Barnwell of Bread Street, merchant;
 John Horton of Old Fish Street, sugar-baker;
 Thomas Smith of Walting Street, linen-draper;
 Godfrey Lowe of Friday Street, draper;
 Edward Burwick of Friday Street, draper;
 Richard Bristow of Bread Street, grocer;
 William Woolley of Cheapside, hosier;
 Richard Bridgeman of Auldgate High Street, grocer;
 Philip Grafton of Auldgate High Street, oil man;
 Samuel Lloyd of Devonshire Square, merchant;
 Henry Hall of St. Helens, merchant; and
 John Tuff of Bishop Gate Street, grocer

— twelve honest, impartial, law-abiding Englishmen, each in turn slowly filed out of their jury box and into the pages of judicial history.

Today, their names appear in letters of gold beside those of Edward Bushel and other courageous jurors in the Roll of Honor of Anglo-American liberty. For those twelve men on that hot July day in 1752 had the courage to stand up to the awesome authority of an omnipotent House of Commons and the dictatorial arrogance of an ermine-robed Chief Justice of England and find William Owen **Not Guilty** of seditious libel. Eighty-two years earlier, they too would have been committed to Newgate Prison. But this time, they were merely menaced by the Court and allowed to return to the humble homes from which they came.

They were common, ordinary men. They came together for a day, reluctantly to be sure, listened to the evidence, consulted their consciences, and rendered an impartial verdict. Then they disbanded, and melted back into the community-at-large. And, yet, they were then, as countless American juries are today, the very essence of justice, the voice of the people, the conscience of the community, the cornerstone of our judicial process and the touchstone of contemporary common sense.

This, my friends, is the vital artery in the bloodstream of democracy which the enemies of liberty now seek to destroy. Contrast their conduct in this case with that of the House of Commons, the supposed guardians of English liberty. Contrast it with the "cold neutrality" of an allegedly impartial English judge, no less than the Chief Justice himself. Were these men irresponsible, or were they, as our American juries are today, an instrument of justice and the embodiment of true democracy?

2. **The Trial of Gideon Henfield (1793).** Having won our independence from Great Britain and established the *Constitution of the United States*, the thoughts of the Founding Fathers naturally turned from independence and individual liberty to national security and economic prosperity. "Treaties of Amity" were soon negotiated with England, France, Prussia and the United Netherlands, providing that "there shall be a firm, inviolable and universal peace" between them and the United States.

Following the French Revolution of 1789, "an open and notoriously public war" broke out between France and England in January of 1793. Those events "violently split American public opinion"[616] and resulted in President Washington's "Neutrality Proclamation" of April 22, 1793, in which he warned the citizens of the United States "carefully to avoid all acts and proceedings" inconsistent with such neutrality and directed federal authorities to prosecute anyone "committing, aiding, or abetting hostilities against any of the said powers."[617]

Unaware of Washington's "Neutrality Proclamation," Gideon Henfield, "a sea-faring man" from Salem, Massachusetts, set sail from Charleston, South Carolina, bound for Philadelphia.

> ... [H]e applied to the master of a packet, who asked him for more passage than he could afford to pay, whereupon he entered on board the Citizen Genet, a French privateer, commissioned by the French Republic and commanded by Pierre Johannen. Captain Johannen, it appeared, promised him the berth of prize-master on board the first prize they should capture, and the ship Williams, belonging to British subjects, having been captured about the 5th of May, he was put aboard her as prize-master, with another person, and arrived in that capacity at Philadelphia.

The seizure of the *Williams* was a matter of great embarrassment to the United States. George Hammond, the British ambassador, wrote to Secretary of State Thomas Jefferson on May 8, 1793, complaining that French privateers, operating out of Charleston, were "for the most part, citizens of the United States," and that he conceived their actions to be in breach of "that neutrality which the United States professes to observe."

---

[616]Presser & Zainalden, *Law and Jurisprudence in American History*, p. 180 (West Publishing Co. 2d ed. 1989).
[617]*Henfield's Case*, 11 *F. Cas.* 1099 (1793).

Gideon Henfield, "a sea-faring man" from Salem, Massachusetts, served as "prize master" of the British ship Williams after its capture by French privateers in May of 1793.

The British ambassador then concluded ominously:

> ... *Under this impression, he doubts not that the executive government of the United States, will pursue such measures as to its wisdom may appear the best calculated for repressing such practices in the future.*

In response, Jefferson wrote to federal prosecutor William Rawle on May 15, 1793, advising him that "there is reason to believe that certain citizens of the United States, have engaged in committing depredations on the property and commerce of some of the nations at peace with the United States."

> ... *I have it in charge to express to you the desire of the government, that you would take such measures for apprehending and prosecuting them as shall be according to law. ...*

Upon receiving these instructions, on May 17, 1793, Rawle wrote to the federal magistrate at Philadelphia as follows:

> *As I have received orders to prosecute, in every instance, those who commit breaches of the neutrality ... of the United States, during the present war ..., it is my duty to request, that you will be pleased ... to issue your warrant for apprehending the said Gideon Henfield, in order that he may be dealt with according to law.*

On May 23, 1793, Chief Justice John Jay convened a federal grand jury at Richmond, Virginia. In substance, he instructed them that "the participation by citizens of a neutral state in an attack by one belligerent power upon another, is an offense against the laws of nations, and may be punished by such neutral states."[618] On July 22, 1793, James Wilson gave similar instructions to a federal grand jury in Philadelphia and, five days later, Henfield was indicted.

> *The prosecution ... was considered of so much importance by General Washington, as to justify a special meeting of Congress, and by Mr. Jefferson as to require a distinct explanation to the British government.*[619]

---

[618] *See Henfield's Case, supra* n.617, at 1120, n.6.
[619] *Henfield's Case, supra* n.617, pp. 1099-1100, n.1.

At his arraignment, Henfield protested that he was a loyal American who would gladly die for his country "and therefore could not be supposed likely to intend anything to her prejudice."

> ... He declared if he had known it to be contrary to the President's Proclamation, or even the wishes of the President, for whom he had the greatest respect, he would not have entered on board. ...

Henfield's prosecution was instituted by Attorney General Edmund Randolph of Virginia before a three-judge panel sitting in Philadelphia, consisting of James Wilson of Pennsylvania and James Iredell of North Carolina, both of whom had been delegates to the Constitutional Convention of 1787, together with Judge Richard Peters. The prosecution argued that any aggression on the subjects of other nations was a violation of President Washington's "Neutrality Proclamation"[620] and the defense contended that the Proclamation created a new offense, which did not exist at the time Henfield committed the acts complained of.[621]

Judge Wilson began his charge to the jury as follows:

> This is, Gentlemen of the Jury, a case of the first importance. Upon your verdict the interest of four millions of your fellow-citizens may be said to depend. But whatever the consequence, it is your duty ... to do only what is right.

Proving that even distinguished American patriot-statesmen do not necessarily adhere to the principle of "cold neutrality" when they don their long black robes and ascend to the federal Bench, Judge Wilson continued:

> ... It is the joint and unanimous opinion of the Court, that the United States, being in a state of neutrality relative to the present war, the acts of hostility committed by Gideon Henfield are an offense against this country, and punishable by its laws. It has been asked by his counsel, in their address to you, against what law has he offended? The answer is, against many and binding laws. As a citizen of the United States, he was bound to take no part which could injure the nation; he was bound to keep the peace in regard to all nations with whom we are at peace. ...

---

[620] *Henfield's Case, supra* n.617, p. 1116.
[621] Presser & Zainalden, *supra* n.616, p. 187.

What chance does a poor, wayfaring seaman from Salem, Massachusetts, who knows nothing of Presidential proclamations, have of acquittal when President George Washington, Secretary of State Thomas Jefferson, Chief Justice John Jay, Attorney General Edmund Randolph, and Judge James Wilson are determined to see him convicted? And, yet, having been instructed that, "whatever be the consequence, it is your duty . . . to do only what is right," an impartial American jury found Gideon Henfield — **Not Guilty**!

> . . . The opposition press hailed the acquittal of Henfield. . . . Indeed, these newspapers suggested that the Henfield victory was as great a triumph for liberty as the verdict in the Seven Bishops' Case. . . .[622]

To illustrate the role of the jury as an instrument of justice, in previous sections we have cited the trial of Sir Nicholas Throckmorton in 1554,[623] the trials of John Lilburne in 1649 and 1653,[624] the trial of William Penn and William Mead in 1670,[625] the trial of the Seven Bishops in 1688,[626] and the trial of John Peter Zenger in 1735.[627] In this section, we have described the trials of William Owen in 1752 and Gideon Henfield in 1793. To borrow the words of British Prime Minister Lord John Russell in his *Essay on the English Government*, published in 1823:

> Many other cases might be mentioned, in which the verdicts of juries have operated to check the execution of a cruel or oppressive law, and in the end to repeal or modify the law itself. . . . Undoubtedly this is a very dangerous authority . . .; yet, exercised as it has been with temper and moderation, the discretion of juries has proved extremely salutary. It has been the cause of amending many bad laws which judges would have administered with exact severity, and defended with professional bigotry; and, above all, it has this important and useful consequence, that laws totally repugnant to the feelings of the community for which they are made, cannot long exist. . . .[628]

---

[622]Presser & Zainalden, *supra n.616*, p. 187.

[623]*See* pp. 100-101 above.

[624]*See* pp. 128-131 above.

[625]*See* pp. 136-139 above.

[626]*See* pp. 144-147 above.

[627]*See* pp. 157-159 above.

[628]Russell, *An Essay on the History of the English Government and Constitution*, pp. 198-199 (2d ed. 1865).

***James Wilson, Presiding Judge in the Trial
of Gideon Henfield (1793)***
*As a delegate to the Pennyslvania Ratification
Convention in 1787, he said that "trial by jury has
excellencies that entitle it to superiority over every other
mode, in cases to which it is applicable."*

3.   The View from the Bar. In 1985, John C. McKenzie of the Chicago Bar wrote "A Defense of the Jury System," in the *American Bar Association Journal*. In it, he said:

> *It should be every man's ambition to go through life without ever having his rights so called into question as to require their submission to a court, but if that unhappy day should come, we can share the conviction and the pride that the jury system makes it possible for each man to present his case with the certainty that the result will be just. . . .*[629]

In 1925, Lester P. Edge of Spokane, Washington, wrote that juries reconcile "the frequently harsh rules of the law with natural and substantial justice."

> *When judgments of the head are tempered by impulses of the heart, justice is not jeopardized, but is sustained.*[630]

In 1961, Robert H. White, Tennessee State Historian, writing in the *Tennessee Law Review*, stated that "the jury is a safeguard against harsh and repugnant laws." He equated the American jury system with justice, borrowing the words of English clergyman Sydney Smith, speaking of justice, in 1824:

> *Truth is its handmaiden. Freedom is its child, peace is its companion; safety walks in its steps, victory follows in its train: it is the brightest emanation of the gospel; it is the greatest attribute of God.*[631]

In 1969, Joseph T. Karcher, writing in the *Chicago-Kent Law Review*, stated that "for almost eight centuries, and despite an occasional miscarriage of justice, trial by jury still remains the best, safest, surest and perhaps the *only* bulwark to the average citizen to protect him in the enjoyment of his basic rights as a free man and a citizen."[632]

---

[629] McKenzie, "What is Truth? A Defense of the Jury System," 44 *ABAJ* 51, 76 (1958).

[630] Edge, "Jury System? Yes," 29 *Law Notes* 151-152 (November 1925).

[631] White, "Origin and Development of Trial by Jury," 29 *Tenn. L.R.* 8, 18 (1961).

[632] Karcher, "The Case for the Jury System," 45 *Chicago-Kent L.R.* 157, 159-160 (1969).

In 1980, E. P. Thompson, in his "classic article" entitled, "The State vs. Its Enemies," wrote:

> When the jurors enter the box, they enter also upon a role . . . inherited as much from our culture and our history as from books of law. . . . The English common law rests upon a bargain between law and the people. . . . The jury attends in judgment . . . upon the justice and humanity of the law. . . . Men and women must consult their reasons and their consciences, their precedents and their sense of who we are and who we have been.[633]

In 1981, English author M.D.A. Freeman, in "The Jury on Trial," wrote that "without the jury we would not be the society we are now." The jury, he believed, "is a mechanism by which the court's output of justice may be balanced with community sentiment."

> Although nominally only a trier of facts the jury probably tries a good many things besides facts behind its closed doors. Without changing legal doctrine, justice according to the community's views, may nonetheless be served.[634]

Finally, in his book *On Juries and Politics*, James P. Levine of the Brooklyn College of the City University of New York wrote in 1992:

> Juries are devoted to justice; it is their beacon. Early empirical research on juries in the 1950s discovered that juries are vitally concerned with handing down morally proper verdicts, and everything that has come to light since then confirms the validity of this finding. Jurors are attuned to the entire context of cases, the whole ranges of circumstances that determine levels of blameworthiness. They are very concerned with seeing to it that people get what they deserve.[635]

---

[633] Quoted by M.D.A. Freeman in "The Jury on Trial," 34 *Current Legal Problems* 89-90 (London 1981).

[634] Freeman, *supra* n.633, p. 90, quoting Bredemeier, *The Sociology of Law*, p. 62 (1969).

[635] Levine, *Juries and Politics*, p. 183 (Brooks/Cole Publishing Co. 1982).

4. **The View from the Bench.** In 1868, Thomas McIntyre Cooley, Professor of Law at the University of Michigan (1859-1884) and Associate Justice of the Supreme Court of Michigan (1864-1885), authored *A Treatise on Constitutional Limitations* in which he wrote:

> *... Jury trial, when considered in all its aspects, — as an instrument in the administration of justice; as an educator of the people in law and politics; and as a means of making them feel their responsibility in government, and the important part they bear in its administration, — is by far the best system of trial yet devised....*[636]

Ninety-nine years later, Judge Irving R. Kaufman, distinguished judge of the Second Circuit Court of Appeals, honored for his forty years of judicial service by an extraordinary session of that Court in November of 1989,[637] wrote "A Fair Jury—The Essence of Justice":

> *... Trial before a jury of one's peers is one of a democratic society's primary techniques for achieving truth. Imperfect though it may be, we have devised no better. When we strengthen that institution we strengthen the framework of our democratic society.*[638]

In the section which follows, we have quoted 116 distinguished authors, writing over a period of more than five centuries, on the nature of the jury as an instrument of justice. The authors quoted in that section and elsewhere in this book include five Chief Justices of England, two Prime Ministers, three English Chancellors, five American Presidents, six Chief Justices and twenty-one Associate Justices of the United States Supreme Court together with many equally-distinguished judges, lawyers, historians and statesmen. As will be seen from their combined wisdom and experience over 500 years of human history, trial by jury is the wisest, safest and most equitable and impartial system of justice known to man.

---

[636]Cooley, *A Treatise on Constitutional Limitations*, p. 326, n.3 (Little, Brown & Co. 1868).

[637]*See* 859 F.2d lxxxiv-ciii (November, 1989); *see also* 508 F.2d 1-27 (November, 1974).

[638]Kaufman, "A Fair Jury—The Essence of Justice," 51 *Judicature* 88, 92 (October, 1967).

Jury trial, as an instrument of justice, as an educator of the people, and as a means of making them feel their responsibility in government, is by far the best system of trial yet devised.
   —**Justice Thomas McIntyre Cooley of Michigan (1868)**

Springing up under the feudal despotism of the Plantagenets, trial by jury has survived alike their rule, that of the House of Tudor and of the House of Stuart; transplanted to a different hemisphere, it struck its roots deep into the new soil, and is, perhaps, the most cherished institution of the greatest exemplar of free and intelligent government that the world has ever seen.

—Justice Theodore Sedgwick of Massachusetts (1813)

T. HOW HISTORY HAS VIEWED THE INSTITUTION OF TRIAL BY JURY

In *The Democracy of Justice* (1918), Delphin M. Delmas wrote that a volume would be required to record the praises of the jury by the "eminent men" of this England and America. Set forth below is a representative selection of what has been said or written in praise of this "vital artery in the bloodstream of the democratic process."

1. Sir John Fortescue (1468). Appointed Chief Justice of the King's Bench in 1442, in 1468, Fortescue wrote *In Praise of the Laws of England*, a book that ranks with Coke's *Institutes* and Blackstone's *Commentaries* as one of the *Bibles* of early English law.[639] In it, he discussed the effectiveness of a jury in eliciting the truth:

> . . . [T]his is a method more powerful and efficient for eliciting the truth than the method of any other law in the world, and more removed from the danger of corruption and subornation. . . .[640]

2. Thomas Williams, *The Excellency and Præheminence of the Laws of England* (1557). Thomas Williams, who served as Speaker of the House of Commons in 1562-1563, delivered a reading on the Statute of Henry VIII, passed in 1557, providing for an improved procedure for summoning jurors.[641] In it, he said that the laws of England were deemed "by men of great learning and judgment to excel all other countries" because trial by jury was "more reasonable, and grounded upon more equity and indifferency, than the manner of trial by any other law." He stressed the impartial selection process and the many safeguards "for avoiding all corruption and sinister affection" and concluded that trial by jury was "of far more justice than the trial of any other human law" and that it was "not to be amended or reformed by the wit of man."[642]

---

[639] Holdsworth has said that its clearness of style and its unique information has made it "the most popular of Fortescue's works." Holdsworth, *A History of English Law*, Vol. 2, p. 570 (4th ed. 1927).

[640] Sir John Fortescue, *De Laudibus Legum Anglae (In Praise of the Laws of England)*, p. 77 (Cambridge Univ. Press 1949).

[641] Holdsworth, *supra* n.639, Vol. 4, pp. 260-261.

[642] Williams, *The Excellency and Præheminence of the Laws of England*, pp. 12, 16-20 (1557) [Garland Pub. Co. 1979].

3. Sir Edward Coke, *Institutes on the Laws of England* (1628). Sir Edward Coke was the most notable English legal scholar in the first half of the 17th century. "English common law won its supremacy over the prerogative power of the Crown and the encroachments of ecclesiastical jurisdiction, largely through [his] efforts."[643] Winston Churchill called him "one of the most learned of English judges" and wrote that it was "at Coke's prompting" that Parliament drafted the *Petition of Right* whose "object was to curtail the king's prerogative."[644] In 1628, Coke published the first volume of his *Institutes on the Laws of England* in which he characterized trial by jury as *a "wise distribution of power" which excels all other modes of trial*.[645]

4. William Walwin, *Juries Justified* (1651). In 1651, British barrister William Walwin, author of *The Manifestors Manifested* (1649), wrote *Juries Justified* in answer to Henry Robinson's *Seven Objections Against Juries* (1651).[646]

> [T]he many good men's lives and estates, that have been preserved by juries, will never be forgotten while England is England.[647]

It is noteworthy that Coke's and Walwin's observations on the superiority of trial by jury as a method of resolving judicial disputes and as a protection of the rights of individual citizens came in the 17th century when the English Crown's attempt to subvert the liberties of the people was at its height. Fortunately for us, the citizens of this country as a whole have not in recent memory encountered a similar experience. Yet, every day that passes sees another citizen subjected to the potential tyranny of those who continually abuse the powers of wealth and position. It is for them that the constitutionally-guaranteed protection of our civil jury system acts as the guardian of their fundamental rights.

---

[643] *Encyclopædia Britannica Macropædia*, Vol. 4, p. 825 (15th ed. 1979).

[644] Churchill, *A History of the English Speaking Peoples*, Vol. 2, pp. 155, 184-185 (Dorset Press 1956).

[645] *Coke's Institutes on the Laws of England*, Vol. 1, §234, p. 155b (1628) [Legal Classics Library 1985].

[646] Allibone, *A Critical Dictionary of English Language and British and American Authors*, Vol. 3, p. 2567 (J. B. Lippincott & Company, Philadelphia 1871).

[647] Walwin, *Juries Justified*, pp. 6, 13 (1651) [Garland Publishing Co. 1978].

LORD CHIEF JUSTICE COKE.
CORNELIUS JANSENS PINXIT.

Trial by jury is a wise distribution of power which excels all other modes of trial.
   —**Sir Edward Coke, Chief Justice of Common Pleas (1628)**

5.   Matthew Hale, *History and Analysis of the Common Law of England* (1676). Matthew Hale, Chief Justice of the King's Bench in the latter half of the 17th century, has been regarded as "one of the greatest scholars in the history of English law." His *History and Analysis of the Common Law of England* was written before 1676 and published in 1713. In it, he describes the many procedural safeguards which the institution of trial by jury affords to a fair and impartial search for the truth. He then explains why "the excellency of this open course of evidence" is preferable to a private hearing "before a commissioner or two, and a couple of clerks, where oftentimes witnesses will deliver that which they will be ashamed to testify publicly." He said that "this excellent order of trial by jury" had "all the helps to investigate the truth" and concluded:

> *It has the unanimous suffrage and opinion of 12 men, which carries in itself a much greater weight and preponderation to discover the truth of a fact than any other trial whatsoever. . . . I might here show the antiquity of this method of trial, both from the Saxon and the British laws, and demonstrate it to have been in use long before the time of [William the Conqueror] and indeed it seems to have been one of the first principles upon which our Constitution was erected and established.*[648]

6.   Henry Care, *English Liberties* (1680). Henry Care's book on *English Liberties* contained a discourse on the advantage of juries in which he wrote that representative government and trial by jury were the "two grand pillars of English liberty."

> *The privilege of trial by jury ranks among the choicest of our fundamental laws, which whosoever shall openly suppress or craftily undermine . . . is an enemy and traitor to his king and country.*[649]

For more than 300 years since Henry Care wrote these words, there have been many who have sought to "openly suppress" and "craftily undermine" trial by jury; and it is the solemn duty of all who have sworn to preserve the *Constitution* to vigorously oppose these attacks upon "the choicest of our fundamental laws."

---

[648] Hale, *History and Analysis of the Common Law of England*, pp. 252-264 (1713) [Legal Classics Lib. 1987].
[649] Care, *English Liberties: Or the Free-Born Subject's Inheritance*, pp. 4-5, 209 (1680).

7. Sir John Hawles, *The English Man's Right* (1680). Sir John Hawles (1645-1716) was "a sturdy Whig" who served in the House of Commons and as Solicitor General from 1695-1702.

> *Besides writing a comment on some of the notable trials of Charles II's reign, he wrote popular accounts of the Grand Jury and Petit Jury . . . [which] give a clear description of the jury's rights and duties. . . . They were popular in America and were reprinted there in 1693, 1772 and 1797. . . .*[650]

In *The English Man's Right* (1680), Sir John Hawles referred to the jury system as the "guardian of our legal liberties against arbitrary injustice" and as "that impregnable fortress wherein the law . . . preserve[s] and defend[s] the just rights and liberties of [this] country."[651]

8. Sir John Maynard, *Serjeant at Law* (1689). As "the most eminent pleader of the latter part of the 17th century," Sir John Maynard (1602-1690) had played "an important part in the professional life of the day." He sat in the Parliaments of Charles I, Oliver Cromwell, Charles II, and James II and served as Commissioner of the Great Seal.

At the age of 87, he represented the legal profession in welcoming William III's ascension to the throne following the "Glorious Revolution" of 1688. He took a leading part in the debates upon the *Bill of Rights* of 1689,[652] in which a number of individual liberties were recognized as the law of the land,[653] including the right to an impartial jury, "duly empaneled and returned," which Maynard considered to be "the subject's birthright and inheritance."

> *Trial by jury is the subject's birthright and inheritance. . . . This way of trial is his fence and protection against all frauds and surprises and against all storms of power.*[654]

---

[650] Holdsworth, *supra n.639*, Vol. 12, pp. 459-460.

[651] Hawles, *The English Man's Right*, pp. 12, 35 (1680) [in *Justices and Juries in Colonial America* (Arno Press 1972)].

[652] Holdsworth, *supra n.639*, Vol. 6, pp. 511-514.

[653] Perry & Cooper, *Sources of Our Liberties*, p. 223 (American Bar Foundation 1952).

[654] Quoted by Judge Henry Clay Caldwell in "Trial by Judge and Jury," 33 *American L.R.* 321, 323 (1899).

9. Giles Duncombe, *The Law of England Concerning Juries* (1725). Originally published in 1682, British barrister Giles Duncombe's *Trials Per Pais* or, *The Law of England Concerning Juries*, had run through nine editions by 1793.[655] In it, he wrote that "in the whole practice of law, there is nothing of greater excellency . . . than trials by juries. . . . [N]either the wisdom of our ancestors could, nor . . . can this present, nor after-ages invent a better."[656]

10. David Hume, *History of England* (1754-1762). David Hume, the famous British philosopher and historian, has been called one of the major figures of the 18th century.[657] His writings are among those of a select group of authors whose works are included in the *Encyclopedia Britannica's Great Books of the Western World*.[658] In his *History of England (1754-1762)*, he refers to trial by jury as "an institution admirable in itself, and, *the best calculated for the preservation of liberty and the administration of justice, that ever was devised by the wit of man.*"[659]

11. Joseph Towers, *Observations on the Rights and Duties of Juries* (1764). In the year preceding that in which Great Britain deprived the colonists of their right to trial by jury by the passage of the infamous *Stamp Act*, Joseph Towers wrote:

> *The right of trial by jury is of infinite importance to the liberty of the subject. It cannot be guarded with too much vigilance, nor defended with too much ardor. . . . If [the people] surrender . . . the right of juries . . . their other rights will inevitably follow.*[660]

---

[655] Allibone, *A Concise Dictionary of English Literature*, Vol. 1, p. 530 (1858).

[656] Duncombe, *Trials Per Pais* or, *The Law of England Concerning Juries*, pp. A3, A5 (1725) [William Hein 1980].

[657] *Encyclopædia Britannica Macropædia*, Vol. 8, p. 1193 (15th ed. 1979).

[658] *See* David Hume, *An Inquiry Concerning Human Understanding* (1748) published in *Great Books of the Western World*, Vol. 35, pp. 445-509 (Encyclopedia Britannica 1952). His works are included along with those of Sir Isaac Newton, John Locke, Montesquieu, Rousseau and John Stuart Mill.

[659] Quoted from Lysander Spooner, *An Essay on the Trial by Jury*, p. 205 (1852) [Legal Classics Library 1989].

[660] Towers, *Observations on the Rights and Duties of Juries* (1764, 1784) [Garland Publishing Co. 1978].

Trial by jury is the best institution calculated for the preservation of liberty and the administration of justice that ever was devised by the wit of man.
—**David Hume, English Philosopher (1762)**

12. Blackstone, *Commentaries on the Laws of England* (1765-1769). Justice William Blackstone was one of the most versatile English scholars of the 18th century. He was architect, poet, Shakespearean scholar, member of Parliament, judge, advocate of prison reform and one of only two Englishmen who "had the motive, the courage, [and] the power, to write a great, readable, reasonable book about English law as a whole."[661] His *Commentaries on the Laws of England* (1765-1769) were the most definitive legal treatise in the history of English law. Edmund Burke said that "nearly as many copies of *Blackstone's Commentaries* had been sold in America as in England."[662]

Blackstone looked upon the institution of trial by jury "as a privilege of the highest and most beneficial nature."

> *Trial by jury . . . seems to have been coeval with the first civil government of England. . . . Its establishment and use in this island . . . was always so highly valued and esteemed by the people, that no conquest, no change of government, could ever prevail to abolish it. In the Magna Carta it is more than once insisted on as the principal bulwark of our liberties. . . . And it was ever esteemed, in all countries, as a privilege of the highest and most beneficial nature.*[663]

"The Liberties of England," he said, "cannot but subsist so long as this palladium remains sacred and inviolate, not only from all open attacks, . . . but also from all secret machinations, which may sap and undermine it;" and he warned that "new and arbitrary methods of trial, however convenient they may appear at first," pose an insidious threat to individual liberty and are "fundamentally opposite to the spirit of our Constitution."[664]

---

[661] Plucknett, *A Concise History of the Common Law*, pp. 285-287 (Little, Brown & Co. 1956). "First it was Bracton, and 500 years later Blackstone. His great skill consisted in affording a reasonable explanation for the state of English law as it then existed."

[662] Connor, "The Constitutional Right to a Trial by a Jury of the Vicinage," 48 *Univ. Penn. L.R.* 197,198 (January, 1909). Blackstone was frequently quoted during the Constitutional Convention debates of May-September, 1787. *See* Madison, *Records of the Debates in the Federal Convention of 1787* (1927).

[663] *Blackstone's Commentaries on the Laws of England*, Vol. III, pp. 349-350 (1768).

[664] Blackstone, *supra*, Vol. 4, pp. 343-344.

13. James Mitchell Varnum, *Trevett v. Weeden* (1786).

A general in the Revolutionary War, James Mitchell Varnum commanded the Rhode Island Regiment at the Battle of Monmouth Courthouse on June 28, 1778, "the last time the two main contending armies were to meet in the field."[665] He returned to Rhode Island after the Revolutionary War to become one of the state's most respected advocates of individual liberty and later served among the first judges in the Northwest Territory.[666]

Varnum, one of "the most prominent lawyers in Rhode Island," appeared for the defendant in *Trevett v. Weeden*, "one of the first cases in which an American state court assumed jurisdiction over the constitutionality of an Act passed by the state legislature."

> At Newport, Rhode Island, a butcher named John Weeden refused to accept at par value the paper money which one of his customers, John Trevett, tendered for the purchase of some meat. Trevett brought an action against Weeden under the Bank Act, one of the numerous legal tender acts of the period which compelled people to accept paper money of the state at par value. This Act also provided that any violation of its provisions should be tried within three days, that there should be no jury, that three judges should constitute a quorum, and that the judges' decision should be final. A heavy penalty was attached to any refusal to accept this money. Since in Rhode Island the judges were subject to recall by the Assembly, there was every reason to believe that the Act would be rigorously enforced by the courts. . . . The general excitement aroused by this case was immense. . . .[667]

Denied the right of trial by jury and convicted in the lower court, Weeden appealed to the Supreme Court of Rhode Island. James Mitchell Varnum's argument before that court in October, 1786, distilled to its essence, is paraphrased below:[668]

---

[665] Lancaster, *The American Revolution*, pp. 196-197 (The American Heritage Library 1987).

[666] Friedman, *A History of American Law*, p. 163 (Touchstone Books 2d ed. 1985).

[667] Chroust, *The Rise of the Legal Profession in America*, Vol. 2, p. 27 n.90 (University of Oklahoma Press 1965).

[668] For the full text of James Mitchell Varnum's argument, *see* Schwartz, *The Roots of the Bill of Rights: An Illustrated Sourcebook of American Freedom*, Vol. 2, pp. 419-429 (Chelsea House Publishers 1980).

> *Trial by jury is a fundamental right, a vital part of our Constitution: the legislature cannot deprive us of its protection. The settlers of this country, from whom we are descended, gloried in their rights: but being persecuted in ways no earthly tribunal could control, they quit their native soil. They conquered the boisterous Atlantic, and settled in a howling wilderness, amidst untamed beasts and dangerous haunts of savage men! Yet they all retained an inviolable attachment to the fundamental rights of their former country.*
>
> *The charters granted to our forefathers guaranteed that we would each enjoy the essential liberties of free men. They fully confirmed the individual liberties guaranteed by the Magna Carta and other fundamental laws of England. The right to trial by jury was sealed with a sacred stipulation that it should never be violated.*
>
> *Have the citizens of this country ever entrusted our legislators with the power of altering their Constitution? Those who snatched their liberty from the jaws of the British lion, amidst the thunder of contending nations, would they submissively surrender it to the perils of error and alarm? As soon may the Great Michael kick the beam, and Lucifer riot in the spoils of angels!*
>
> *The right of trial by civil juries has always been a vital, fundamental right. The laws of our legislature cannot change our Constitution. The very idea is dangerous; it borders upon treason! The moment the basic rights of the people are dependent upon our legislatures for their preservation, there will be an end to individual liberty.*

When the Supreme Court reversed Weeden's conviction, the General Assembly was "dismayed by the decision" and cited the judges to appear and explain why they had declared an Act of the "Supreme Legislature" to be unconstitutional.

> *The defense of the court was made by David Howell, who laid down the principle that judges were not accountable to the Assembly, and that the right to trial by jury, denied under the Bank Act, was a fundamental right which the Assembly could not abolish.*

Trial by jury is a fundamental right, a vital part of our Constitution: the legislature cannot deprive us of its protection. The moment the basic rights of the people are dependent upon our legislature for their preservation, there will be an end to individual liberty.
   —**James Mitchell Varnum**, *Trevett v. Weeden* **(1786)**

14.   Thomas Erskine (1788). In the latter half of the 18th century, Thomas Erskine was the leading lawyer of the English Bar. He thought so highly of the institution that he chose "Trial by Jury" as his family motto.[669] In arguing that it should be for the jury, not the judge, to determine whether a publication is libelous, he quoted *Blackstone's Commentaries* on "the excellence of trial by jury in civil cases" stating:

> [T]he liberties of England cannot but subsist so long as [trial by jury] remains sacred and inviolate not only from all open attacks, . . . but also from all secret machinations, which may sap and undermine it.[670]

15.   Charles Pratt, Lord Camden, Chancellor of England (1792). Charles Pratt (1713-1794), "a learned lawyer," was appointed Attorney General in 1757, served as Chief Justice of the Court of Common Pleas from 1761 through 1766 and as Chancellor of England from 1766 through 1770.[671] In his first speech before the House of Lords in 1765, he attacked the Stamp Act and his continued opposition to taxation of the American colonists without representation in Parliament resulted in his dismissal as Chancellor in 1770.[672]

He supported the legislative independence of Ireland, Parliamentary reform, and the right of English juries to return a general verdict in prosecutions for criminal libel. In his last two speeches in the House of Lords in 1792 in support of Fox's Libel Act,[673] that "great constitutional lawyer" exclaimed:

> Trial by jury is indeed the foundation of our free Constitution; take that away and the whole fabric will soon moulder into dust.[674]

This prophetic warning, delivered 200 years ago, is one which we cannot afford to ignore today.

---

[669] Mullins, *In Quest of Justice*, p. 259 (London 1931).

[670] *Speeches of Lord Erskine*, Vol. I, pp. 291-292 [Legal Classics Library 1984]: The preface calls Lord Erskine the "greatest advocate . . . who ever appeared in any age."

[671] Holdsworth, *supra n.639*, Vol. 12, pp. 304-310.

[672] *Encyclopædia Britannica Micropædia*, Vol. II, p. 479 (15th ed. 1979).

[673] Holdsworth, *supra n.639*, Vol. 12, p. 309.

[674] Caldwell, "Trial by Judge and Jury," 33 *American L.R.* 321, 323 (1899).

16.   Thomas Jefferson, *First Inaugural Address* (March 4, 1801). On March 4, 1801, Thomas Jefferson delivered his first inaugural address. In it, he said:

> *Equal and exact justice to all . . . ; freedom of religion, freedom of the press, and freedom of person under the protection of the habeas corpus, and trial by juries impartially selected. These principles form the bright constellation which has gone before us and guided our steps through an age of revolution and reformation. The wisdom of our sages and the blood of our heroes has been devoted to their attainment. They should be the creed of our political faith, the text of civil instruction, the touchstone by which we try the services of those we trust; and should we wander from them in moments of error or alarm, let us hasten to retrace our steps and to regain the road which alone leads to peace, liberty and safety.*[675]

17.   Theodore Sedgwick (1746-1813). Theodore Sedgwick graduated from Yale University and was admitted to the Massachusetts Bar in 1766. He was elected to the Continental Congress and appointed to the Massachusetts Ratification Convention. He represented Massachusetts in the House of Representatives (1789-1796), and in the U.S. Senate (1796-1799), and then returned to the House (1799-1801) when he served as Speaker. He was appointed Justice of the Supreme Judicial Court of Massachusetts in 1802 and served through 1813. He called trial by jury "the most cherished institution" of free government that the world has ever seen:

> *Springing up under the feudal despotism of the Plantagenets, it has survived alike their rule, that of the House of Tudor and of the House of Stuart, and now flourishes with all its original vigor . . . ; while during the same period, transplanted to a different hemisphere, it has struck deep its roots into the new soil, and is, perhaps, the most cherished institution of the greatest exemplar of free and intelligent government that the world has ever seen.*[676]

---

[675] *Annals of America*, Vol. 4, p. 145 (Encyclopædia Britannica 1976).

[676] Quoted from the Dedication Page in Lesser, *The Historical Development of the Jury System* (Lawyers Cooperative Pub. Co. 1894).

18.   Lord John Russell, *On the English Government* **(1823).** John Russell (1792-1878) was "a rebel against aristocracy" whose "liberalism was ahead of his time." Elected to Parliament at age 21, his first speech was an attack on the suspension of the *Habeas Corpus Act.* He served as Prime Minister of England from 1846 to 1852 and from 1865 to 1866. He was the chief promoter of liberal reform of the Whig party and led the fight for the *Parliamentary Reform Act of 1832.*[677] Russell "championed the cause of religious freedom for both English dissenters and Irish catholics," reduced the number of crimes subject to capital punishment, pushed for increased support of public education, established a 10-hour work day for factory workers and founded the National Board of Health. In addition to these worthy accomplishments, "among the English prime ministers, few wrote so copiously — biography, history, poetry — as Russell."[678]

In his treatise, *On the English Government* (1823), Russell defended the institution of trial by jury as the chief instrument through which the people share in the government of the country.

> *It is to trial by jury . . . more than even by representation . . . that the people owe the share they have in the government of the country; it is to trial by jury, also, that the government mainly owes the attachment of the people to the laws; a consideration which ought to make our legislators very cautious how they take away this mode of trial by new, trifling, and vexatious enactments.*[679]

The tendency of our legislatures to undermine our constitutional right to trial by jury "by new, trifling, and vexatious enactments," has been a constant threat to the rights of the citizen since John Russell wrote those words more than 150 years ago. Those who would defend the *Bill of Rights* must maintain a constant vigil to preserve the right of trial by jury for our children and their descendants.

---

[677] *Encyclopædia Britannica Macropædia,* Vol. 16, p. 38 (15th ed. 1979).

[678] *Encyclopædia Britannica Macropædia, supra,* Vol. 16, p. 38.

[679] Russell, *On the English Government,* p. 394 (1823), quoted by Forsythe, *History of Trial by Jury,* p. 358 (Lenox Hill Publishing Company 2d ed. 1878). *See* Russell, *An Essay on the History of the English Government and Constitution* (New ed. London 1865) [Kraus Reprint Co., New York 1971].

It is to trial by jury, more than even by representation that the people owe the share they have in the government of the country; a consideration which ought to make our legislators very cautious how they take away this mode of trial by new, trifling and vexatious enactments.
—**Lord John Russell,** *On the English Government* **(1823)**

19. **Henry Hallam, *The Constitutional History of England* (1827).** Henry Hallam was "an enlightened lawyer, an accomplished scholar, and a steady assertor of the best interest of mankind."[680] In what W. S. Holdsworth calls an accurate and impartial account of English constitutional history from the reign of Henry VII (1485-1509) through the reign of George II (1727-1760),[681] Henry Hallam referred to an Englishman's "sacred privilege" of "trial by his peers" and said:

> . . . That primeval institution, those inquests by twelve true men, the unadulterated voice of the people, responsible alone to God and their conscience, . . . should have been heard in the sanctuaries of justice, as fountains springing fresh from the lap of earth. . . .[682]

20. **Chancellor James Kent, *Commentaries on American Law* (1827).** James Kent became the first professor of law at Columbia University in 1793. In 1798, he was appointed to the Supreme Court of New York and became Chief Justice in 1804. In 1814, he was appointed Chancellor of the Court of Chancery, at that time the highest judicial office in New York.[683] *Kent's Commentaries*, published in four volumes from 1826 to 1830 was the most comprehensive treatise on American law available at that time. In Volume 2, published in 1827, he wrote:

> . . . [A]ll the colonies were parties to the National Declaration of Rights in 1774, in which the trial by jury, and the other rights and liberties of English subjects, were peremptorily claimed as their undoubted inheritance and birthright. It may be received as a self-evident proposition, universally understood and acknowledged throughout this country, that no person can be . . . deprived of life, liberty, or property, unless by . . . the judgment of his peers. . . .[684]

---

[680] Allibone, *A Critical Dictionary of English Literature*, Vol. 1, p. 769 (1858).

[681] Holdsworth, *supra n.639*, Vol. 15, pp. 275-276.

[682] Hallam, *The Constitutional History of England From the Accession of Henry VII to the Death of George III*, Vol. 1, pp. 47-48, 233 (1827) [Garland Publishing Co. 1978].

[683] *Encyclopædia Britannica Micropædia*, Vol. V, p. 761 (15th ed. 1979).

[684] James Kent, *Commentaries on American Law*, Vol. 4, p. 10 (New York: 1826-1830) [Legal Classics Library 1986].

21.   Henry Peter Brougham (1828). Henry Peter Brougham was one of the leaders of the English bar in the early 19th century. As a member of the House of Commons and later of the House of Lords, he proposed a statute guaranteeing freedom of the press in 1816, sponsored the public education bill of 1820 and was a leader in forcing the Parliamentary Reform Act of 1832. He served as Chancellor of England from 1830 through 1834.[685]

He said that the jury system "is above all praise."[686] In his now-famous address to the House of Commons on February 7, 1828, "that gave direction to the reform of English civil procedure later in the 19th century," he spoke of his experience with the jury system:

> *Speaking from experience, . . . I must aver that I consider the method of juries a most wholesome, wise, and almost perfect invention, for the purpose of judicial inquiry. In the first place, it controls the judge, who might . . . have a prejudice against one party or a leaning toward another . . . or, what is as detrimental to justice, their counsel or attorneys. In the second place, it supplies that knowledge of the world . . . which judges seldom possess. . . .*
>
> *In the third place, what individual can so well weigh conflicting evidence, as twelve men indifferently chosen from . . . the community, of various habits, characters, prejudices and ability? . . .*
>
> *Lastly, what individual can so well assess the amount of damages which a plaintiff ought to recover for any injury he has received [than] . . . an intelligent jury? . . .*[687]

This question posed by Chancellor Brougham is at the heart of the present controversy over the preservation of the civil jury. If we accept the wisdom and experience of those who are quoted throughout this book, the answer is that no individual, no panel, no commission and no institution yet devised by the mind of man can so well assess the amount of a victim's damages as an impartial American jury.

---

[685]*Encyclopædia Britannica Micropædia*, Vol. II, p. 305 (15th ed. 1979).
[686]Mullins, *In Quest of Justice*, p. 259 (London 1931).
[687]*See* Lesser, *supra* n.676, pp. 223-224.

22. Sir Francis Palgrave, *The Rise and Progress of the English Commonwealth* (1832). Sir Francis Palgrave was a noted historian who made a significant contribution to the publication of English public records and was instrumental in the establishment of the Rolls of Parliament.[688] In his two-volume treatise on *The Rise and Progress of the English Commonwealth* (1832), he traced the evolution of "trial by the country" from the ancient policy of the Anglo-Saxons to the Legislation of Henry II (1154-1189). Calling this "great bulwark of English liberty" the "best safeguard of a free *Constitution*," Palgrave wrote that "during the whole of that period of the infancy of liberty," trial by jury served as the "mainspring of the machinery of remedial justice." He said that the jury system "brings the law home to every man's door" and that "both in its form and its consequences, it had a material influence upon the general *Constitution* of the realm."[689]

23. Jeremy Bentham (1748-1832). As an English utilitarian philosopher, Jeremy Bentham (1748-1832) "exerted a predominant influence on reforming of the 19th century."[690] His many publications included *A Fragment on Government* (1776), *An Introduction to Principles of Morals and Legislation* (1789), *The Rationale of Reward* (1825), *The Rationale of Punishment* (1830), and *The Rationale of Judicial Evidence*. According to the *Encyclopedia Britannica*, the fame of his *Principles of Morals and Legislation* (1789) "spread widely and rapidly," and "his advice was respectfully received in several of the states of Europe and America."[691] Of the English system of trial by judge and jury, he wrote:

> *The law of England has established the trial by judge and jury, in the conviction that it is the mode best calculated to ascertain the truth, and do the greatest amount of justice, in the great majority of cases.*[692]

---

[688] Holdsworth, *supra n.639*, Vol. 2, pp. 328, 423; Vol. 15, p. 351.

[689] Palgrave, *The Rise and Progress of the English Commonwealth*, Vol. 1, pp. 243-244, 276-277 (London 1832).

[690] *Encyclopædia Britannica Macropædia*, Vol. 2, pp. 837-839 (15th ed. 1979). *See* Stephen B. Presser's essay on Jeremy Bentham in *The Guide to American Law Encyclopedia*, Vol. 2, pp. 71-73 (West Publishing Co. 1984).

[691] *Encyclopædia Britannica*, *supra n.690*, p. 838.

[692] Quoted from the dedication page in Lesser, *supra n.676*. The quote is apparently from *The Rationale of Judicial Evidence* which is also cited in Lesser, p. 11 n.35.

The law of England has established the trial by judge and jury, in the conviction that it is the mode best calculated to ascertain the truth, and do the greatest amount of justice, in the great majority of cases.
—**Jeremy Bentham, English Philosopher (1832)**

24. **Justice Joseph Story (1833).** Joseph Story was born in Marblehead, Massachusetts, on September 18, 1779. He was elected Speaker of the Massachusetts House of Representatives and served one term in Congress prior to his appointment to the United States Supreme Court by President James Madison in November, 1811. He taught concurrently at Harvard Law School (1829-1845) and was a prolific author. His publications included *Commentaries on the Constitution of the United States* (3 vols., 1833), *The Conflict of Laws* (1834), and *Equity Jurisprudence* (2 vols., 1836).[693]

> *His opinion . . . in Martin v. Hunter's Lessee (1816) established the appellate authority of the Supreme Court over the highest state courts in all civil cases involving the federal constitution . . . [and] was called "the keystone of the whole arch of federal judicial power. . . ." His works on equity made him, along with Chancellor James Kent of New York, a founder of equity jurisprudence in the United States, and Story also came to be authoritative in England. . . .*[694]

In *United States v. Wonson* (1812), Justice Story wrote:

> *. . . At the time when the Constitution was submitted to the people for adoption, one of the most powerful objections urged against it was, that in civil causes it did not secure the trial of facts by a jury. . . . The advocates of the Constitution endeavored to remove the weight of this objection by showing, that it was within the authority of Congress to provide in all cases for the trial by jury. . . . Whoever will read . . . The Federalist, will learn how deeply the subject at the time interested the several states of the Union, and with what singular zeal and acuteness it was discussed. . . .*[695]

---

[693] *See Encyclopædia Britannica Micropædia*, Vol. IX, p. 593 (15th ed. 1979). Justice Story's *Commentaries on Equity Jurisprudence* were republished by the Legal Classics Library in 1988.

[694] *Encyclopædia Britannica*, supra. *See also* Stephen B. Presser's essay on Joseph Story in *The Guide to American Law*, Vol. 9, pp. 406-413 (West Publishing Co. 1984). Presser wrote that "of all U.S. judges, it was Joseph Story who probably exerted the greatest influence on the formation of the U.S. common law."

[695] *U.S. v. Wonson*, 28 Fed. Cas. 745, 750 (1812).

In his *Commentaries on the Constitution of the United States* (1833), Justice Story wrote that the language of the *Constitution* that "the Supreme Court shall have appellate jurisdiction, both as to law and fact" caused "no small alarm" because the people feared that it conveyed upon the Court "the power to review the decision of a jury in mere matters of fact; and thus, in effect, to destroy the validity of their verdict, and to reduce to a mere form the right of trial by jury in civil cases." He said that this objection "had a vast influence upon public opinion" and led to the adoption of the *Seventh Amendment*.[696]

> *... It is a most important and valuable amendment; and places upon the high ground of constitutional right the inestimable privilege of trial by jury in civil cases, a privilege scarcely inferior to that in criminal cases, which is conceded by all persons to be essential to political and civil liberty.*[697]

Of our constitutional right to trial by jury, Justice Story said:

> *Trial by jury is justly dear to the American people. It has been an object of deep interest and solicitude, and every encroachment upon it has been watched with great jealously....*[698]

In an article on our American jury system published in *Encyclopedia Americana* in 1831, Justice Story wrote:

> *It is not too much, then, to affirm that the trial by jury is justly the boast of England and America; and we may hope that, by the goodness of Providence it may be perpetual.*[699]

---

[696] Seven of the first eight states to ratify the *Constitution* proposed amendments guaranteeing the right of trial by jury in civil cases. *See* Schwartz, *The Roots of the Bill of Rights*, Vol. 7, p. 1167 (Chelsea House Publishers 1980).

[697] Story, *Commentaries on the Constitution of the United States*, Book III, pp. 653-654 (1833).

[698] *See* Forsythe, *History of Trial by Jury*, pp. 291-292 (Lenox Hill Publishing Co. 2d ed. 1878) [New York Public Library Reprint 1971].

[699] Hogan, "Joseph Story on Juries," 37 *Ore. L.R.* 234, 255 (1958).

25.   Justice William Johnson, The First Dissenter (1833). William Johnson of South Carolina was the first appointment to the United States Supreme Court by President Thomas Jefferson in 1804. Known as the "First Dissenter," he was "a man of unusual independence" who has been described as "one of the outstanding minds of the early Supreme Court" and who "stood firmly for the right of jury trial."[700] In 1833, he said that the right to trial by jury was among the "most inestimable privileges" of an American citizen.[701]

> *As a judge, he was concerned immediately with individual rights and accordingly deprecated the state's interference with trial by jury. In its precipitate course toward nullification, South Carolina had, by binding jurors to conform with its Ordinance, impaired a right Johnson deemed fundamental. The exponents of extreme states rights have thus ended by abridging an individual right. It was the protection of the lowliest individual, Johnson had said, for which the Union existed.*[702]

Justice Johnson was, in essence, a true defender of civil liberty.

> *. . . In opposition to the majority of his neighbors, he persevered in thinking that even slaves were entitled . . . to "due course of law." Rights of this sort, like trial by jury, had express footing in the Constitution. Johnson deemed them fundamental. These rights it was the special province of the judiciary to protect.*[703]

Not only is it "the special province" of our judiciary to protect the right of trial by jury, but it is also "the special province" of our President, our senators, our congressmen, our governors, our state legislators, and everyone who has taken a solemn oath to preserve, protect and defend the *Constitution of the United States*.

---

[700] *See* Morgan, *Justice William Johnson, The First Dissenter: The Career and Constitutional Philosophy of a Jeffersonian Judge,* pp. v, vii, 271 (University of South Carolina Press 1954).
[701] *Lessees of Livingston v. Moore,* 7 Pet. 469, 552 (1833).
[702] Morgan, *supra,* pp. 276-277.
[703] Morgan, *supra,* p. 296.

Trial by jury is among the most inestimable privileges of an American citizen. It is a fundamental right which protects the lowliest individual for which our union exists.

—**Justice William Johnson of South Carolina (1833)**

26. Alexis de Tocqueville, *Democracy in America* (1835).

In 1835, the famous French political scientist Alexis de Tocqueville wrote *Democracy in America*, a book which was "universally regarded as a sound, philosophical, impartial and remarkably clear and distinct view of our political institutions in the United States."[704] In it, he considered trial by jury both as a judicial and as a political institution, concluding that, particularly in civil cases, trial by jury was "one of the forms of sovereignty of the people" which affords "the most energetic means of making the people rule."[705]

What is unique about de Tocqueville's view of the civil jury is that, being native to a country whose civil justice system was based upon civil law as opposed to the English common law, he had the opportunity to view the civil jury system as a fair and impartial outside observer. Not having lived under the system, he had no opportunity to take it for granted as many in America do today. His was, in short, a fresh view upon the subject.

From the nature of his observations,[706] it is obvious that he studied his subject carefully with an insight seldom seen among the political scientists of today.

> *Of trial by jury, considered as a judicial institution, I shall here say but very few words. When the English adopted trial by jury they were a semi-barbarous people; they have become, in course of time, one of the most enlightened nations of the earth; and their attachment to this institution seems to have increased with their increasing cultivation. . . . A judicial institution which obtains the suffrages of a great people for long a series of ages, which is zealously renewed at every epoch of civilization, in all the climates of the earth, and under every form of human government, cannot be contrary to the spirit of justice.*

---

[704] *See* Preface to the American edition in de Tocqueville, *Democracy in America*, p. i (New York: 1838) [Legal Classics Library 1988].

[705] de Tocqueville, *supra*, pp. 281, 287, from the Alfred A. Knopf Company translation (1935). All of the cites to *Democracy in America* are to the 1838 edition [*see* n.704 above], so the translation and page citations may vary slightly.

[706] de Tocqueville, *supra*, pp. 262, 264-267.

... The system of the jury, as it is understood in America, appears ... as extreme a consequence of the sovereignty of the people, as universal suffrage.... All the sovereigns who have chosen to govern by their own authority, and to direct society instead of obeying its direction, have destroyed or enfeebled the institution of the jury....

When ... the influence of the jury is extended to civil causes, ... it affects all the interests of the community; everyone co-operates in its work: it thus penetrates into all the usages of life, it fashions the human mind to its particular forms, and is gradually associated with the idea of justice itself.

The institution of the jury, ... when once it is introduced into civil proceedings ... defies the aggressions of time and man. If it had been ... easy to remove the jury ... from the laws of England, it would have perished under Henry VIII and Elizabeth [I]; and the civil jury did in reality, at that period, save the liberties of the country. In whatever manner the jury be applied, it cannot fail to exercise a powerful influence upon the national character; but this influence is prodigiously increased when it is introduced into civil causes. The jury, and more especially the civil jury, serves to communicate the spirit of the judges to the minds of all citizens; and this spirit, with the habits which attend it, is the soundest preparation for free institutions. It imbues all classes with a respect for the thing judged, and with the notion of right.... It teaches men to practice equity; every man learns to judge his neighbor as he would himself be judged: and this is especially true of the jury in civil causes.... The jury teaches every man not to recoil before the responsibility of his own actions, and impresses him with that manly confidence without which political virtue cannot exist. It invests each citizen with a kind of magistracy; it makes them all feel the duties which they are bound to discharge toward society; and the part which they take in government. By obliging men to turn their attention to affairs which are not exclusively their own, it rubs off that individual egotism which is the rust of society.

The jury contributes most powerfully to form the judgment and to increase the natural intelligence of the people; and this is, in my opinion, its greatest advantage.... I think that the practical intelligence and political good sense of the Americans are mainly attributable to the long use which they have made of the jury in civil causes.... I look upon it as one of the most efficacious means for the education of the people, which society can employ....

... [I]n civil causes ... the judges appear as a disinterested arbiter between the conflicting passions of the parties. The jurors look up to him with confidence, and listen to him with respect.... Thus the jury, which is the most energetic means of making the people rule, is also the most efficacious means of teaching it to rule well.

Alexis de Tocqueville was a man of great understanding, a man of great wisdom, and a man of great insight into the foundations of free government. In the American jury system, he saw all that was good and valuable in a democratic institution. He found in it not only an institution unmatched in the enlightened and impartial administration of civil justice, but also an institution which strengthened the very fabric of a democratic society through citizen participation in the administration of justice.

We in America profess to be the greatest remaining fortress of free government on the face of the earth. Our ability to maintain that position depends on the support of our people and their elected and appointed officials for the preservation of our democratic institutions. As the renowned philosopher George Santayana and many others rightfully have said, trial by jury is pure, unvarnished, and unalloyed democracy. Shall we give it up now so that corporate America can supposedly become more prosperous? Has the destruction of democracy ever proved productive of economic prosperity?

Will we listen to William Blackstone and Patrick Henry, or to the insurance industry? Will we listen to Thomas Jefferson and James Madison, or to the editors of *Fortune* magazine? Will we listen to Alexis de Tocqueville and Winston Churchill, or to the National Association of Manufacturers and the American Medical Association? These are the questions we must answer, realizing that upon our answer rests the future of our country and the ultimate fate of the free world.

The civil jury is the most effective form of sovereignty of the people. It defies the aggressions of time and man. During the reigns of Henry VIII (1509-1547) and Elizabeth I (1558-1603), the civil jury did in reality save the liberties of England.

—French Political Scientist, Alexis de Tocqueville (1835)

27. **John Quincy Adams (1839).** John Quincy Adams served as a U.S. senator, as ambassador to Russia, as Secretary of State and as the sixth President of the United States (1825-1829). He has been called "one of America's greatest diplomats."[707] On April 30, 1839, he delivered an address to the New York Historical Society on the 50th anniversary of the inauguration of George Washington. Speaking of the spirit of the American Revolution, he said that "in the bosoms of this people . . . there was burning . . . one clear, steady flame of LIBERTY."

> *Resistance, instantaneous, unconcerted, sympathetic, inflexible resistance like an electric shock startled and roused the people of all the English colonies on this continent.*

For what did our forefathers fight? According to John Quincy Adams, it was, first and foremost, for trial by jury.

> *This was the first signal of North American Union. The struggle was for chartered rights — for English liberties — . . . for trial by jury — the habeas corpus and Magna Carta.*

> *But the English lawyers had decided that Parliament was omnipotent — and Parliament in their omnipotence, instead of trial by jury . . . enacted admiralty courts in England to try Americans for offenses charged against them as committed in America — instead of the privileges of Magna Carta. . . .*

> *English liberties had failed them. From the omnipotence of Parliament the colonists appealed to the rights of man and the omnipotence of the god of battles. . . .*

> *Independence was declared. The colonies were transformed into states. Their inhabitants were proclaimed to be one people . . . [with] all claims to chartered rights as Englishmen. Thenceforth their charter was the Declaration of Independence. Their rights, the natural rights of mankind. . . .*[708]

---

[707] *Encyclopædia Britannica Micropædia*, Vol. I, p. 79 (15th ed. 1979).

[708] Stedman, *Our Ageless Constitution*, pp. 215-216 (W. David Stedman Associates 1987).

28.   Henry John Stephen, *New Commentaries on the Laws of England* (1844). Henry John Stephen was a member of that select group of English advocates called Serjeants at Law,[709] and author of a four-volume treatise called *New Commentaries on the Laws of England*. In this work, he traced the history and procedure of "one of the most celebrated of English institutions" and concluded that "trial by jury ever has been looked upon as the glory of English law" and that "sensible and upright jurymen, chosen by lot from among those of the middle rank, will be found the best investigators of truth, and the surest guardians of public justice."

> ... It may be truly affirmed, that the most transcendent privilege which any subject can enjoy or wish for is, that he cannot be affected either in his property, his liberty, or his person, but by the unanimous consent of twelve of his neighbors and equals; and there can be no doubt that this Constitution has secured the just liberties of this nation for a long succession of ages. And therefore a celebrated French writer who concludes, that because Rome, Sparta and Carthage have lost their liberties, therefore those of England in time must perish, should have recollected that Rome, Sparta and Carthage, at the time when their liberties were lost, were strangers to trial by jury.[710]

Daniel Webster has said that "justice is the great interest of man on earth" and "the ligament which holds civilized beings and civilized nations together." John Greenleaf Whittier called justice "the hope of all who suffer" and "the dread of all who wrong." And Robert Maynard Hutchins wrote that equality and justice are "the two distinguishing characteristics of democracy" which "follow inevitably from the conception of men, *all men*, as rational spiritual beings." So if Henry John Stephen is right that "sensible and upright jurymen" are "the surest guardians of public justice," what do we do for public justice if we undermine our civil jury system? What do we do to "the great interest of man on earth" and "the ligament which holds civilized beings and civilized nations together" and to "the hope of all who suffer" if we tamper with "the most transcendent privilege" of an American citizen? We risk its total destruction and the untimely end of equal justice under law.

---

[709] *See* Holdsworth, *supra* n.639, Vol. 2, pp. 485-493.
[710] Stephen, *New Commentaries on the Laws of England*, Vol. III, pp. 588, 622-623 (1844) [Garland Pub. Co. 1979].

29. **Levi Woodbury, *Trial by Jury in Admiralty Cases* (1847).** Levi Woodbury (1789-1851) served as Associate Justice of the New Hampshire Superior Court, Speaker of the State House of Representatives and Governor of New Hampshire (1823-1824). He served two terms as U.S. Senator and was appointed Secretary of the Navy by President Andrew Jackson. He served as Secretary of the Treasury under President Martin Van Buren and was appointed Associate Justice of the United States Supreme Court in 1845 by President James K. Polk.

Dissenting in *Waring v. Clarke* (1847), he argued that citizens involved in disputes within the Admiralty jurisdiction were entitled to be tried by a jury of their fellow citizens. Referring to those "great principles, dear to the subject and his rights and liberties," he argued that the colonists had "remonstrated early and late, and complained of this abridgment of trial by jury even in the *Declaration of Independence* and as one prominent cause of the Revolution." He said that "our ancestors, both English and American, have resisted" non-jury Admiralty tribunals "for reasons most vital to public liberty." He wrote of those principles "dear to free men of the Saxon race — preferring the trial by jury, and the common law, to a single judge in admiralty . . . [which] could be no less highly prized by our American fathers than their English ancestry."

Without intending to enter with any minuteness into the origin and history of admiralty jurisdiction abroad, it will be sufficient . . . to say that the trial by jury and the common law, so ardently adhered to by the Anglo-Saxons . . . where a jury could easily be summoned, and where the principles of the common law had ever in England been accustomed to prevail . . . , it was sufficient to make them look on the admiralty as a foreign and odious interloper . . . ; and it was regarded by the commons and barons of England as an intruder into that realm, and without the sanction of Parliament.

In the course of a few years, that same sturdy spirit, . . . in Magna Carta was unwilling to let the laws of England be changed. . . . And they have ever since retained it there . . . , from the highest principles of safety to the common law, English liberties, and the inestimable trial by jury — principles surely no less dear in a republic than a monarchy.[711]

---

[711] Dissenting Opinion of Justice Woodbury in *Waring v. Clarke*, 5 How. (46 U.S.) 441, 467-503 (1847).

Our ancestors, both English and American, have resisted non-jury tribunals for reasons most vital to public liberty. They remonstrated on the abridgment of trial by jury even in the Declaration of Independence and it was a prominent cause of the Revolution.
—**U.S. Supreme Court Justice Levi Woodbury (1847)**

30. William Forsythe, *History of Trial by Jury* (1852).

According to W. S. Holdsworth, William Forsythe (1812-1899) was "a famous man of his day." He served as Queen's Counsel, Treasurer of the Inner Temple, a member of the House of Commons, and Secretary of State for India. As a prolific author, he wrote *A History of the Captivity of Napoleon*, *A Life of Cicero* and *A History of Advocacy in Ancient Greece*. His most important legal treatises included *Cases and Opinions on Constitutional Law* (1869) and "a careful and learned summary" regarded as "the standard history of the jury."[712] In his "classic treatise,"[713] *History of Trial by Jury* (1852), William Forsythe considered the jury "as a social, political and judicial institution."

> ... Now the very essence of jury trial is its principle of fairness. The right of being tried by his equals, that is, his fellow citizens, taken indiscriminately from the mass, who feel neither malice nor favor, but simply decide according to what in their conscience they believe to be the truth, gives every man a conviction that he will be dealt with impartially, and inspires him with the wish to mete out to others the same measure of equity that is dealt to himself.[714]

Considering the jury's contribution to the establishment and preservation of our other fundamental rights, Forsythe wrote that freedom of the press, "which we justly prize as one of the first social blessings, is chiefly indebted to the jury for its vigorous existence."[715] He called the jury system our best "means of protecting innocence" and asserted that "the concurrence of the people in the administration of the law, through the medium of the jury, greatly increases the respect and reverence paid to the judges." He concluded that "the jury acts as a constant check upon, and correction of, that narrow subtlety to which professional lawyers are so prone, and subjects the rules of rigid technicality to be construed by a vigorous common sense."

---

[712] Holdsworth, *supra n.639*, Vol. 15, pp. 273, 346-347, 374. Holdsworth called Forsythe's *Cases and Opinions on Constitutional Law* the most important case-book on that subject.

[713] *Encyclopædia Britannica Macropædia*, Vol. 10, pp. 360-362 (15th ed. 1979).

[714] Forsythe, *History of Trial by Jury*, p. 354 (2d ed. 1878).

[715] Forsythe, *supra*, p. 364.

> *. . . Calling the English jury that "great court of appeal," Forsythe wrote: For to what end is the machinery of the Constitution employed, but to give every man his due, and protect all in the enjoyment of their property, liberty, and rights? And the twelve men in the jury box are in this country the great court of appeal, when in the case of the humblest as well as the most exalted citizen, these or any of these are attacked. Long may it be so! And while other nations are heaving with the throes of revolution, and regard their polity with discontent, long may the characteristics of England be her attachment to the institutions handed down to us by our forefathers — her confidence in the pure and upright administration of justice — and her reverence for the law.*[716]

31.   Lysander Spooner (1852). Lysander Spooner was a Massachusetts lawyer and an ardent abolitionist. In 1852, he published *An Essay on the Trial by Jury* in which he wrote that inherent in that institution was "that first and indispensable requisite in a judicial tribunal, *integrity*."

> *Legislators and judges are necessarily exposed to all the temptations of money, fame, and power, to induce them to disregard justice between parties and sell the rights, and violate the liberties of the people. Jurors, on the other hand, are exposed to none of these temptations. They are not liable to bribery, for they are unknown to the parties until they come into the jury-box. They can rarely gain either fame, power, or money, by giving erroneous decisions. Their offices are temporary, and they know that when they shall have executed them, they must return to the people, to hold all their rights in life subject to the liability of such judgments . . . as they themselves have given an example for. The laws of human nature do not permit the supposition that twelve men, taken by lot from the mass of the people, and acting under such circumstances, will all prove dishonest. . . . A jury, therefore, ensures to us — what no other court does — that first and indispensable requisite in a judicial tribunal, integrity.*[717]

---

[716]Forsythe, *supra n.714*, pp. 366, 378-379, 382.
[717]Lysander Spooner, *An Essay on the Trial by Jury*, pp. 124-125 (Boston: 1852) [Legal Classics Library 1989].

32. Justice Joseph N. Whitner of South Carolina (1856). Justice Whitner served in the South Carolina General Assembly, as a circuit solicitor, circuit judge and as a justice on the South Carolina Court of Appeals from 1850 through 1859. His biographer, Governor B. F. Perry, described him as "one of the kindest, most amiable and best of men."[718] In *McCoy v. Lemmon* (1856), for a unanimous court, Judge Whitner wrote:

> *The Constitutions adopted by the different States of this Union, as well as the whole current of legislation and adjudication, demonstrate the great jealousy of the American people on the subject of jury trial. So universally regarded as a great palladium in England and America, we may well be cautious of any innovation.... [T]he judgment of a panel of twelve men has been incorporated as an indispensable element in the judicial administration of the country. Our notions may well be pronounced inveterate as to this mode of securing rights and redressing wrongs.*[719]

33. John Norton Pomeroy, *An Introduction to Municipal Law* (1863). John Norton Pomeroy (1828-1885) "achieved prominence as a jurist, educator, and legal author during the latter part of the 19th century."[720] He served on the faculty of New York University and later at Hastings College in San Francisco. He created and edited the *West Coast Reporter* during the 1880's and authored many publications. "His first book, *An Introduction to Municipal Law*, was considered an important text book for law students."[721] In it, he wrote:

> *... We are bound to the jury trial by all the holiest traditions of our past history; we esteem it as the very bulwark of our liberties....*[722]

---

[718]"Joseph N. Whitner by Governor B. F. Perry," in Brooks, *South Carolina Bench and Bar*, Vol. 1, pp. 121-124 (State Publishing Co. 1908).

[719]*McCoy v. Lemmon*, 11 Rich. (45 S.C.L.) 165, 176 (1856).

[720]*The Guide to American Law Encyclopedia*, Vol. 8, pp. 232-233 (West Publishing Co. 1984).

[721]*Guide to American Law, supra.*

[722]Pomeroy, *An Introduction to Municipal Law*, § 6 (1864), quoted on the Dedication Page to Maximus A. Lesser, *The Historical Development of the Jury System* (Lawyers Cooperative Publishing Co. 1894).

We are bound to the jury trial by all the holiest traditions of our past history; we esteem it as the very bulwark of our liberties.
—American Author John Norton Pomeroy (1863)

34. Eli K. Price, *Discourse on the Trial by Jury* (1863).
Of Eli K. Price of Philadelphia (1797-1884), it has been written that "few if any American lawyers devoted so much of their time and experience to the improvement of the law." In an address to the American Philosophical Society in 1863, he called trial by jury a "time honored institution" which has served the American citizen as "a bulwark of liberty and justice."[723]

> . . . Such an immunity in ages of violence and insecurity, must have been regarded as of inestimable value, and as no age or country is exempt from the violence of prejudice and excitement, and the partialities of similar social condition, this security of trial by one's peers should forever be regarded as an inappreciable inheritance.
>
> Justice is always administered with the highest satisfaction to the citizen, when he is satisfied with those who are to adjudge his rights. When assured that the jury are his equals, possessing a common interest with himself in the laws to which they are to give effect, he is best prepared to yield his confidence, and to abide their verdict. . . .
>
> This institution of trial by jury . . . since an unknown antiquity has been consecrated in the affections of the only nations of the earth truly free. . . .
>
> Trial by jury is necessarily a public proceeding, and that publicity is the strongest guarantee against judicial favoritism and corruption. . . . And thus too . . . the whole public are learning the principles of law by which they hold their property and enjoy their rights. . . . Supersede this system by cheaper modes . . . and we shall . . . soon lose those characteristics which make us a nation of free men.
>
> . . . God grant in his goodness that, in the words of our Constitution, it may forever remain inviolate.[724]

---

[723]*Dictionary of American Biography*, Vol. 3, p. 212 (1963).
[724]Price, *A Discourse on the Trial by Jury*, pp. 6-8, 23-24 (Caxton Press, Philadelphia 1863).

35.   Jeremiah S. Black, *Argument for the Petitioner in Ex Parte Milligan* **(1866).** By Proclamation dated September 15, 1863, President Lincoln suspended the privilege of the *Writ of Habeas Corpus* where, by his authority, military or civil officers held persons in their custody "either as prisoners of war, spies, or aiders or abettors of the enemy." On October 5, 1864, Lamdin P. Milligan, a civilian, was arrested at his residence in Indiana, charged with "affording aid and comfort to rebels against the authority of the United States," tried by a military tribunal and sentenced to death by hanging.

On May 10, 1865, Milligan petitioned the Circuit Court of the United States for the District of Indiana for a *Writ of Habeas Corpus* and his claim for the right of trial by jury was argued before the Supreme Court of the United States by Jeremiah S. Black, former Chief Justice of Pennsylvania (1851-1857), Attorney General of the United States (1857-1860), and Secretary of State (1860-1861). In Milligan's behalf, Black argued that the military commission had no jurisdiction to try him "and that the right of trial by jury was guaranteed to him by the *Constitution of the United States.*"[725] In his argument to the court, Black maintained that trial by jury "is the best protection for innocence, and the surest mode of punishing guilt, that has yet been discovered."

> *. . . It has borne the test of a longer experience, and borne it better than any other legal institution that ever existed among men. England owes more of her freedom, her grandeur, and her prosperity to that than to all other causes put together. It had the approbation not only of those who lived under it, but of great thinkers who looked at it calmly from a distance, and judged it impartially. Montesquieu and de Tocqueville speak of it with admiration as rapturous as Coke and Blackstone. . . .*
>
> *Those colonists of this country who came from the British Islands . . . regarded it as the most precious part of their inheritance. The immigrants from other places, where trial by jury did not exist, became equally attached to it as soon as they understood what it was. There was no subject upon which all the inhabitants of the country were more perfectly unanimous than they were in their determination to maintain this great right unimpaired. . . .*

---

[725] *Ex Parte Milligan*, 71 U.S. (4 Wall.) 2, 108 (1866).

> *If the men who fought our revolution . . . had failed to insert a provision making trial by jury perpetual and universal, they would have . . . proved themselves basely recreant to the principles of that very liberty of which they professed to be the special champions. But they were guilty of no such treachery. . . .*
>
> *But our fathers were not absurd enough to . . . take away the protection of law from the rights of individuals. . . . They went over the Magna Carta, the Petition of Right, the Bill of Rights, and the Rules of the Common Law, and whatever was found there to favor individual liberty they carefully inserted in their own system, improved by clearer expression, strengthened by heavier sanctions, and extended by a more universal application. . . .*
>
> *If these provisions exist in full force, . . . every citizen may safely pursue his lawful calling in the open day; and at night, . . . he may lie down in security, and sleep the sound sleep of a free man.*[726]

36. Justice David Davis, *Opinion in Ex Parte Milligan* (1866). Appointed Associate Justice of the United States Supreme Court in 1862 by President Lincoln, *Ex Parte Milligan* was Justice David Davis' "most significant opinion."[727] In reversing Milligan's conviction by a military tribunal, Justice Davis wrote that "the importance of the main question presented by this record cannot be overstated; for it involves the very framework of the government and the fundamental principles of American liberty." Calling the right of trial by jury "one of the most valuable in a free country," Justice Davis wrote that all citizens "are guaranteed the inestimable privilege of trial by jury," a "vital principle, underlying the whole administration of criminal justice." In a separate, concurring opinion, Chief Justice Salmon P. Chase wrote:

> *We assent, fully, to all that is said, in the opinion, of the inestimable value of the trial by jury, and of the other constitutional safeguards of civil liberty.*[728]

---

[726] *See* Rousse, "Trial by Jury," *The University of Texas Bulletin* No. 3028, pp. 121-124 (July 22, 1930).

[727] de Gregorio, *The Complete Book of U.S. Presidents*, pp. 240-241 (Dembner Books 2d ed. 1984).

[728] *Ex Parte Milligan*, 71 U.S. (4 Wall.) 2, 109, 123, 137 (1866).

The right of trial by jury involves the very framework of the government and the fundamental principles of American liberty. The inestimable privilege of trial by jury is one of the most valuable in a free country.
—U.S. Supreme Court Justice David Davis (1866)

37. Emory Washburn, *Lectures on the Study and Practice of Law* (1871). Emory Washburn (1800-1877) graduated from Harvard Law School in 1820, was a member of both Houses of the Massachusetts legislature (1826-1842), presided over the Court of Common Pleas (1844-1847), and served as governor of the state (1854-1855). In his later years, he joined the faculty of Harvard Law School where he authored *Sketches of the Judicial History of Massachusetts from 1630 to 1775* (1840), *A Treatise on the American Law of Real Property* (1860-1862); and *A Treatise on the American Law of Easements and Servitudes* (1863).[729] In his *Study and Practice of Law* (1871), he wrote of the superiority of "the honest instincts of a juror" in the judicial fact-finding process:

> . . . *The people have no safeguard or protection on which they can so confidently rely for life or property, as upon an enlightened and independent judiciary. But when men talk gravely of substituting the learning and experience of the court for the good sense, practical experience and unbiased instincts of an impartial jury, they do violence to history, and injustice to the cause of personal liberty and right. . . . [F]or trying and settling disputed questions of fact, through the instrumentality of human testimony, where men and their motives are to be weighed and scrutinized, and balances are struck between conflicting witnesses, I had rather trust to the verdict of twelve fair-minded men of average shrewdness and intelligence in a jury box. . . . I had rather trust to the honest instincts of a juror, than the learning of a judge. . . .*[730]

38. Justice Ward Hunt on the Superiority of a Civil Jury (1873). An opponent to the expansion of slavery, Ward Hunt served in the New York legislature (1838-1840) and was elected mayor of Utica in 1844. He was appointed to the New York Court of Appeals in 1865 and became Chief Justice in 1868. President Ulysses S. Grant nominated him to the United States Supreme Court in 1872 where he served for five years. In *Railroad Co. v. Stout*, 84 U.S. 657, 664 (1873), speaking in support of a unanimous Supreme Court, Justice Hunt wrote:

---

[729]*The Guide to American Law Encyclopedia*, Vol. 10, p. 315 (West Publishing Co. 1884).

[730]Washburn, *Lectures on the Study and Practice of the Law*, pp. 177-178 (1871) [Fred B. Rothman & Co. 1982].

344

. . . Twelve men of the average of the community, comprising men of education and men of little education, men of learning and men whose learning consists only in what they have themselves seen and heard, the merchant, the mechanic, the farmer, the laborer; these sit together, consult, apply their separate experience of the affairs of life to the facts proven, and draw a unanimous conclusion. This average judgment thus given is the great effort of the law to obtain. It is assumed that twelve men know more of the common affairs of life than does one man, that they can draw wiser and safer conclusions from admitted facts thus occurring than can a single judge.

39.   John Proffatt, *A Treatise on Trial by Jury* (1877).

John Proffatt (1845-1879) compiled the 11-volume series, *The American Decisions 1760-1869* and authored *A Treatise on Trial by Jury* (1877). In it, Proffatt reported that, since the *Magna Carta*, the right of trial by jury has been regarded as an "inestimable privilege by the English race."

The English colonists settled here with a deep-rooted regard for this right. It had been, no doubt, to them in the Mother Country a valuable protection. They brought it with them and established it and cherished it as one of their dearest privileges, and in every enumeration of their rights and immunities it takes a conspicuous place. . . . Ever since Magna Carta, the right of trial by jury has been esteemed a peculiarly dear and inestimable privilege by the English race; . . . and whenever an invasion or violation of individual rights was threatened, the security afforded by this guaranty was relied on as an effectual safeguard either to repel the attack or nullify its effect.[731]

It is significant that the invasion of individual rights which is threatened today is to the institution of trial by jury itself. Should we lose it, what security will we have against the next invasion? Paraphrasing Patrick Henry, is our economy so sweet and our prosperity to dear to be purchased by the surrender of our most democratic institution? *Forbid it, Almighty God!*

---

[731]Proffatt, *A Treatise on Trial by Jury*, §§ 81, 82, pp. 120-122 (Hurd & Houghston 1877).

40.   Edward P. Wilder, "The Clown of the Law," (1879).
In 1879, Edward P. Wilder of the New York Bar responded to a recent contributor to the *Albany Law Journal* who had characterized the jury as "the clown of the law." Calling a typical jury "a fair sample of the community at large," Wilder wrote:

> . . . But for downright common sense, unsophisticated by too much learning, and for that sort of shrewdness which discerns the truth hidden in the bowels of a complicated dispute, commends us to a jury of twelve plain men of affairs. It is typical of our democratic institutions. . . .[732]

41.   John Duke, Lord Coleridge, Chief Justice of England, *On the Jury System* (January 4, 1879). John Duke, Lord Coleridge (1820-1894), was appointed Judge of the King's Bench in 1853, became Attorney General in 1871, rose to Chief Justice of the Common Pleas in 1873 and Lord Chief Justice of England in 1880. An article in *The Solicitor's Journal* on January 4, 1879, reported Lord Coleridge's views on the English jury system:

> The interesting of a great number of persons in the discharge of justice, the education to a certain extent which the jury system affords to a large number of persons in our community, is a matter that is far too much lost sight of. . . . I believe that much of the satisfaction which I hope and trust does exist, with our administration of justice as a whole . . . may to a great extent be traced to the large infusion of what I may call the popular element, and the popular element in the administration of our system of justice is the jury. . . .[733]

What will happen to public confidence in our American system of civil justice if the people are deprived of their only voice in its administration? At a time when public confidence in government has reached a record low, is it wise to consolidate the reins of power in the hands of the privileged few who are subject to the same corrupting influences to which other public officials have succumbed? The answer is obvious.

---

[732]Wilder, "The Clown of the Law," 20 *Albany Law J.* 45, 47 (1879).
[733]23 *The Solicitor's Journal* 178 (1879).

The jury system involves a great number of persons in the discharge of justice. Much of the satisfaction with our administration of justice as a whole may be traced to the large infusion of the popular element which the jury adds to the administration of our system of justice.
—John Duke, Lord Coleridge, Chief Justice of England (1879)

42. Sir James Fitzjames Stephen, *A History of the Criminal Law of England* (1883). James Fitzjames Stephen (1829-1894) was a distinguished criminal lawyer, jurist and judge whom W. S. Holdsworth considered to be "*the historian* of our criminal law." He authored *A General View of the Criminal Law of England* (1863), "the most original of all books on the criminal law." His edition of *Blackstone's Commentaries* has been called "the most important of student's books."[734]

During his service on the High Court of Justice (1879-1891),[735] Judge Stephen published his 3-volume treatise entitled *A History of the Criminal Law of England* (1883). In it, he wrote of the institution of trial by jury as follows:

> ... The public at large feel more sympathy with jury-men than they do with judges, and accept their verdicts with much less hesitation and distrust than they would feel towards judgments however ably written or expressed. ... Trial by jury interests large numbers of people in the administration of justice and makes them responsible for it. It is difficult to overestimate the importance of this. It gives a degree of power and popularity to the administration of justice which could hardly be derived from any other source.[736]

43. Justice Stanley Matthews (1885). Stanley Matthews (1824-1889) was "a large, strongly built, earnest man" who spoke with "dignity and precision" and was "brimful of intense, stalwart courage and imperial determination."[737] He was admitted to the Bar at age 18 in 1842 and appointed prosecuting attorney for Cincinnati at age 20 in 1844. He served as Clerk of the Ohio House of Representatives, Judge of the Court of Common Pleas, a member of Ohio Senate, U.S. Attorney and U.S. Senator (1877-1879). He was nominated to the United States Supreme Court first by President Rutherford B. Hayes and then by President James A. Garfield where he served from 1881 until his death in 1889.[738]

---

[734]Holdsworth, *supra* n.639, Vol. 13, p. 287; Vol. 15, pp. 147, 290, 368.

[735]*Guide to American Law, supra* n.729, Vol. 9, p. 392.

[736]Stephen, *A History of the Criminal Law of England*, Vol. 1, pp. 572-573 (Macmillan & Co. 1883).

[737]Donovan, *Modern Jury Trials and Advocates*, p. 471 (4th ed. 1911).

[738]*Guide to American Law, supra* n.729, Vol. 7, pp. 306-307.

On the Supreme Court, Justice Matthews "clearly won the respect of his colleagues." He was "a believer in the sanctity of the law" who "exhibited an independence and clarity of thought considered brilliant for his day."[739] His most notable opinion was in *Yick Wo v. Hopkins* (1886), where he held that "the discriminatory administration of otherwise just laws violated the equal protection clause of the 14th amendment."[740] On the subject of the *Seventh Amendment*, he wrote:

> *The right of trial by jury in the courts of the United States is expressly secured by the Seventh Article of Amendment to the Constitution. . . . This constitutional right this court has always guarded with jealousy. . . .*[741]

44.   D. H. Chamberlain, *The American System of Trial by Jury* (1887). In an address before the Annual Convention of the American Social Science Association on September 8, 1887, D. H. Chamberlain of New York, formerly Attorney General (1868-1872) and Governor of South Carolina (1874-1876),[742] described the development of the institution of trial by jury in England and its adoption in this country as one of the fundamental rights of the American citizen.

> *Embedded thus in the historical foundations of the civil government and jurisprudence of the English people, entrenched behind the strongest and most permanent defenses which the people of this country can erect — the organic laws and Constitutions of the United States and of the several states — trial by jury presents itself as one of the foremost features of the system of jurisprudence under which the English race has been trained, concurrently with which it has gained its liberties, and through which it is believed, as is evident, those liberties will in the future be preserved.*[743]

---

[739]Filler, "Biography of Stanley Matthews," pp. 1351, 1360, Vol. II, *Justices of the United States Supreme Court 1789-1969: Their Lives and Major Opinions* (1969).

[740]de Gregorio, *The Complete Book of U.S. Presidents*, p. 302 (2d ed. 1989). See Yick Wo v. Hopkins, 118 U.S. 536 (1886).

[741]*Baylis v. Travelers Ins. Co.*, 113 U.S. 316, 321 (1885).

[742]*Encyclopedia of Southern History*, p. 194 (1979).

[743]Chamberlain, *The American System of Trial by Jury*, pp. 17-21 (George E. Crosby Press, Boston 1887).

45. Elihu Root, *Addresses on Government and Citizenship* **(1894).** Elihu Root (1845-1937) served as Secretary of War under President McKinley, Secretary of State under President Theodore Roosevelt, U.S. Senator, Chief Counsel for the United States before The Hague Tribunal, and President of Carnegie Endowment for International Peace. He received Honorary Doctor of Law degrees from Harvard, Yale, Princeton, Columbia, California, NYU and Oxford.[744] He led a U.S. diplomatic mission to Russia in 1917 and, "for these and other contributions to peace and world harmony" he was awarded the Nobel Peace Prize in 1912.[745]

"Root also achieved prominence for his numerous publications, including *Experiment in Government and The Essentials of the Constitution* (1913) and *Russia and the United States* (1917)."[746]

Elihu Root, in supporting trial by jury as one of our most cherished institutions, stressed the system's effectiveness in protecting the people against judges.[747]

As floor leader of the New York Constitutional Convention of 1894, he said:

. . . I believe that [trial by jury] is one of the most important, most vital, most sacred of the institutions which maintain our free and popular government. I believe that it serves to bring the people . . . into immediate participation in the administration of the law. I believe that it mitigates the severe logic of the law, and makes its administration tolerable. . . . [Trial by jury is] the most vital matter in the administration of the law . . . ; and I will never consent, if I vote alone, against overwhelming majorities, to take away one jot or tittle of the strength, stability and the perpetuity of that safeguard.[748]

---

[744] *Guide to American Law, supra n.729,* Vol. 9, pp. 67-68.
[745] *Encyclopædia Britannica Micropædia,* Vol. VIII, pp. 666-667 (15th ed. 1979).
[746] *Guide to American Law, supra n.729.*
[747] Meagher, "Trial by Jury Deserves a Fair Trial," 36 *N.Y.S.B.J.* 303, 307 (August, 1964).
[748] Elihu Root, as quoted in *Addresses on Government and Citizenship,* pp. 122-123 (Harvard University Press 1916).

Trial by Jury is one of the most important, most vital, most sacred of the institutions which maintain our free and popular government. It serves to bring the people into immediate participation in the administration of law and makes its administration tolerable.

—**Nobel Peace Prize Winner Elihu Root (1894)**

46. Maximus A. Lesser (1894).

In 1894, Lawyers Cooperative Publishing Company published one of the most thorough investigations of the historical development of trial by jury in existence at that time. Authored by Maximus A. Lesser, of the New York Bar, *The Historical Development of the Jury System* traces the origins of the modern American jury through the *Dikasts* of Greece, the *Judices* of Rome, the tribunals of the ancient Germans, the institutions of the early Britons, the legal system of the Anglo-Saxons, and the customs of William the Conqueror to the refinement of the civil jury system under Henry II (1154-1189). He summarizes his findings in the concluding chapter entitled, "Present Aspects of the Jury."[749]

> *We have thus traced the history of the jury ... and submit the following conclusions: first, that an institution resembling the modern jury in various respects must have existed in England — brought thither by the Romans, and originating among the Greeks — at the earliest civilized period; ... and ... that ... it was formally established by positive legislation as an ingredient of our jurisprudence in the reign and by the will of [Henry II (1154-1189)]. ...*[750]

Observing that our civil jury system was under attack even then,[751] Lesser noted that "its champions contend" that civil jury service provides the citizen a lesson in applied civics.[752] He quotes the French author, Sikyes, as saying that "*the judgment by jurors is the true guaranty of individual liberty in England, and in every other country in the world where men aspire to freedom.*"[753]

---

[749] Maximus A. Lesser, *The Historical Development of the Jury System*, Ch. 12, pp. 171-224 (Lawyers Cooperative Publishing Co. 1894).

[750] Lesser, *supra*, p. 171.

[751] "The great point of attack, however, is the civil jury. ..." Lesser, *supra*, p. 176.

[752] "[I]ts champions contend that 'one marked benefit' of the system, which has done much to distinguish English and American civilization from that of other countries is, that it affords a school for the more intelligent and responsible citizens in the principles and details of the municipal law. ..." Lesser, *supra*, p. 173.

[753] Lesser, *supra*, Dedication page.

47. J.E.R. Stephens, *The Growth of Trial by Jury in England* (1896). J.E.R. Stephens, Barrister at Law of London, served as Magistrate for Her Majesty's Court of Zanzibar, Judge of Kingston Court, Jamaica, Senior Prison Judge of the Supreme Court of Kenya, and a member of the Court of Appeal for East Africa.[754] In an 1896 article for the *Harvard Law Review*, he traced the growth and development of the English jury system from Henry I (1100-1135) through George I (1714-1727). He concluded that "the very essence of trial by jury is its principle of fairness" which is "the reason why the English jury flourishes still in its pristine vigor."

> ... [T]he distinguishing characteristic of the system is that the jury consists of a body of men taken from the community at large, and summoned for the purpose of finding the truth of disputed facts, who are quite distinct from the judges of the court. Their duty is to decide upon the effect of evidence, so that the court may be able to pronounce a right judgment. Twelve men of ordinary ability are just as capable of deciding today on the effect of evidence as they were in the infancy of the institution....[755]

48. James Bradley Thayer, *A Preliminary Treatise on Evidence at Common Law* (1898). James Bradley Thayer served as professor at Harvard Law School from 1874 to 1902 and "was regarded as an expert on Constitutional law and the law of evidence." He "received acclaim for several important publications" and was instrumental in the development of the case method of teaching law.[756]

In his *Preliminary Treatise on Evidence at Common Law* (1898), Professor Thayer devoted 136 pages to "Trial by Jury and its Development." Noting that England was substantially populated by Germanic races, he commented that "nothing among them was more ancient than the idea and practice of popular justice." He praised the jury system for its "intrinsic fairness" and called it the most "rational mode of determining questions of fact."[757]

---

[754] *Who Was Who Among English and European Authors*, Vol. 3, p. 1343 (1978).

[755] J.E.R. Stephens, "The Growth of Trial by Jury in England," 10 *Harv. L.R.* 150, 152, 160 (1896).

[756] *Guide to American Law, supra* n. 729, Vol. 10, p. 77.

[757] Thayer, *A Preliminary Treatise on Evidence at Common Law*, pp. 8, 59-60 (Little, Brown & Co. 1898). *See also* Thayer, "The Jury and its Development," Parts I, II and III, 5 *Harv. L.R.* 249, 296, 357 (1892).

49. Joseph Choate, The Value of the Jury (1898). By the close of the 19th century, attacks upon the civil jury had escalated to such an extent that, in 1898, distinguished trial lawyer Joseph H. Choate devoted his annual address as President of the American Bar Association to the virtues of the civil jury system. Mr. Choate said that the jury has proved itself to be "an invaluable security for the enjoyment of life, liberty and property for so many centuries" that it is "justly appreciated" as the best means for "admitting the people to a share . . . in the administration of justice" and it is "an indispensable factor in educating them in their personal and civil rights."[758]

> *It is for the integrity, efficiency, and utility of trial by jury in civil causes that I am chiefly concerned. . . . For I cherish as the result of a life's work . . . that the old fashioned trial by jury of twelve honest and intelligent citizens remains today . . . the best and safest practical method for the determination of facts . . . , and that all attempts to tinker or tamper with it should be discouraged as disastrous to the public welfare.*[759]

Mr. Choate concluded his remarks to the American Bar Association as follows:

> *Give us then competent jurors, able judges, and honest, fearless and learned advocates, and trial by jury, which . . . [to] the people of America . . . will . . . be the best safeguard of their lives, their liberties and their property.*[760]

What Joseph Choate said in 1898 is equally true today. Able judges, honest and fearless advocates, and trial by jury are the best safeguard of our lives, our liberties and our property. Seven and a half centuries after King John sealed the *Magna Carta*, trial by jury is still "the citadel of freedom," "the conscience of the community," "the cornerstone of our judicial process," and "the touchstone of contemporary common sense."

---

[758] Joiner, *Civil Justice and the Jury*, pp. 113-120 (Prentice Hall 1962) [reprinted by Greenwood Press 1972, 1977], reprinted from the *Report of the 21st Annual Meeting of the American Bar Association*, Vol. 21 (Dando Publishing Co. 1898).

[759] Joiner, *supra*, p. 114.

[760] Joiner, *supra*, pp. 120-121.

Trial by jury in civil causes remains today the best and safest practical method for the determination of facts, and all attempts to tinker or tamper with it should be discouraged as disastrous to the public welfare.

—ABA President Joseph Choate (1898)

50. Sir Frederick Pollock, *The History of English Law* (1899). Frederick Pollock (1845-1937) "played a prominent role in the advancement of the study of English law and in the resurgence of interest in English legal history during the late 19th and early 20th centuries." As a prolific author, his major works included *Principles of Contract at Law and in Equity* (1876) and a companion work on *The Law of Torts* (1877), "the standard text used by English legal educators for many years." He served as Professor of Jurisprudence at Oxford University and as Visiting Professor at Harvard and Columbia Law Schools. He helped draft the English *Partnership Act of 1890*, was editor of the *Law Quarterly Review* and was "a major supporting influence in the establishment of the Selden Society." He served as Judge of the Admiralty Court, King's Council and Chairman of the Royal Commission on Public Records.[761] His other works included *A First Book of Jurisprudence* (1896), *The Expansion of the Common Law* (1904), *The Genius of the Common Law* (1912) and *The League of Nations* (1920).

He co-authored with Frederic William Maitland *The History of English Law Before the Time of Edward I* (1895) in which they traced the origin of the modern jury to "the Frankish Empire of the 9th century," later brought to England by William the Conqueror in 1066 A.D.[762] One hundred years after trial by jury crossed the English Channel, its use and acceptance was broadly expanded during the reign of Henry II (1154-1189). Pollock & Maitland referred to Henry II's expansion of the jury system as one of his "most durable and the most fruitful" legacies "which modern Englishmen will be apt to think of as the most distinctive" contribution of his reign. Pollock & Maitland maintained that "the English jury has been so highly prized by Englishmen [and] so often copied by foreigners" that it could correctly claim to be the "*palladium of our liberties*."[763]

> *. . . The verdict of the jurors . . . [was] deemed to be the voice of the countryside. . . . [It] was associated with the protection of the weak against the strong . . . [and] became a cherished institution [which] was connected in their minds with all the liberties they held dear.*[764]

---

[761] *A Guide to American Law Encyclopedia*, Vol. 8, pp. 235-236 (West Publishing Co. 1984).

[762] Pollock & Maitland, *The History of English Law*, Vol. 1, p. 141 (2d ed. 1899) [Legal Classics Library 1982].

[763] Pollock & Maitland, *supra*, Vol. 1, pp. 138-142.

[764] Pollock & Maitland, *supra*, Vol. 2, pp. 624, 632.

51. Judge Henry Clay Caldwell, *Trial by Judge and Jury* **(1899).** Henry Clay Caldwell (1832-1915) was admitted to the Iowa Bar in 1852. He was elected to the state legislature in 1858 and in 1860, he was a delegate to the Republican National Convention which nominated Abraham Lincoln for President. He served as a major in the Iowa Cavalry and in June, 1864, while yet on active service, he was appointed by President Lincoln United States District Judge for the District of Arkansas.

> *The people of Arkansas viewed Caldwell at first with suspicion, if not aversion, as a northern . . . intruder. Displaying, however, great firmness and courage, and resolutely resisting political pressure, he administered justice with scrupulous impartiality, and by his tact, common sense, and expedition gradually obtained the respect and confidence of the populace. It was said of him that "during the six years that the carpet-bag régime lasted he was the greatest protection that the people of the state had." . . . He remained district judge for 25 years, and was appointed circuit judge for the 8th Federal District in 1890 by President Harrison. . . . His scrupulous honesty of mind and conduct was exemplified in his declining the appointment of Chief Justice of the United States Supreme Court, offered him by President Cleveland, assigning as a reason his lack of the necessary qualities of training and legal equipment.*[765]

In 1888, Caldwell authored an article entitled, "The American Jury System" in which he declared that:

> *The jury is an indispensable part of the machinery of justice. Liberty cannot exist without trial by jury, and despotism cannot long survive with it. . . .*[766]

Eleven years later, Judge Caldwell delivered an address to the Annual Meeting of the Missouri State Bar Association in 1899 on the subject of "Trial by Judge and Jury." In it, he insisted that while "it is undeniable that there are powerful influences at work to undermine the constitutional right of trial by jury," complaints against the jury were "groundless."

---

[765] *Dictionary of American Biography*, Vol. 2, p. 408 (1958).
[766] Caldwell, "The American Jury System," 22 *American L.R.* 853 (1888).

> *When you impeach the impartiality and integrity of the jury, you impeach the impartiality and integrity of the whole body of the people from whom they are drawn, and of which they are a representative part....*

He said that "it is a curious and significant fact" that the reasons given for denying the right of trial by jury "are precisely those given for the establishment of the Court of Star Chamber;" and he quoted Edmund Burke for the proposition that although the Star Chamber had been abolished during the reign of Charles I, "the spirit of the Star Chamber has transmigrated, and lives again."

He called trial by jury "the most valuable right "secured by" the English *Constitution* which had been resolutely and inexorably incorporated into our own:

> *When the framers of the Declaration of Independence came to make a formal statement of the grievances of the colonists against King George, one of the chief counts in the indictment was "for depriving them in many cases of the benefit of trial by jury." While trial by jury was an undoubted heritage of the people of this country, they were unwilling that such a supreme and vital right should rest on the unwritten common law. They were stern and inflexible in their demand that the right should be anchored in the Constitution in terms so explicit and peremptory as to make any evasion or denial of it impossible, except by overthrowing the Constitution itself. When the several provisions of the Constitution are read in connection we are amazed at their fullness and completeness. No more resolute and inexorable purpose to accomplish a particular end ever found expression on paper....*

Judge Caldwell then ended his remarks as follows:

> *For a free people, trial by judge and jury is immensely superior to any other mode of trial that the wit of man has ever yet devised, or is capable of devising; and evil will be the hour for the people of the country when, seduced by any theory however plausible, or deluded by any consideration of fancied emergency or expediency, they supinely acquiesce in its invasion or consent to its abolition.*[767]

---

[767] Caldwell, "Trial by Judge and Jury," 33 *American L.R.* 321, 322, 326, 330, 332-333, 340, 343, 346 (1899).

Trial by judge and jury is immensely superior to any other mode of trial that the wit of man has ever devised; and evil will be the hour when the people of this country supinely acquiesce in its invasion or consent to its abolition.
　　—**Judge Henry Clay Caldwell, U.S. Court of Appeals (1899)**

52. Justice John Marshall Harlan (1900). John Marshall Harlan was Attorney General of Kentucky and served as Associate Justice of the United States Supreme Court from 1877-1911. Noted for his dissenting opinions, he "established himself as a resolute supporter of civil rights."[768] In *Hodges v. Easton* (1882), he said that "trial by jury is a fundamental guarantee of the rights and liberties of the people"[769] and in *Maxwell v. Dow* (1900), he wrote:

> It is not difficult to understand why the [founding] fathers entrenched the right of trial by jury in the supreme law of the land. They regarded the recognition and exercise of that right as vital to the protection of liberty against arbitrary power....

Regarding to the guarantee of a trial by jury in the *Bill of Rights*, Justice Harlan wrote that "the privileges and immunities enumerated in these amendments belong to every citizen of the United States."

> ...I take it no one doubts that the great men who laid the foundations of our government regarded the preservation of the... first ten Amendments as vital to the personal security of American citizens. To say of any people that they do not enjoy those privileges and immunities is to say that they do not enjoy real freedom.[770]

He called trial by jury one of the "guarantees of life and liberty that English speaking people have for centuries regarded as vital to personal security, and which the men of the Revolutionary period universally claimed as the birthright of free men."

> ...Liberty, it has been said, depends not so much upon the absence of actual oppression, as on the existence of constitutional checks upon the power to oppress....[771]

---

[768] *The Guide to American Law Encyclopedia*, Vol. 6, pp. 6-7 (West Publishing Co. 1984). His most memorable dissent came in *Plessy v. Ferguson* (1896) where he proclaimed that under our *Constitution*, the humblest citizen is equal in the eyes of the law to the most powerful.

[769] *Hodges v. Easton*, 106 U.S. 408, 412 (1882).

[770] Dissenting Opinion of Justice John Marshall Harlan in *Maxwell v. Dow*, 176 U.S. 581, 605, 609, 615 (1900).

[771] *Maxwell v. Dow*, supra, 176 U.S. 617 (1900).

53.   Alfred C. Coxe, *The Trials of Jury Trials* (1901). In the inaugural edition of the *Columbia Law Review*, Alfred C. Coxe wrote of the "trials of jury trials." He said that the foundations of trial by jury "are laid in the organic law of the nation" and "deeper still, in the hearts of all liberty loving Anglo-Saxons." He said that "it is the best system yet devised for the settlement of disputed questions of fact" and that "without it the Republic would be deprived of one of its most effective weapons against absolutism, intolerance and greed."

> *The jury system can never be permanently corrupted. Individual jurors may yield to improper influences, but the system will remain free, pure and honest so long as the community at large venerates freedom, purity and honesty. . . .*[772]

54.   Justice David J. Brewer, *The Jury* (1902). David J. Brewer (1837-1910) served on the Kansas Supreme Court from 1870 to 1884 and as Associate Justice of the United States Supreme Court from 1889 through 1910. He achieved recognition as an author with four publications, including *The Pew and the Pulpit* (1897), *The Twentieth Century from Another Viewpoint* (1899), *American Citizenship* (1902), and *The United States as a Christian Nation* (1905).[773]

In an article in the *International Monthly*, reprinted in the inaugural edition of the *Canadian Law Review* in 1902, Justice Brewer wrote that the jury "has been one of the most valuable institutions in our history." Stating that "the preservation of the jury is a matter of great importance," he wrote:

> *It is of importance that the people as a whole should realize that the administration of justice is a part of their work. . . . If popular government is to continue, all must take an interest therein, and realize that upon each one rests some share of the responsibility; and the administering of justice is one of the peculiar duties of government. . . .*[774]

---

[772]Coxe, "The Trials of Jury Trials," 1 *Columbia L.R.* 286, 289-290 (1901). Coxe wrote that "in all lands and in every age there are conspicuous instances of judges who have proved arbitrary, ignorant, bigoted and corrupt." *Id.* at 290.

[773]*The Guide to American Law Encyclopedia*, Vol. 2, pp. 155-156 (West Publishing Company 1984).

[774]Brewer, "The Jury," 1 *Canadian L.R.* 302-306 (1902).

55.   William H. Holt, *The Jury System* (1905). William H. Holt presided over the United States Court in Puerto Rico for the first four years of its existence. Responding to allegations that the jury system had proven to be a failure in Puerto Rico, he wrote that the same criticisms generally heard against the jury "may be urged as to the right of suffrage, or of legislative representation."

> The Magna Carta . . . provided that no free man should be condemned but by the lawful judgment of his peers. The Constitution of the United States . . . has secured it to all the people of our country, . . . and our courts . . . have always guarded the right with the most jealous care. All this . . . impresses its wisdom.

> Like the right of suffrage, [trial by jury] is one of the instruments of the sovereignty of the people. . . . It is a school; it increases their intelligence, and educates them; extends a knowledge of the law among them; creates the idea of right, impresses them with the duties of citizenship, and is essential to both civil and political liberty.[775]

56.   John F. Geeting, *Trial by Jury Must be Preserved* (1907). Writing in the Chicago *Sun Times*, March 10, 1907, John F. Geeting proclaimed that "trial by jury must be preserved."

> The trial by jury comes to us from remote antiquity. It has withstood the reign of tyrants, survived the overthrow of dynasties, refuted the criticisms of its enemies, and remains as one of the best expressions of free government by the people in their original and sovereign capacity.

> The question as to whether or not this bulwark of free government by the people shall be dismantled now is a vital question before the public. . . . This heritage, coming from our free-born liberty-loving ancestors, seasoned by the experience of centuries, [and] adorned with the triumphs of justice, . . . form[s] one of the foundation stones of our commonwealth.[776]

---

[775]Holt, "The Jury System," 67 *Albany L.R.* 298-300 (1905).

[776]Geeting, "Trial by Jury Must Be Preserved," 69 *Albany Law J.* 134-135 (1907).

The Magna Carta itself is in substance but a constrained declaration of our original, inherent, indefeasible natural rights as citizens.

—Samuel Adams (1772)

57.   Justice E. C. O'Rear, *The Jury* (1910). In 1910, Justice E. C. O'Rear of the Kentucky Court of Appeals wrote that "the jury is part of the machinery of the government" and that its brief existence "is the best security against its abuse."

> *Of the first importance in government I would place the elective franchise. But next to the elective franchise, and so close to it as to admit of no other to intervene, is the right of trial by jury. No future constitution of a popular government can safely be drawn that does not include that right as one inalienable, and beyond every other power to abrogate.*

Calling trial by jury in England "the greatest and safest power in that realm," Justice O'Rear declared that the "heroism and sturdy spirit" of jurors has been one of "the strongest and most eloquent chapters in the history of this remarkable people":

> *... It was not only a triumph of the people over oppression, but of virtue over vice in a judicial proceeding. They vindicated, not only their personal independence, but the pre-eminent power of the prerogative of a jury trial, the inheritance and shield of every Englishman, and from that time called the palladium of English liberty.*[777]

58.   Sam M. Wolfe, *A Defense of the Jury* (1911). In the May, 1911, issue of *Case and Comment*, Sam M. Wolfe of the Anderson, South Carolina, Bar defended the jury system, stating:

> *... It is essentially a child of freedom. Where the scepter of the tyrant rules, it has no home. The system was inaugurated in the effort to thwart the power of the despot. It is the greatest safeguard of liberty, and the greatest protector of its privileges.*[778]

The critical question today is whether we will preserve this "child of freedom" handed down to us by those who built this sacred republic and sanctified our fundamental liberties in the *Bill of Rights*. If we continue to ignore the lessons of history, its future prospects are extremely bleak.

---

[777] O'Rear, "The Jury," 17 *Central Law J.* 65-66 (1910).
[778] Wolfe, "A Defense of the Jury," *Case and Comment* 599-601 (May, 1911).

59.   Justice James A. McBride, *A Coal from the Altar of Liberty* **(1912).** When Oregon was admitted to the Union as the 33rd state in 1859, its *Constitution* provided that "in all civil cases the right of trial by jury shall remain inviolate."[779] When George Tobias Myers, a Seattle salmon packer domiciled in Portland, died in July of 1907, he disinherited his daughter and left a considerable inheritance to his son. The daughter contested the will in the Portland Probate Court and demanded a trial by jury in reliance upon the provisions of the Oregon *Constitution*.[780]

The probate court's denial of the daughter's demand for a jury trial was affirmed on appeal by the Supreme Court of Oregon on the grounds that the provisions of the Oregon State *Constitution* guaranteeing the right of trial by jury in civil cases did not apply to equitable actions pending in the probate court. Justice James A. McBride, who served continuously on the Supreme Court of Oregon from 1909 through 1930, dissented, stating in part as follows:

> *I regard it as established by the great weight of authority that, when the framers of the Constitution used the language, "In all civil cases the right of trial by jury shall remain inviolate," they meant that the system of trial by jury, which was then in existence, and which had been in existence for years, and which had been tried and found satisfactory, should remain intact. . . .*

Calling the right of trial by jury in civil cases a "valuable bulwark of our liberties," Justice McBride wrote:

> *. . . The fathers of free government in Oregon were jealous of any encroachment on the right of jury trial, and carefully preserved that right in the matter of contests in regard to the validity of wills by providing for a hearing in a court where juries were permitted.*

---

[779] *See* Tongue, "In Defense of Juries as Exclusive Judges of the Facts," 35 *Ore. L.R.* 143, 150 (April, 1956).

[780] *See Stevens v. Myers*, 62 Ore. 372, 121 Pac. 434 (1912), opinion on petition for rehearing, 62 Ore. 272, 126 Pac. 29, 35-37 (1912). For a comparison of the provisions of the *Oregon State Constitution* regarding guarantees of the right of trial by jury to those of other states, *see* Appendix A on pages 469-476 below.

> *...It may be true... that the provisions of the Constitution... which, in my judgment, give such right in cases of this kind have been generally overlooked [in probate actions]; but, "though the law hath slept, it is not dead," and the right of trial by jury is one so precious, so vital to the preservation of our liberties, that we can well afford to search a little to find it, even to the extent of raking the dead ashes of the past 50 years. It is a coal from the altar of liberty, and we should rather blow it into a flame than seek to extinguish it.*[781]

60. Frederic William Maitland, *Collected Papers* (1912). Frederic William Maitland (1850-1906) "is considered by many to be the greatest historian English law has ever known."

> *... His inspired historical writing, his pioneering work with early English records, and his imaginative historical method have provided the foundations upon which most subsequent scholarship in the early history of English law has been based.*[782]

Maitland was one of the principal contributing editors to the publications of the Selden Society and authored many treatises on English legal history, including *Bracton's Notebook* (1887), *The History of English Law* (1895), *Domesday Book and Beyond* (1897), *English Law and the Renaissance* (1901) and *The Constitutional History of England* (1908). In his *Collected Papers*, published posthumously, Maitland wrote:

> *For a long time past Englishmen have been proud of their trial by jury, proud to see the nations of Europe imitating as best they might this "palladium of English liberties," this "bulwark of the British Constitution." Their pride... need not be diminished by any modern discoveries of ancient facts, even though they may have to learn that in its origin trial by jury was rather French than English.... We may well say, therefore, that trial by jury, though it has its roots in the Frankish Inquest, grew up on English soil....*[783]

---

[781] *Stevens v. Myers, supra* n.780, 126 Pac. at 29, 35 & 37.
[782] *Guide to American Law, supra* n.773, Vol. 7, pp. 241-243.
[783] Fisher, ed., *The Collected Papers of Frederic William Maitland*, Vol. 2, pp. 445, 454 (Cambridge U. Press 1911).

For a long time past Englishmen have been proud of their trial by jury, proud to see the nations of Europe imitating as best they might this "palladium of English liberties," this "bulwark of the British Constitution."
—Frederic William Maitland, *Collected Papers* (1912)

61. Delphin M. Delmas, *The Democracy of Justice — The Jury* (1918). Delphin M. Delmas (1844-1928) graduated from Yale Law School in 1865 and soon became one of the leaders of the California Bar. Known as the "silver-tongued spell-binder of the Pacific Coast," he was a master of the art of cross-examination who achieved nationwide notoriety.[784]

In one of the most eloquent defenses of trial by jury, he wrote substantially as follows:

> *Trial by jury is the most ancient and has been the most enduring of all the political and judicial institutions which have flourished among the English-speaking peoples. The hand of time, beneath which all other institutions underwent alteration or decay, left it untouched. The march of ages served to confirm it. The wars and revolutions, which uprooted weaker growths, endured its trunk to defy still mightier storms. In the long unfolding of centuries, it saw kingly houses rise, flourish and vanish; it saw the feudal system crumble into dust; it saw the scepter of empire and of rule, fallen from the nerveless grasp of the nobility, snatched up by the strong hand of Parliament; it saw the kingly office decline; it saw the material wealth of the realm transferred from the landed aristocracy to the counting houses of merchants; it saw the whole frame of legal procedure recast and remolded, and the whole fabric of the judicial hierarchy rebuilt from turret to foundation stone — all this it saw, and, amid the universal wreck of things which seemed endowed with enduring life, it alone, defying time and change, stands in all the essentials of a popular tribunal, as it stood in the years when Edward the Confessor sat upon the throne of England.*
>
> *No other institution ever struck its roots so deep into the hearts of the English speaking races. As long as the people continue to govern themselves, so long shall it endure among them. Its decay will mark the decadence, and its overthrow the end of popular liberty.*[785]

---

[784]*Dictionary of American Biography*, Vol. 3, p. 226 (1959).
[785]Delmas, "The Democracy of Justice — The Jury," 6 *Kentucky Law J.* 245-246 (1918). [Ellipsis omitted].

62. Austin Wakeman Scott, *Trial by Jury and the Reform of Civil Procedure* (1918). Austin Wakeman Scott (1848-1922) gained prominence as an historian, a law professor, and President of Rutgers College. He graduated from Yale University in 1869 and was awarded a Doctor of Laws degree from Princeton. He taught at the University of Michigan and Johns Hopkins and was elected President of Rutgers College in 1890. He authored a history of the State of New Jersey and assisted George Bancroft in the preparation of his *History of the United States*.[786]

In "Trial by Jury and the Reform of Civil Procedure," published in the *Harvard Law Review* in 1918, he wrote that "perhaps the most striking phenomenon in the history of our procedural law is the gradual evolution of the institution of trial by jury." Noting that trial by jury in civil cases is guaranteed by the *Seventh Amendment*, he asked:

> *Now what is this trial by jury, the right to which was so highly prized by our ancestors as to be put beyond the power of the legislature to abolish? The Constitution does not define it. Its meaning must be ascertained by a resort to history.*

The answer, he found, was in the growing desire of the American colonists to increase citizen participation in the administration of justice by means of an institution the people regarded as a "bulwark of liberty." He observed that initially the jury was regarded as "a protection against the despotic power of the Crown" as a result of which "in the American colonies during the 18th century there was a gradually increasing enthusiasm for trial by jury and a popular desire to strictly limit the powers of judges and to give the jury great latitude."

> *At the time when the first permanent settlements were being established in America there was a great deal of popular enthusiasm in England for trial by jury. This enthusiasm was based chiefly on the value of the institution as a bulwark of liberty....*[787]

In his first inaugural address, George Washington said that "the preservation of the sacred fire of liberty," has been "justly entrusted into the hands of the American people." It is our duty to ensure that no power on earth shall ever snuff it out.

---

[786]*Guide to American Law, supra* n.773, Vol. 9, p. 123.
[787]Scott, "Trial by Jury and the Reform of Civil Procedure," 31 Harv. L.R. 669, 671, 676-677 (1918).

63. Charles T. Coleman, *Origin and Development of Trial by Jury* (1919).

In 1919, Charles T. Coleman wrote that trial by jury, "venerable with age, and splendid in the history of its achievement, has won the esteem of *all classes of people*, and found a guaranty in every American *Constitution*."

> *The jury system appeals with peculiar force to the great masses of the common people. Inspired by the rich heritage of the common law, and by the history of the long struggle of the English people for civil liberty, they revere the jury as the Ark of the Covenant, which not only contains the Tables of the Law, but brings those laws down to the level of their own comprehension, and makes them speak, so far as their interpretation and execution is concerned, through the voice of the "country-side," the voice of the people themselves. Trial by jury is justly prized as the cornerstone of our free institutions. It shields individual rights from the encroachment of governmental power; it imbues the ordinary citizen with an important part in the administration of governmental affairs; and it makes the people of a state the keepers of the conscience of the laws of that state. But above all, the jury system is especially dear to the heart of the masses, because service on the jury is the simple but transfiguring ceremony which the shoulder of every citizen, whatever the accident of his birth or station, tingles with the accolade of that matchless precept of the law that all men are born free, equal and independent.*[788]

In honor of those great principles of freedom, equality, and independence, in 1883, Emma Lazarus wrote "The New Colossus" which closes with the motto inscribed upon our *Statue of Liberty*:

> *Give me your tired, your poor,*
> *Your huddled masses yearning to breathe free,*
> *The wretched refuse of your teeming shore.*
> *Send these, the homeless, the tempest tossed to me,*
> *I lift my lamp beside the golden door!*

Will we remain faithful to these words, or will we dim that lamp, or take it down? *The choice is ours.*

---

[788] Coleman, "Origin and Development of Trial by Jury," 6 *Va. L.R.* 77-78, 86 (1919).

The Statue of Liberty
The jury system appeals with peculiar force to the great masses of common people. It brings the laws down to the level of their own comprehension, and makes them speak through the voice of the people themselves.
—Charles T. Coleman (1919)

64.   James L. Coke, *On Jury Trial* (June, 1922). Less than 20 years before the "Day of Infamy" on which the Empire of Japan bombed Pearl Harbor, the Chief Justice of the Territory of Hawaii was invited to address the faculty and students of the Tokyo Imperial University of Japan on the American jury system. The address of Chief Justice James L. Coke was translated into the Japanese language and printed in pamphlet form for distribution throughout Japan.

In his address, Justice Coke stated:

If any human work ought to be cherished and regarded with sanctity by the American and English people it is those guarantees contained in the fundamental laws of those countries guaranteeing the right of trial by jury. These are bulwarks of national life, of general prosperity and of countless blessings, primal lights shining with steadfast fidelity of the North Star and the Southern Cross.

Many years of practice in the courts as well as a rather extended tenure on the Bench has strengthened my regard for the jury system and leaves me to remark that in my opinion judges are not preeminently fitted over other men of good judgment in business affairs to decide upon mere questions of disputed fact.

When these remarks were later published in the *Oregon Law Review* in June of 1922, an editorial note stated:

... Since the address was given the adoption of the jury system in Japan has become a very live question. A bill to adopt the jury system . . . has been introduced in the Japanese Diet, has passed the House of Representatives, but has been held up in the House of Peers.[789]

Unfortunately for us all, "the democracy of justice" did not take hold in the *Land of the Rising Sun.*[790]

---

[789] Coke, "On Jury Trial," 1 *Ore. L.R.* 177, 179 (June, 1922).

[790] According to the *Encyclopædia Britannica*, after a brief flirtation with the concept of popular justice, the Empire of Japan "did away with its short-lived jury courts in 1943." *Encyclopædia Britannica Macropædia*, Vol. 10, p. 361 (15th ed. 1979).

65.   A. C. Umbreit, *Trial by Jury as an Instrument of Democracy* (1924). In an article in the April, 1924, edition of the *Marquette Law Review*, Professor A. C. Umbreit of the Marquette University Law School wrote that "trial by jury plays a large part in the social and political life of a community."

> *Trial by jury also tends to foster respect for our courts, the last and final protecting tribunal of our liberties. Abolish this institution and you have taken away practically the last opportunity the great mass of the people have of participating in any way in any of the activities of government, of being in any way concerned in the political life of the community and have left them only the right of exercising the elective franchise, a privilege which all too many of our citizens at present do not appreciate.*

> *Trial by jury is too deeply rooted in our civilization, is too important to our judicial system, is of too great value to our social and political life to be rudely condemned and unceremoniously abolished at the request and behest of disappointed litigants and their attorneys, and to be replaced by an experiment in judicial procedure which history has shown to be a failure whenever tried and to replace which trial by jury was instituted.*

Professor Umbreit also acknowledged "perverse verdicts" are, in fact, occasionally rendered by juries, but are, more often than not, corrected by judicial review:

> *Perverse verdicts have been rendered by juries, but the damage done to the administration of justice by such verdicts, has been greatly minimized, if not entirely neutralized, by the power of the court to set aside such verdicts and grant new trials. . . .*[791]

The intricate system of checks and balances built into our civil justice system makes the so-called "excessive verdict" extremely rare. Like catastrophic events, large verdicts are always well publicized, but they are no more typical than the notion that the average airplane crashes. Safe landings and modest verdicts are simply not newsworthy.

---

[791]Umbreit, "Is Trial by Jury: An Ineffective Survival?" 8 *Marquette L.R.* 125, 132-133 (April, 1924).

66. Francis L. Wellman, *Gentlemen of the Jury* (1924).

Francis Wellman, valedictorian of his class at Harvard Law School in 1876, was an immensely successful prosecutor, a prolific author, and one of the preeminent civil jury trial lawyers of his day. Author of the great classic *The Art of Cross Examination* (1903),[792] he also wrote *Day in Court* (1910), *Gentlemen of the Jury* (1924), *Luck and Opportunity* (1938), and *Success in Court* (1942). In the words of his biographer, as a trial lawyer his "overall impact was feral" and "the game that he hunted and destroyed was the perjurer."[793]

Armed with the experience of hundreds of jury trials, in *Gentlemen of the Jury* (1924), he traced the history of "that ancient and honorable institution of Trial by Jury" which he said was "universally considered the bulwark of our system of jurisprudence." He called the jury system "a great popular university" which "has done a large part to perpetuate democracy and to train our citizens in the art of self government." He wrote that the courage of juries during the reign of the Tudors and Stuarts had "won for the petit jury much of its prestige and glory in English history" as an "effective barrier" against "the wrath and tyranny of kings."

> *. . . The [English jury] system was so valued by the people that no conquest, no change of government, no attempted upheaval of public opinion could ever succeed in abolishing it.*

As a fitting tribute to our American jury system, he concluded:

> *. . . We Americans are in the main educated and intelligent people, living under and governed by laws of our own making; and it is of vital importance to us that these laws should be fairly administered by ourselves under the old, time honored method of trial by jury.*[794]

---

[792] Wellman, *The Art of Cross Examination* (Macmillan Co., 2d ed. 1904) [Legal Classics Library 1983].

[793] *See* Biographical Introduction to the Legal Classics Library's 1983 edition of *The Art of Cross Examination* by Thomas G. Barnes, p. 17 (1983).

[794] Wellman, *Gentlemen of the Jury: Reminiscences of 30 Years at the Bar*, pp. x, 23-24, 27, 28, 53 (2d ed. 1936).

The ancient and honorable institution of trial by jury has been universally considered the bulwark of our system of jurisprudence. It is a great popular university which has done a large part to perpetuate our American democracy and to train our citizens in the art of self government.
    —Francis L. Wellman, *Gentlemen of the Jury* (1924)

67.   Lester P. Edge, *Jury System? Yes.* (November, 1925). Noting that his practice had been "devoted considerably to trial work — much of it in the defense of personal injury cases before juries," Lester P. Edge of the Spokane Bar wrote that our American jury system is "as fundamental as freedom of speech, *habeas corpus*, due process of law, or any of the other guarantees of the *Bill of Rights*." Its failings, he asserted, "are common to all humanity, its infirmities are those of the race." Responding to those who criticize juries for their compassion, Edge wrote:

> *It is true that juries are occasionally moved by sympathy or compassion. All properly balanced human machinery is so moved. Why censure the jury for being consistent with the finest motives of humanity? The jury is inclined to favor the underdog, and when it can, will aid the oppressed. Are these faults in the system? Surely not, but on the other hand are positive virtues, reconciling the frequently harsh rules of the law with natural and substantial justice. When judgments of the head are tempered by impulses of the heart, justice is not jeopardized, but is sustained.*[795]

68.   John E. Wall, *Efficacy of Trial by Jury* (April, 1926). Responding to critics of the educational level of the average jury, John E. Wall of the Quincy, Illinois, Bar responded that "the fallacy of that position lies in the assumption that education and intelligence are synonymous."

> *. . . If the educated possessed, more than the uneducated, intelligence, good sense, sound judgment and homely wisdom, which they do not, the point would not be without merit. Frequently, however, jurors are more intelligent than the lawyer trying the case. Moreover, since the contested points in most cases center around the ordinary affairs of life, it follows, as a necessary corollary, that ordinary intelligence ought to be amply adequate to meet the situation. . . . If the fact that juries make mistakes is a point against the system, how will the condition be bettered with another form of trial, which experience has shown to be equally fallible?*[796]

---

[795] Edge, "Jury System? Yes," 29 *Law Notes* 151-152 (November, 1925).

[796] Wall, "Efficacy of Trial by Jury," 30 *Law Notes* 7 (April, 1926).

69. W. S. Holdsworth, *A History of English Law* **(1927).** In 1927, W. S. Holdsworth, professor of English law at the University of Oxford, published the 4th edition of his 12-volume treatise entitled *A History of English Law.* In Volume 1, he devoted 52 pages of text to the origin, history, development and impact of the institution of trial by jury on the common law. "The jury is, as Blackstone terms it, 'The principal criterion of truth in the law of England.'"[797] Holdsworth concluded this section of his famous treatise with a discussion of "the legal and political effects of the jury system":

> *The defects of the jury system are obvious. They are twelve ordinary men . . . [and] they give no reasons for their verdict. The verdict itself is not subject to any appeal. . . . But in spite of these obvious defects, distinguished judges who have spent many years working with juries, have combined to praise the jury system. Fortescue, Coke, Hale, Blackstone and Steven are witnesses whose evidence should be conclusive. . . . In fact the jury system works well from the point of view of the litigant, the judge, the jury itself, and the law.*
>
> *The litigant gets a body of persons who bring average common sense to bear upon the facts of the case. "A jury," says Chalmers, "is a far better tribunal than a judge for dealing with questions of fact. The more I see of juries the higher is the respect I have for their decisions. . . . They have a marvelous faculty for scenting out a fraud." Their findings create no precedent; and thus they can decide hard cases equitably without making bad law. . . .*
>
> * * *
>
> *The jury itself is educated by the part which it is required to take in the administration of justice. The jury system teaches the members of the jury to cultivate a judicial habit of mind. It helps to create in them a respect for law and order. It makes them feel that they owe duties to society, and that they have a share in government. . . .*

---

[797]W. S. Holdsworth, *A History of English Law*, Vol. 1, p. 298 (Methuen & Co., London, 4th ed. 1927) [The 1972 edition contains 17 volumes].

> *The effects of the jury system upon the law are no less remarkable and no less beneficial. It tends to make the law intelligible by keeping it in touch with the common facts of life. . . . The jury system has for some hundreds of years been constantly bringing the rules of law to the touchstone of contemporary common sense. . . .*[798]

At every stage of our history, there have been those who have attacked the basic concepts of democratic self-government. In 1913, Theodore Roosevelt wrote that "even a democrat like myself must admit" that "there is something to be said for government by a great aristocracy."[799] But what can be said for government by aristocracy is simply this: the concept is not only foreign to our American *Constitution*, but it won't work.

On the other hand, our civil jury system works well. From 26 years of trial experience on both sides of the aisle, I have been constantly impressed by the collective wisdom, common sense and good judgment of American juries. They are, in my experience, remarkably adept at cutting through the haze and smoke of dubious claims and unsubstantiated arguments to reach the true justice of a civil dispute. Their mere presence and the promise of their forthcoming verdicts brings about the settlement of the vast majority of civil cases. Those that are tried are generally decided in a predictable way.

Non-jury trials are a different matter. Their outcome generally depends on the philosophical predisposition and the past professional experience of the trial judge. Fewer verdicts are just and reasonable and fewer settlements are fair and equitable. While jury deliberations are over in a matter of hours, non-jury decisions may be marinated for months. The level of a man's formal education is a poor measure of his fairness, his judgment and his common sense. Few, if any, judges are more intelligent, more astute or better informed than a six, eight or twelve-member jury.

Ralph Waldo Emerson defined "common sense" as "genius dressed in working clothes,"[800] and, with appropriate apologies to college-educated intellectuals, I have found it as often in overalls as in coat and tie. There is a great genius in the common people of America. They are the backbone of democracy and, as W. S. Holdsworth has said, in their service as jurors, "the touchstone of contemporary common sense."

---

[798]Holdsworth, *supra n.797*, pp. 347-349.
[799]*Bartlett's Familiar Quotations*, p. 846b (1968).
[800]*Webster's New World Dictionary of Quotable Definitions*, p. 97 (Prentice Hall Press 2d ed. 1988).

The jury system has for some hundreds of years been constantly bringing the rules of law to the touchstone of contemporary common sense.
—**English Author W. S. Holdsworth (1927)**

70.   Harold Corbin, *The Jury on Trial* (1928). In an article in the *American Bar Association Journal*, Harold H. Corbin of the New York Bar wrote that "elimination of trial by jury of civil cases is being urged and predicted by several eminent members of the Bench and Bar." Responding to this challenge, he wrote:

> I want to record an emphatic dissent from these views. I believe in the jury. I believe in its present day efficiency. I believe it is the most practical and most satisfactory arbiter of issues of fact in civil actions....
>
> ... The jury's homely experience, its touch with human affairs, its contact in everyday society with the types of men and women who appear as litigants, endow it with a special ability, an inherent intuition, an innate acumen to see and know what the real facts are.... The experience of every trial lawyer teaches him a profound respect for the jury.[801]

71.   Frederick Edwin Smith, Lord Birkenhead, Chancellor of England (1929). F. E. Smith (1872-1930) served as a member of the House of Commons, Solicitor General, Attorney General, Chancellor of England and Secretary of State for India. He sponsored major legal reforms and was instrumental in the passage of the *Law of Property Act* (1922), the *County Courts Act* (1924) and the *Supreme Court Consolidation Act* (1925).[802] "No man has had a larger experience with juries."[803] In *Law, Life and Letters*, he wrote:

> The traditions of English jurisprudence ... are the admiration of the world. They depend upon the broad and simple principle that what twelve ordinary men think of the facts is on the whole more likely to be right than a very highly instructed legal functionary. The liberties of England are required to be construed, where the issues are those of fact, not by technical persons very highly instructed, but by ordinary men who lead ordinary lives and think ordinary thoughts of ordinary people.[804]

---

[801] Corbin, "The Jury on Trial," 14 *ABAJ* 507, 509 (1928).
[802] *Encyclopædia Britannica Micropædia*, Vol. II, p. 38 (1979).
[803] Crane, "Judge and Jury," 15 *ABAJ* 201-203 (1929).
[804] Smith, *Law, Life and Letters*, Vol. 1, pp. 255-256 (London 1927).

72. Judge Frederick E. Crane, *Judge and Jury* (1929).
Frederick E. Crane, Judge of the Court of Appeals of the State of New York, delivered an address to the judicial section of the Ohio State Bar Association published in the *American Bar Association Journal* in 1929. In it, he defended the jury system as "far superior in its results to any other method."

> *There is no better or healthier system . . . than to have disputed questions of fact, both in civil and criminal cases, passed upon by ordinary citizens of ordinary intelligence. . . . The law is more or less rigid and the jury, being human beings, with all the feelings that the rest of us have, give to the law an elasticity which . . . saves our legal institutions. . . . [I]n the vast majority of cases they see through sham, fraud and deceit or fake claims and defenses and try to do the right thing. . . .*
>
> *A democracy should be very slow in abolishing the jury. . . . The jury determines what care a reasonably prudent man should and would exercise in a given case. These men constituting our jury, engaged daily in the active pursuits of business, traveling all over the city and country, in and out of subways, elevators, factories, machine shops, know more about the care usually exercised than a judge whose days are spent in more peaceful pursuits.*[805]

73. Robert Von Moschzisker, *Trial by Jury* (1930).
Robert Von Moschzisker was a successful trial lawyer who served as a public prosecutor, Judge of the Pennsylvania Court of Common Pleas, and Chief Justice of the Pennsylvania Supreme Court. In 1921, he delivered a series of lectures on trial by jury at the University of Pennsylvania Law School. In his comprehensive treatise on *Trial by Jury*, Justice Von Moschzisker analyzed the ancient tribunals of Greece, Rome, Denmark, Norway, Sweden, Iceland, France and Germany and traced the development of the jury system in England. From his own experience, he wrote that trial by jury "may be viewed as an ideal institution . . . for determining disputes between private parties, as well as for the proper administration of the criminal law."[806]

---

[805] Crane, "Judge and Jury," 15 *ABAJ* 201, 202-203 (1929).
[806] Von Moschzisker, *Trial by Jury*, pp. 67-68 (George T. Bisel Co. 2d ed. 1930).

As judges of the credibility of witnesses, the weight of evidence in the average case, or the guilt or innocence of those charged with criminal offenses, and for ascertainment of unliquidated damages, my experience convinces me that jurors, through the general verdict, can render better service than is possible by any fixed tribunal, composed of one or more members with professionally trained minds. . . . [T]he general finding of a jury is the most acceptable device so far conceived for the practical administration of law and justice. I have taken part in one capacity or another, in the trial or review of thousands of cases, and this experience has given me faith in the jury system. . . .

When twelve men are gathered together from all walks of life and placed in the responsible position of jurors, in the sum total they are better judges of parties and witnesses, of the way people look on everyday affairs, and of the motives which move men, than the trained judge. . . . Moreover, the juror brings a certain spontaneity of judgment to bear on the decision of matters before him; whereas the trained official constantly thinks of rules and precedents, which are apt to control him, even when determining questions of fact. In other words, by employing the casual tribunal, we command a more general use of the common-sense way of getting at the real facts, as distinguished from the scientific method of drawing inferences, making deductions, and reaching conclusions.[807]

74. ABA President Clarence E. Martin on the Jury System (1934). Clarence E. Martin of West Virginia, President of the American Bar Association 1932-1933, wrote of trial by jury in 1934:

The system is one of our cherished institutions. Often, in times of stress, it has stood as a bulwark against oppression. It is the layman's contribution to the administration of justice. It is his duty, his honor. . . . It should, and, in most cases, it does make him a better citizen.[808]

---

[807] Von Moschzisker, *supra* n.806, pp. 67-70.
[808] Clarence E. Martin, Foreword to Brewster, *Twelve Men in a Box* (Callahan & Co. 1934).

The general finding of a jury is the most acceptable device so far conceived for the practical administration of law and justice. I have taken part in the trial or review of thousands of cases and this experience has given me faith in the jury system.
—Chief Justice Robert Von Moschzisker of Pennsylvania (1930)

75.   Justice George Sutherland (1935). Justice George Sutherland, one of the staunchest defenders of individual liberty ever to grace the bench of the United States Supreme Court,[809] believed strongly that that Court was "in a very special sense . . . charged with the duty of construing and upholding the *Constitution*." And ever alert not to weaken or subvert "the fundamental law of the land," he firmly believed that this rule "applies with particular force" to the right of trial by jury. In *Dimick v. Schiedt* (1935), he wrote:

> *The right of trial by jury is of ancient origin, characterized by Blackstone as "the glory of the English law" and "the most transcendent privilege which any subject can enjoy"; and as Justice Story said, "the Constitution would have been justly obnoxious to the most conclusive objection if it had not recognized and confirmed it in the most solemn terms." . . . Maintenance of the jury as a fact finding body is of such importance and occupies so firm a place in our history and jurisprudence that any seeming curtailment of the right to a jury trial should be scrutinized with utmost care. . . .*[810]

76.   Justice Hugo Black on the Need to "Scrupulously Safeguard" Trial by Jury (1939). The eighth child of a farmer from Clay County, Alabama, Hugo Black was born on February 27, 1886. He graduated from the University of Alabama Law School in 1906 and practiced law in Birmingham for 20 years prior to his election to the United States Senate in 1927. During this time, he served as a part-time police court judge, prosecuting attorney and a trial lawyer. His first verdict was for $137.50.

As United States Senator between 1927 and 1937, he sponsored the *Fair Labor Standards Act*, investigated governmental subsidies and exposed "false front" lobbyist organizations. Investigating utility lobbies in 1936, he found that they "were in fact subsidized by a small group of major financiers. For illustration, what purported to be a farmers group was in fact financed by the DuPont Company, the Sun Oil Company, Swift & Company, and General Motors. . . . The Black investigation discovered that over one million dollars had been contributed by approximately ten organizations or groups to finance false front organizations around the country."

---

[809]For Justice Sutherland's views on the *Bill of Rights*, see Vol. 1, pp. 52-55 above.

[810]*Dimick v. Schiedt*, 293 U.S. 474, 485-486 (1935).

He was appointed Associate Justice on the United States Supreme Court by President Franklin D. Roosevelt on August 12, 1937, where he was "without doubt the most influential of the many strong figures who have sat during the 30 years that . . . passed in his justiceship." During more than 30 years on the Court, Justice Black "sat with a quarter of all the justices since George Washington's time, and a third of all the Chiefs."

As a Supreme Court Justice, Hugo Black maintained a solid commitment to civil liberties and battled the monopolization of big business. He also believed "that the law of personal injury cases was truly important, as important as any other part of the law of the United States." In the words of Senator George W. Norris of Nebraska, he was "a worthy representative of the common people. He underst[ood] their hopes and ambitions, and their liberties in his hands [were] safe."[811]

In *Lyon v. Mutual Benefit Health & Acc. Assn.*, 305 U.S. 484, 492 (1939), Justice Black wrote that "it is essential that the right to trial by jury be scrupulously safeguarded." Later, in his dissenting opinion in *Galloway v. United States*, 319 U.S. 372, 396-411 (1943), Justice Black wrote:

. . . The founders of our government thought that trial of fact by juries rather than by judges was an essential bulwark of civil liberty. . . .[812]

Speaking of the battle over ratification of the *Constitution* between the federalists and the anti-federalists, Justice Black said: ". . . [I]n response to widespread demands from the various state constitutional conventions, the First Congress adopted the *Bill of Rights* containing the *Sixth and Seventh Amendments*, intended to save trial in both criminal and common law cases from legislative or judicial abridgment. . . ."[813]

---

[811] John P. Frank, "Biography of Hugo L. Black," pp. 2321-2347 in Vol. 3, *The Justices of the United States Supreme Court 1789-1969: Their Lives and Major Opinions* (Chelsea House Publishers 1969). *See also In Memoriam: Honorable Hugo Lafayette Black*, 92 S. Ct. 5-83 (October 4, 1971).

[812] *Dissenting opinion* of Justice Hugo Black in *Galloway v. United States*, 319 U.S. 372, 397 (1943).

[813] *Galloway v. United States, supra,* 319 U.S. at 398. In footnote 3, Justice Black states that "of the seven states which, in ratifying the *Constitution*, proposed amendments, six included proposals for the preservation of jury trial in civil cases. . . ."

Justice Black observed that when our *Constitution* was ratified in 1789, "juries occupied the principal place in the administration of justice." He said that "*trial by jury is a fundamental guaranty of the rights of the people*":

> *The call for the true application of the Seventh Amendment is not to words, but to the spirit of honest desire to see that constitutional right preserved. . . . Our duty to preserve this one of the Bill of Rights . . . is a matter of high constitutional importance. . . .*[814]

In a tribute to Justice Black's defense of the jury system, University of Texas Law Professor Leon Green called the history of jury trial "a constant struggle" to "preserve the integrity of the political ideal of laymen's justice."

> *To citizens generally, jury trial has given a sense of political freedom; a feeling of being a part of government. It offers an assurance of judgment by neighbors who understand the community climate of values, a bulwark against the petty tyrannies of headstrong judges, and a means of softening the cold letter of the law in cases of hardship. . . .*[815]

Just as it was in 1943, it remains "a matter of high constitutional importance" today that our legislators, as well as our judges, respect the right of trial by jury and develop "the spirit of honest desire to see that constitutional right preserved." This importance increases as our court administrators rush to computerize their dockets in an age of automation where names are replaced by numbers and statistics count more in the minds of many than individual liberty and the due administration of civil justice.

It was the "*Liber Primus*" or "First Book" of the *Institutes of Justinian* (533 A.D.) that "justice is the constant and perpetual wish to render *every one* his due."[816] *Justice* is not subject to mass production. Litigants cannot be herded like cattle through the courtroom door. *Every case* is important and *justice* must be administered on an *individual basis*.

---

[814] *Galloway v. U.S., supra* n.812, 319 U.S. 399, 407.

[815] Green, "Jury Trial and Mr. Justice Black," 65 *Yale Law J.* 482, 483 (1956).

[816] *The Institutes of Justinian*, p. 5 (Greenwood Press 7th ed. 1970).

Our duty to preserve the Seventh Amendment is a matter of high Constitutional importance. The founders of our country thought that trial by civil jury was an essential bulwark of civil liberty and it must be scrupulously safeguarded.

—Supreme Court Justice Hugo Black (1939, 1943)

77.   Ashton File, *Right of Trial by Jury in Civil Actions* (August 8, 1940). In an address to the Virginia and West Virginia Bar Associations, Ashton File, President of the West Virginia Bar Association, said that "never before has it been more important to guard the ancient institutions of our state" at a time when "the combined enemies of all democratic institutions are seeking to undermine their foundations."

> *. . . The guardians of our jury system are found in that great army of patriots whose faith in our state and its institutions is anchored to the faith of the fathers, and who cherish the right of trial by jury as one of the great bulwarks of our liberties. The combined wisdom and experience through the centuries since Magna Carta have demonstrated that trial by judge and jury is the best that has ever been devised, and the best machinery for bringing out a true result.*[817]

78.   Justice Frank Murphy on the Need to Jealously Guard the Civil Jury (1942). Clarence Darrow described Frank Murphy as "the kindliest and most understanding man I have ever happened to meet on the bench." He graduated from Michigan Law School in 1914 and served as Assistant U.S. Attorney, criminal court judge, Mayor of Detroit, Governor General of the Philippines, Governor of Michigan and Attorney General of the United States. He was appointed Associate Justice of the United States Supreme Court in January of 1940 and was described as "one of the most totally independent figures in the Court's history." His "most distinguishing intellectual quality" was "his dedication to the cause of civil liberties."[818]

In *Jacob v. City of New York*, 315 U.S. 752 (1942), he wrote:

> *The right of jury trial in civil cases at common law is a basic and fundamental feature of our system of federal jurisprudence which is protected by the Seventh Amendment. A right so fundamental and sacred to the citizen . . . should be jealously guarded by the courts. . . .*

---

[817] File, "Right of Trial by Jury in Civil Actions," *Proceedings of the 51st Annual Meeting of the Virginia State Bar Association*, pp. 240, 243, 246, 258 (1941).

[818] John P. Frank, "Biography of Frank Murphy," pp. 2493-2506 in Vol. 4, *The Justices of the United States Supreme Court 1789-1969: Their Lives and Opinions* (Chelsea House Publishers 1969).

79. The Boston Bar Association on Trial by Jury (1943). According to a symposium on trial by jury published in the *New York State Bar Bulletin*, "the position of the jury in our democracy was well stated by the Boston Bar Association in a resolution quoted and approved by a committee of the American Bar Association:"

> *The jury is more than the mere decider of cases. It is a balance wheel in the administration of justice, it has been the protector of the people against tyranny, and it may be so against a militant bureaucracy. It serves to give laymen an insight into the functioning of the judicial machine and in this sense is an educational institution. It is a buffer for our courts, protecting them from the full effect of the blasts of popular emotion. In a heterogeneous nation such as ours, the jury is called upon to pass upon matters involving every class in the community, on disputes between rich and poor, between employers and employees, between corporations and individuals, between property owners and wage earners, between those of different races and creeds.*[819]

80. William Seagle, *The Citadel of Freedom* (1946). In *The History of Law*, William Seagle describes the historical origins of the rules of law and their maturity into the modern legal philosophy of the 20th century. He notes that "one group of jurists is convinced that a new day would dawn if only the presumption of innocence could be abolished" while "still another concentrates on lambasting the jury system." Quoting Frederick Pollock for the proposition that one virtue of the common law "is that freedom is her sister," Seagle concludes that trial by jury is one of the "*the chief technical glories of the common law.*"

> *... Indeed, all the characteristics of the common law are merely phases of its solicitude for freedom: a war on individualism presupposes a yearning for social justice; the adherence to precedent is a guarantee against arbitrary action; and trial by jury has been the subject of countless [eulogies] as the very citadel of freedom.*[820]

---

[819] "Jury Trial on Trial — A Symposium," 28 *N.Y.S.B. Bulletin* 322, 330 (1956).

[820] Seagle, *The History of Law*, pp. 246, 75 & 157 (Tudor Publishing Co. 1946) [Seagle uses the term "panegyrics"].

81.   Justice Bernard Botein, *This Right Was Dearly Won* (1946). The son of Russian immigrants, Bernard Botein (1900-1974) graduated from Brooklyn Law School in 1924, served as an assistant district attorney and was appointed Justice of the New York Supreme Court in 1941. Governor Thomas Dewey nominated him to the Appellate Division in 1953, where he became Presiding Justice in 1957, serving until his retirement in 1968. "During this period, he sponsored many administrative reforms and became recognized as one of the country's foremost administrative judges."[821] On the opening of a term of court in 1946, he said:

> *The right to equality before the law — this principle that everyone is entitled to the same even-handed justice in the courts as everyone else, without regard to the color of his skin, the place of worship he attends — this right was dearly won. Men had to fight and many men had to die so that this liberty might be ours. Too much blood has been spilt over it, too many tears shed, for us to be careless about it.*
>
> *It is precious not only because of the sacrifices wrought on its behalf, but because of the security it spells for each of us. It guarantees to all of us that, if ever we have occasion to enter these halls as litigants, our claims will be decided on their merits.*
>
> *. . . It is here, no less than in the polling booth, that every day the American way of life is either given its rebirth or condemned to ineffectuality. In your role as jurymen you are the custodians and guarantors of the democratic ideal.*[822]

82.   René Wormser, *The Law* (1949). René Wormser was a prolific writer and a member of the New York bar. In 1946, he published a one-volume text entitled simply *The Law*. Beginning with the Law of Moses, he traced the contributions to our modern legal system by the Greeks, the Romans, the Germans, the churchmen, the western Europeans, the English, and the Americans. He referred to the jury system as "one of our treasured legacies" and concluded that, "to date, no finer or more just system of law . . . has been devised anywhere."[823]

---

[821] *The National Cyclopædia of American Biography*, Vol. 57, p. 751 (1977).
[822] Botein, *This Right Was Dearly Won* (1946).
[823] Wormser, *The Law*, pp. 37-38, 251, 312 (1949).

In the jury box, no less than in the polling booth, every day the American way of life is given its rebirth. American jurymen are the custodians and guarantors of the democratic ideal.
—Justice Bernard Botein of New York (1946)

83. Clinton Rossiter, *Seedtime of the Republic* (1953). Clinton Rossiter's book examines "the origin of the American tradition of political liberty." Beginning with the pattern of colonial government, "popular participation in politics" and "the factors of freedom," Rossiter discusses the circumstances,[824] the men,[825] and the heritage[826] that led to the American Revolution. Concerning "that firmest Barrier of English liberty, *The Trial by Juries*," Rossiter wrote:

> *It is difficult to exaggerate the esteem in which the colonists held the representative legislature and jury trial. The vehemence of their defense of these two bulwarks of freedoms was, of course, a direct reaction to the ministry's assault upon them in the Sugar and Stamp Acts. Yet colonial devotion to these ancient techniques was more than just occasional. Few Americans believed that representative assembly and jury trial could ever be improved upon as instruments of popular government. . . .*[827]

Rossiter wrote that the right of representative government and trial by jury "are not only rights, but the means of defending all other rights" and that "the solid foundation of all free government is some form of equal representation and impartial trial."[828]

It is this "solid foundation of all free government" that we must preserve today by protecting "the twin pillars of liberty" — representative democracy and trial by jury — from *any infringement, however slight*.

---

[824] Colonial government, colonial religion, colonial economy, colonial society and "the colonial mind" and their influence on "the rise of liberty." Rossiter, *Seedtime of the Republic: The Origin of the American Tradition of Political Liberty*, Chaps. 1-5 (Harcourt Brace 1953).

[825] Including, Richard Bland (1710-1776), an 18th century Virginia aristocrat who believed that "trial by jury was hardly less important than representation itself" [p. 276].

[826] The effect of *The Chain of Political Events (1765-1776)* [pp. 313-325], *American Political Writing (1775-1776)* [pp. 326-361], and *American Political Thought (1765-1776)* on "The Rights of Man" [pp. 362-401] and "The Pattern of Government" [pp. 402-439].

[827] Rossiter, *supra*, p. 391.

[828] Rossiter, *supra*, p. 443.

84. Justice William O. Douglas, *An Almanac of Liberty* (1954). Born October 16, 1898, in Maine, Minnesota, William O. Douglas (1898-1980), "served longer (36 years) and wrote more opinions (1,500) than any other Justice in the Court's history."[829] He was a member of the faculty of Yale Law School and later Chairman of the Securities and Exchange Commission prior to his appointment as Associate Justice by Franklin D. Roosevelt in 1939. During his tenure on the Court, he was "a champion of civil liberties"[830] who "consistently applied the tenets of the *Bill of Rights* to protect individual freedoms."[831]

Justice Douglas was also a prolific author, his significant works including *Of Men and Mountains* (1950), *Beyond the Himalayas* (1952), *An Almanac of Liberty* (1954), *The Right of the People* (1958), and *Democracy's Manifesto* (1962). In *The Right of the People*, Justice Douglas wrote that "the jury trial is the institution through which the community's sense of justice has through the years tempered the strictness of the law" by bringing to the Bar of Judgment "the quality of mercy."[832] He believed that the right of trial by jury was "an indispensable part of a free government"[833] and in *An Almanac of Liberty*, he said that trial by jury is "the inherent and invaluable right" of every American citizen. Echoing the First Continental Congress' *Letter to the People of Quebec* (October 26, 1774) declaring that "the first grand right" is representative government and "the next great right" is trial by jury, Justice Douglas wrote:

> *These were "the invaluable rights" — the rights "without which a people cannot be free and happy." . . . These were the rights in the forefront of events leading to the Declaration of Independence.*[834]

---

[829]de Gregorio, *The Complete Book of U.S. Presidents*, p. 502 (Dembner Books 2d ed. 1989).

[830]de Gregorio, *supra*, p. 502.

[831]*The Guide to American Law Encyclopedia*, Vol. 4, p. 184 (West Publishing Co. 1984). Lieberman called Douglas a true apostle of individual liberty. *See* Lieberman, *Milestones! Two Hundred Years of American Law*, pp. 249-251 (West Publishing Co. 1976).

[832]Douglas, *The Right of the People*, pp. 183-184 (Greenwood Press 1958).

[833]Statement of Mr. Justice Black and Mr. Justice Douglas on the Rules of Civil Procedure and the Proposed Amendments, 374 U.S. 865 (1963).

[834]Douglas, *An Almanac of Liberty*, pp. 121-122 (Doubleday & Co. 1954).

85. Winston Churchill, *The Birth of Britain* (1956).

As an orator, statesman, prime minister, and intense English patriot,[835] Winston Churchill knew no equal. It was as an accomplished author and historian, however, that he won the *Nobel Prize*. His *History of the Second World War* was published in six volumes between 1948 and 1954 and his four-volume *History of the English Speaking Peoples* was published from 1956 through 1958. The first volume of the latter publication is entitled *The Birth of Britain*. In it, Churchill traces the history of his country from Julius Caesar's midnight raid across the English Channel in August of 55 B.C. to conquer and subdue that "brave, warlike race" of "uncouth" Celtic tribesmen called Britons. Volume I concludes with the death of King Richard III on Bosworth Field in August of 1485.[836]

In a chapter on the historical development of the English common law, he "illuminates" the origin of the jury and "the part it played in the triumph of the common law," concluding that the "idea of the jury" was one of the "great contributions" to the English legal system. His most lavish praise was saved for the civil jury system in which "plaintiff and defendant alike have a safeguard from arbitrary perversion of the law."

> *The jury system has come to stand for all we mean by English justice, because so long as a case has to be scrutinized by twelve honest men, defendant and plaintiff alike have a safeguard from arbitrary perversion of the law. . . . Thus amidst the great process of centralization the old principle was preserved, and endures to this day, that law flows from the people. . . .*[837]

---

[835] *Encyclopædia Britannica Macropædia*, Vol. 4, pp. 595-600 (15th ed. 1979), describes Winston Churchill as an "author, orator, and statesman" [p. 595] who served as a member of the House of Commons, as Under-Secretary of State, as President of the Board of Trade, as Home Secretary, Cabinet Minister, Chief Minister of the Admiralty, Lieutenant of the Sixth Royal Scots Fusiliers, Chief of the Colonial Office, Chancellor of the Exchequer, editor of the *British Gazette*, "an intense patriot" [p. 598], "the popular architect of victory" in World War II [p. 599], coiner of the phrase "Iron Curtain," recipient of the Nobel Prize for literature, and "father" of the House of Commons [p. 600].

[836] Churchill, *A History of the English Speaking Peoples*, Vol. 1, pp. 1-17, 479-500 (Dorset Press 1956).

[837] Churchill, *supra*, Vol. 1, pp. 217, 219.

The jury system has come to stand for all we mean by English justice. The scrutiny of 12 honest jurors provides defendant and plaintiff alike a safeguard from arbitrary perversion of the law and preserves the old principle that law flows from the people.
—**Sir Winston Churchill (1956)**

86.   Theodore Plucknett, *A Concise History of the Common Law* (1956). As literary director of the Selden Society and distinguished Professor of Legal History at the University of London, Theodore Plucknett's *Concise History of the Common Law* is one of the most widely distributed historical treatises on the common law currently in publication. In it, he gives the "representative character" of the English jury system much of the credit for the development of our Anglo-American system of representative government.

> . . . [I]n its origin the jury is of a representative character; the basis of its composition . . . was clearly the intention to make it representative of the community. . . .[838]

Plucknett recognized that trial by jury has long been considered "a safeguard of political liberty."

> Ever since the 17th century when juries began to express sentiments against the government, there has been a tendency for the jury to become, at least in popular thought, a safeguard of political liberty.[839]

As author of the 11th edition of *Taswell-Langmead's English Constitutional History* (1960), Plucknett called trial by jury the "most democratical of juridicial institutions" and "the cherished bulwark of constitutional liberty."[840]

87.   Albert Averbach, *Tampering with the Jury System* (1956). Noting that "jury trials are a precious heritage for which our forefathers fought," Albert Averbach of the New York Bar wrote that "the public regards the retention of jury trials as a matter of constitutional safeguard of their rights and liberties."

> Since it was first recognized in the Magna Carta, trial by jury has been a prized shield against oppression. It is a right treasured by the American people.[841]

---

[838] Plucknett, *supra n.763*, pp. 127, 136-137. *See also* Stubbs, The Constitutional History of England, Vol. 1, pp. 697-698 (1880).

[839] Plucknett, *supra*, p. 107.

[840] Plucknett, *Taswell-Langmead's English Constitutional History*, p. 101 (11th ed. 1960).

[841] Averbach, "Tampering with the Jury System," *Insurance Law J.* 99, 102, 104 (1956).

88. Judge David Edelstein, "A Kind Word for the Civil Jury" (1956). In the same year that Winston Churchill paid tribute to trial by jury on the far side of the Atlantic, Judge David Edelstein[842] defended it here at home. Noting that jurors listen carefully and appear to understand the testimony, Judge Edelstein was "not convinced that the usual battle of experts presents an undue challenge to the jury." He concluded that "jurors, like other human beings, make mistakes" but felt that their mistakes were no different than those of "legislators, administrators and judges which equally may affect the life and security of the individual citizen."

> *I can only insist that I am well satisfied that the juries in my experience have acted responsibly. . . .*

From his experience, Judge Edelstein believed that jurors provided safety in numbers with less likelihood of distortion "based on the reconciliation of twelve varied temperaments and minds."

> *Moreover, a jury of twelve brings a valuable array of experience in the problems of mankind and acquaintance with the trials and obstacles that confront men in the pursuit of life, peace and security. No single judge . . . can bring to bear so varied and valuable an experience as can any jury.*

Judge Edelstein also felt that "jury service serves . . . to spread among the community at large a respect for the decisions of law" and compared a citizen's jury service to his right to vote. Since the voter and the juror are one in the same, if the juror is unqualified to understand and apply complicated expert testimony then —

> *. . . the mere voter is no longer qualified to vote, but should stand by for one who knows more about the true interests of society. For ultimately, the fact determinations involved in voting for a mayor, a governor, a congressman or a president are more complex and infinitely more significant than any fact determinations called for from the jury box.*[843]

---

[842] Appointed U.S. District Judge, Southern District of New York, April 8, 1952, and serving continuously since.

[843] Edelstein, "A Kind Word for the Civil Jury," 17 *NACCA L.J.* 302-313 (1956).

89.   Clarence R. Runals, *Trial by Jury is a Cherished Right* (1956). One of the most spirited defenses of the jury system was delivered by Clarence R. Runals, Vice President of the New York State Bar Association. In 1956, he wrote that "every constitution adopted by the people of this state since those fateful days of the American Revolution" provided that trial by jury "shall remain inviolate forever." Calling it "a cherished right," he concluded:

> To the American people the right to trial by jury is and has been a symbol of democracy — a bulwark against intemperate, arbitrary, capricious action, whether of state or judge. The reason is not difficult to discern... Every school child knows of the "bloody Assizes" presided over by Judge Jeffries. His name has become a byword of infamy. It is a symbol of merciless severity, mockery of justice, heinous inequities — a reminder that an alert citizenry must not permit his history to repeat itself. Every school child is taught the guarantees of liberty wrested from King John on the field at Runnymede and the basic phrase in Magna Carta that "no free man shall be deprived of life, liberty and property, but by the judgment of his peers and the law of the land." The jury box and the ballot box frequently have been called "the twin pillars of liberty." With some force has the jury system been termed "the most venerated institution in Anglo-Saxon law."[844]

90.   Sir Patrick Devlin, *The Lamp of Freedom* (1956). In 1956, that "distinguished English barrister and judge," Sir Patrick Devlin delivered the Hamlyn Lectures on trial by jury. Calling trial by jury the "lamp of freedom," Devlin said:

> ... The [second] object of any tyrant ... would be ... to overthrow or diminish trial by jury, for no tyrant could afford to leave a subject's freedom in the hands of twelve of his countrymen. So that trial by jury is more than an instrument of justice and more than one wheel of the Constitution: it is the lamp that shows that freedom lives....[845]

---

[844]Runals, "Jury Trial on Trial — A Symposium," 28 *N.Y.S.B. Bulletin* 322, 329-331 (October, 1956).

[845]Devlin, "Trial by Jury," the Hamlyn Lecture Series (London 1956), reprinted in Joiner, *supra* n.758, pp. 124-134.

The object of any tyrant would be to overthrow or diminish trial by jury, for it is more than an instrument of justice and more than one wheel of the Constitution: it is the lamp that shows that freedom lives.

—British Judge, Sir Patrick Devlin (1956)

91. Judge William J. Palmer, *On Trial: The Jury Trial* (1958). Noting that "trial by jury" is on trial before the ultimate Supreme Court, *the Court of Public Opinion,*" Judge William J. Palmer of the Superior Court of California examined the evolution of "this idea of democratic justice" in an article published in *Federal Rules Decisions.*

> *At the outset we ought to face thoughtfully the fact that 500 years . . . of human history, is a very long time for a specific pattern of judicial procedure continuously to exist. That fact alone . . . requires a good deal of respect for the institution. . . . Indeed, for those 500 years the jury trial has been . . . regarded with the same near-religious zeal as have the "unalienable rights" and basic civil liberties cherished in the thinking of free and freedom seeking peoples.*

Judge Palmer believed that "the germ-ideas of the jury trial were the same as those from which democracy itself evolved." Observing from his own experience that jurors "show an amazing resistance to pure sympathy, a conscientious faithfulness to the court's instructions, and a remarkably intelligent and sensible disposition of the issues," Judge Palmer concluded that "the right to trial by jury is yet a refuge from tyranny":

> *Being realistic, we shall not imagine that the constitutional provisions for trial by jury trial would save us from . . . a national tyranny. . . . But little tyrannies have been coming and going through the years, and they will continue to do so. They are not limited . . . to bureaucrats or the underworld. They have been plotted behind hypocritical fronts in well respected places, in places theoretically dedicated to the preservation of the basic civil liberties. Against all these tyrannies, existent or to come, trial by jury stands today as ever, a sheltering institution promising a sincere, though human, effort to deal justly with all who seek its ministrations.*[846]

These "little tyrannies" persist. No matter how sophisticated we may become, graft, greed and corruption will remain. *Our only practical protection is trial by jury.*

---

[846]Palmer, "On Trial: The Jury Trial," 20 *F.R.D.* 65-82 (1958).

92. W. S. Martin, *The Role of the Civil Jury* (1959). In 1959, W. S. Martin, a Canadian Queen's Counsel well-versed in trial techniques, wrote "The Role of a Jury in a Civil Case." In defense of the civil jury, he stated:

> *The right to trial by jury is the heritage of our common law — it has served well for countless generations. In the perspective given us by history we can see it as an institution protecting our citizens against the harshness of outdated laws. The man in the street looks on the jury as a bulwark against injustice — that will protect him from the insolence of those in public office — will shield the weak against the strong.*[847]

Concerning the capacity of the civil jury as "a tribunal for dispensing justice," Martin wrote:

> *... They may be ignorant of the law, but in their common wisdom they are fully aware of the dangers and tribulations of ordinary life. They are patient and generous to counsel who appear before them, but they resent bitterly anything which they think is a trick. They will tolerate no subterfuge. They will listen for interminable periods to common sense, but will become uneasy and restless under a barrage of ill-advised words. They will be annoyed at an ill-timed jest and they will detest the smallest attempt to bully a witness or themselves.*
>
> *But as a tribunal for dispensing justice, the centuries have proved them to be without equal.*[848]

As to its impartiality, Martin relates that a jury "is independent of politicians and outside influences." It brings to the decision of each case an approach fresh from the community.

> *... Truly the jury guarantees that the law shall belong to the people."*[849]

---

[847] Martin, "The Role of a Jury in a Civil Case," reprinted in Joiner, *Civil Justice and the Jury, supra n.758*, pp. 142-143.

[848] W. S. Martin, "The Role of a Jury in a Civil Case," Joiner, *supra n.758*, p. 143.

[849] Joiner, *supra n.758*, p. 146.

93. Chief Justice Earl Warren on the Excellence of Juries (1962).

Earl Warren (1891-1974), three-term governor of California (1943-1953) and Chief Justice of the United States for 16 years, "stamped his named indelibly on that period of the Court's history — from 1953 to 1969 — when great and enduring constitutional principles were forcefully enunciated."[850]

> *Although the Court under Warren had many of the usual cases that occupy the highest court of the nation, cases involving individual rights seem to be the hallmark of the Warren era. In addition to desegregation, legislative reapportionment, and the rights of the accused, the Warren Court underlined citizenship as a basic constitutional right. . . . . It also insisted that the military be kept subordinate to the civil government . . . and in general, it "read into" the Fourteenth Amendment, applicable against the states, most of the provisions of the Bill of Rights. . . .*[851]

On the standard of excellence maintained by American juries, Chief Justice Warren wrote:

> *Freedom and justice for the individual — grounded upon a just system of laws and protected by the courts — are the keystones of America's strength. This is the American concept, and it is our main claim to moral leadership in the world community.*
>
> *The men and women who are called upon to serve on juries in both our federal and state courts have maintained a standard of fairness and excellence throughout the history of our country. They have demonstrated a vision and a will toward the administration of justice that is a wellspring of inspiration. . . .*[852]

---

[850] Lieberman, *Milestones! Two Hundred Years of American Law*, p. 239 (West Publishing Co. 1976). *See also Encyclopædia Britannica Micropædia*, Vol. X, p. 552 (15th ed. 1979).

[851] *The Guide to American Law Encyclopedia*, Vol. 10, pp. 302-304 (West Publishing Company 1984).

[852] Chief Justice Warren's Foreword to Joiner, *Civil Justice and the Jury*, pp. v-vi (Prentice Hall 1962).

ILLUSTRATION BY ROBERT WEAVER

The men and women who serve on juries have maintained a standard of fairness and excellence throughout the history of our country and a vision toward the administration of justice that is a wellspring of inspiration.

—**Chief Justice Earl Warren (1962)**

94. Charles W. Joiner, *Civil Justice and the Jury* **(1962).** Born February 14, 1916, in Maquoketa, Iowa, Charles W. Joiner served on the faculty of the University of Michigan Law School (1947-1968) and as Dean of the Wayne State University Law School (1968-1972). He was appointed United States District Judge for Detroit in 1972 and was Chairman of Fellows of the American Bar Foundation (1978-1979).[853]

Reporting on the University of Chicago Jury Project financed by the Ford Foundation, Joiner authored *Civil Justice and the Jury* in 1962 in which he investigated the jury as a judicial and social institution, evaluated the basic strengths of a civil jury, examined the arguments of its critics and reflected upon what others had written about its intrinsic value. Characterizing the civil jury as "the conscience of the community," Joiner listed among the basic strengths of the civil jury its capacity for obtaining a sense of the community in interpreting general legal standards, a reduction of the inherent prejudice of the decision-making process, its tendency toward greater citizen participation in government, and its "carefully developed" system of checks and balances.[854]

> *The laws by which all of us live are not [a] series of hard and fast rules but, on the whole, a number of general statements. . . . These general standards must be interpreted in individual cases in a way that is understood by the community, otherwise, it will not live by them. The very purpose of using general language is to permit interpretation by the community from which the jury is chosen and . . . to obtain a sense of that community in interpreting these general standards.*[855]

Regarding the inherent prejudices and judges and jurors, Joiner asserted:

> *Everybody . . . carries with him a certain number of prejudices and biases, some strong and some weak. Jurors are not exempt from them, nor are judges. In one respect, however, jurors bring fewer prejudices to the decision making process. . . .*[856]

---

[853] Evory, ed., *Contemporary Authors*, Vol. 1, p. 307 (1976).
[854] Joiner, *supra* n.852, pp. 35-38, 65-68.
[855] Joiner, *supra*, p. 65.
[856] Joiner, *supra*, p. 66.

With respect to the educational value of jury participation, Joiner noted:

> *Because of the jury a great many people are involved in responsible governmental decision making.... More than any other single institution, the jury has brought people into government.... This valuable education in government cannot be underestimated as a significant strength of the civil jury.*[857]

Finally, concerning the carefully developed system of checks and balances inherent in our civil jury system, Joiner declared:

> *Trial by juries involve a trial before a judge and jury, the jury consisting of twelve reasonably impartial people, and a unanimous verdict under the instructions from the judge who has the power to set aside a verdict if it is erroneous. This is the traditional and constitutional concept of jury trial, involving a series of checks and balances which have been devised to obtain justice for litigants in the final judgment entered by the court. In no other method of trial are these checks and balances so carefully developed....*[858]

95.   Harry Kalven, Jr., *The Dignity of the Civil Jury* (1964). As Director of the University of Chicago Jury Project, Professor Kalven wrote that "the jury is almost by definition an exciting and gallant experiment in the conduct of serious human affairs." He wondered how it was that so many detractors of the civil jury could "cherish the criminal jury" at the same time they attacked the civil jury and concluded:

> *... In the course of the many years of [this] study it should be clear that I, personally, have become increasingly impressed with the humanity, strength, sanity, and responsibility of the [civil] jury....*[859]

---

[857] Joiner, *supra n.852*, pp. 66-67.
[858] Joiner, *supra n.852*, pp. 67-68.
[859] Kalven, The Dignity of the Civil Jury, 50 Va. L.R. 1055, 1067, 1075 (1964).

96.   Jefferson F. Meagher, *Trial by Jury Deserves a Fair Trial* (1964). Writing in the *New York State Bar Journal*, Jefferson F. Meagher, "an articulate upstate New York lawyer who has a long trial experience behind him," wrote that trial by jury had been "created for the protection of the individual in his rights and freedoms over the long pull of history."

> *Traditionally considered one of the bulwarks of our system of jurisprudence, trial by jury has become one of the hallmarks of our civilization...*[860]

Commenting on the insurance industry's longstanding campaign to undermine our civil jury system, Meagher wrote:

> *Many lawyers cannot dispel the nagging thought that there is more to the campaign against jury trials than meets the eye. While the bulk of personal injury actions are between individual litigants, the insurance company is an omnipresence brooding over the trial. The nature and extent of the propaganda campaign... does little to exorcise the lurking conviction that no small part of the pressure against the perpetuation of the democratic institution of trial by jury is corporate in inspiration. The nation's press, swallowing the statistical releases of the public relations agencies, finds little motivation for defense of the people's institution, when under attack.*[861]

Calling trial by jury "a vital artery in the bloodstream of the democratic process," Meagher concluded:

> *To abolish trial by jury is to rupture a vital artery in the bloodstream of the democratic process. Without such an organic link with the people, the continuity of our system is threatened. And in the struggle facing us, commitment by those who believe, who care very much, is our chief hope for survival.*[862]

---

[860] Meagher, "Trial by Jury Deserves a Fair Trial," 36 *N.Y.S.B.J.* 303-304 (August, 1964). Born October 19, 1908, and admitted to the New York Bar in 1935, Mr. Meagher has served as president of the Broome County Historical Society (1947-1948) and of the New York State Bar Association (1949-1950).

[861] Meagher, *supra*, 36 *N.Y.S.B.J.* 307-308.

[862] Meagher, *supra*, 36 *N.Y.S.B.J.* at 309-310.

Created for the protection of individual rights and freedoms over the long pull of history, trial by jury has become one of the hallmarks of our civilization. To abolish trial by jury is to rupture a vital artery in the bloodstream of the democratic process.
—**Jefferson F. Meagher,** *A Fair Trial for Trial by Jury* (1964)

97. Donald K. Ross, *Trial by Jury — Preserve It* (1965). Donald K. Ross, Public Relations Director of the Defense Research Institute, wrote in 1965 that "the right to trial by jury was gained through the blood of revolution," and "is part of the *Constitution* which has truly made this the land of the free." He said that "jurors are chosen for their open minds" and that "their newness to a situation leaves them open to legitimate persuasion." He said that "twelve minds balance the prejudice found in each, prejudice that is bound to respective background, state of life and emotional makeup."

> *The finger has been pointed at the United States as the only major country which retains the civil jury and the only one which suffers serious delays in the trial of lawsuits. . . . America has [also] been singled out . . . as the major country engaged in preserving freedom for the free world. . . . A just result is more important than a quick one; it matters not that other countries have abandoned civil juries. There is no outcry from the people to abolish the Seventh Amendment to the Constitution.*[863]

98. Stanley E. Sacks, *Preservation of the Civil Jury System* (1965). A 1948 graduate of Washington and Lee Law School, in 1965, Stanley E. Sachs of Norfolk, Virginia, authored an article on the civil jury system in the *Washington and Lee Law Review*. In it, he said that trial by jury was not only "a matter of constitutional mandate, but it is the only civil right guaranteed in three separate places in the *Constitution*." Calling the civil jury "one of our most cherished democratic institutions," he wrote:

> *The evolution of the jury in this country to the present day should be a matter of common knowledge. Its role as an independent fact finding body, working along with the impartial judge constituting the jury trial, has come down through the years as an ingenious and cherished element of Anglo-American jurisprudence. Its own performance record has proved vividly its valuable place as a bulwark of liberty and a cornerstone of democracy.*[864]

---

[863] Ross, *Trial by Jury — Preserve It*, pp. 5-7 (A pamphlet published by The Defense Research Institute 1965).

[864] Sachs, "Preservation of the Civil Jury System," 22 *Washington & Lee L.R.* 76-77 (1965).

99.   H. H. Grooms, "The Origin and Development of Trial by Jury" (1965). H. H. Grooms, United States District Judge for the Northern District of Alabama, found evidence that "something in the nature of trial by jury was employed," in England "as far back as Hlothar and Eadrick, Kings of Kent (673-680)," and concluded that trial by jury was "deeply imbedded in our *Constitutions*, state and federal." He believed that the development of the jury system was the inevitable result of "the excessive penalties of the law, the severity of punishment, the crudeness of the systems of justice, and the tyranny and servility of judges." We have our jury system today, he wrote, because our ancestors "struggled so mightily to achieve" it.

> We have the jury system as we know it today, with all that it means to our institution of government, because of those who have gone before and treasured it as an instrument of justice and a safeguard of liberties, which we enjoy, and for which they struggled so mightily to achieve.
>
> It can hardly be disputed that the stability of peoples of common law heritage may be attributed in a wholesome part to trial by jury, because it has brought justice close to the people and put its dispensation largely in their keeping.[865]

100.   Maurice Rosenberg, ***The Trial Judge's Verdict on the Civil Jury*** **(January, 1966).** Maurice Rosenberg of the Columbia Law School and a member of the faculty of the National College of State Trial Judges, reported in the January, 1966, issue of *The Trial Judge's Journal* that "among state trial judges — whether new to the bench or seasoned by years of service — the verdict on the civil jury is overwhelmingly 'not guilty' of deserving extinction or major curtailment." Among the major causes for the trial judge's overwhelming approval of the civil jury listed by Professor Rosenberg, were the following: (a) "the jurymen are *of* the community and may be better aware than judges of the norms which it expects prudent people to observe"; (b) that "jury service is a good exercise in democracy"; (c) that the "people have more confidence in jury verdicts"; and (d) the greater "neutrality" of juries when compared with judges.[866]

---

[865]Grooms, "The Origin and Development of Trial by Jury," 26 *Ala. Lawyer* 162-163, 164, 171 (1965).

[866]Rosenberg, "The Trial Judge's Verdict on the Civil Jury," 5 *Trial Judge's Journal* 11 (January, 1966).

101. Justice Tom C. Clark, *The American Jury: A Justification* (1966). Born in Dallas on September 23, 1899, Tom C. Clark was admitted to the Texas Bar in 1922. He was District Attorney for Dallas and Assistant U.S. Attorney General before being appointed Attorney General by President Truman in 1945. In 1949, he was nominated to the United States Supreme Court where he served until his retirement in 1967.[867]

Selected to author the lead article in the inaugural edition of the *Valparaiso Law Review*, Justice Clark took as his topic trial by jury, asserting that "700 years of jury verdicts without a change in procedure is heavy weight to overcome."

> *The demands of the law are strict while those of the jury depend upon its collective conscience. It is the jury, therefore, which is able to make the best accommodation between the law and the merits. It adds a humanistic touch to the law relaxing it at times so as to allow a more equitable judgment....*
>
> *It was also thought that the jury was "the reasonable man" about which the law often speaks. Should not the collective judgment of 12 people be more reasonable than that of one?*
>
> *... History has proven that trial by jury has been a bulwark of liberty.... In our own times, the jury often has served as a deterrent to ambitious officials who wish to crush before them those who stand in their way....*

Observing that juries "exert tremendous influence on the molding of the national character," Justice Clark concluded:

> *In conclusion, it is submitted that the jury system improves the quality of justice.... It is, therefore, the sole means of keeping the administration of justice attuned to community standards. Daniel Webster tells us that justice is the great interest of man on earth. Let us not cut its jugular vein!*[868]

---

[867] *The Guide to American Law Encyclopedia*, Vol. 2, pp. 372-373 (West Publishing Co. 1984).

[868] Clark, "The American Jury: A Justification," 1 *Valparaiso L.R.* 1-7 (Fall 1966).

The collective conscience of the jury adds a humanistic touch to the strict demands of the law so as to allow a more equitable judgment. The jury system improves the quality of justice and is the sole means of keeping its administration attuned to community standards.
—**U.S. Supreme Court Justice Tom C. Clark (1966)**

102. Morris J. Bloomstein, *Verdict: The Jury System* (1968). Born in Brooklyn in 1928, Morris J. Bloomstein authored *The Consumer's Guide to Fighting Back* in 1976.[869] In his 1968 text on the jury system, he called the institution of trial by jury "the cornerstone of our judicial process."[870]

103. Joseph T. Karcher, *The Case for the Jury System* (1969). In 1969, Joseph T. Karcher wrote that avowed opponents of our American jury system are "marshalling their forces for battle."

> *The struggle of the so-called average man . . . to secure the protection of his individual rights to life, liberty and property had been dearly fought. It had not been easily won. The fight had been long and bitter. He had suffered for centuries under the tyranny of despotic Kings. It had taken a revolution and almost a miracle to secure these rights. The memory of the cruel injustice he had suffered prior to the advent of the jury system was still fresh in his mind three or four centuries later. The rights were not to be given up lightly. It was only logical that he should cling to these precious rights and fight a war, if necessary, to secure them for himself and his descendants.*

"Justice," he said, "is a precious commodity" and must be preserved, whatever the cost.

> *It is the considered judgment of most members of the Bench and Bar that the right of trial by jury is as good, as useful, as sacred as it ever was. It is still a bulwark against tyranny. It is still the surest guarantee of the protection of the average citizen to life, liberty and property. It is still the "Lamp of Liberty." It is still worth every cent that it costs . . . [and] it must be preserved. . . .*
>
> *Is there a better way to administer justice than through the jury system? If there is, no one has yet found it. . . .*[871]

---

[869]Nasso, ed., *Contemporary Authors*, Vols. 25-28, p. 78 (1st Rev. 1977).
[870]Bloomstein, *Verdict: The Jury System*, p. 29 (1968).
[871]Karcher, "The Case for the Jury System," 45 *Chicago-Kent L.R.* 157, 159-1962 (1969).

**104.	Henry Marsh, *British Documents of Liberty* (1971).**
Henry Marsh traced the evolution of democracy in England from the 10th century Saxon kings to universal suffrage, concluding that the concept of the British jury system began with the selection of two knights from every shire who, in turn, "chose upon their oath ten knights of every 100."

> *Their familiarity with local folk and customs made it likely that they would reach decisions through sound common sense rather than through the too fine logic of legal niceties; while their remoteness from the king's court (and, in the modern context, from the central government), ensures that measure of independence which is essential to true justice.*

Of the *Magna Carta*, Marsh wrote that the rebel barons of Runnymede were "anxious that the royal power should be exercised with moderation" and that no man should be placed on trial based solely upon the "unsupported statements" of the king or his officers.

> *From such particular matters the barons moved to the statement of broad rules as to how justice was to be administered. They had in mind no wider aim than to check current abuses, but in fact they laid down principles of government from which the English people have never departed and which other nations have been eager to follow. No free man was to be punished except by the lawful judgment of his equals or by the law of the land. (Clause 39). By that simple phrase — "the lawful judgment of his equals" — the king and his judges were prevented from using the courts to oppress their enemies, or disguise tyranny in the cloak of justice. Trial by jury was thus secured, and it has been demonstrated in modern times how such a system protects the citizen from the tyrannies of governments. Justice can easily be banished from courts where juries are absent. Governments may bring a man into the courts out of fear or envy. Sycophantic judges may try them. But while the verdict of the court is in fact the verdict of a group of ordinary men, independent of judge and ruler, liberty can never be totally extinguished.*[872]

---

[872]Henry Marsh, *British Documents of Liberty*, p. 332, 352 (Fairleigh Dickinson University Press 1971).

105. Lloyd E. Moore, *The Jury: Tool of Kings, Palladium of Liberty* (1973). Lloyd E. Moore's classic traces the development of the jury system from the Inquisitio of Charlemagne[873] to the *Constitution* of the United States. In conclusion, he states:

> ... Jury trial ensures the common citizen of receiving very nearly the same justice as the others in society. ... When the jury is fairly representative of the community, it is the best protection against judicial injustice. But, the overriding reason for retaining and expanding the jury system is the belief that, ... the sovereign power of judgment ought to be vested directly in the people. ...[874]

106. Justice E. L. Haines, *The Role of the Jury in the Control of the Abuse of Power* (1979). In a series of special lectures of the Law Society of Upper Canada, Justice E. L. Haines spoke of the role of the jury in the control of the abuse of power. He called trial by jury "a remarkable institution because it represents a deep commitment to the use of laymen in the administration of justice." Therein, he said, "lies its strength against tyranny." As "a bulwark against the abuse of power," it is, he said, "our oldest and strongest fortress."

> Trial by jury is the ultimate protector of individual liberties. ... It is the only real check against abuse of power. ... The integrity and independence of the jury has a significant impact on the way we are governed and the kind of laws under which we operate. A jury ensures that our leaders are responsive and responsible. The power of wealth, status and the state with its vast resources and enforcement agencies must be subject to the scrutiny of the average citizen in a democratic and just society.[875]

---

[873] Known as "Charles the Great," Charlemagne served as king of the Franks from 768-814 A.D. and as emperor of the Holy Roman Empire from 800-814 A.D.

[874] Moore, *The Jury: Tool of Kings, Palladium of Liberty*, p. 82 (1973).

[875] Haines, "The Role of the Jury in the Control of the Abuse of Power," in *The Abuse of Power and the Role of an Independent Judicial System in Its Regulation and Control*, pp. 31, 34, 48 (The Law Society of Upper Canada 1979).

Those twelve men [and women] in the jury box are the cornerstone of our judicial process.
  —**Morris J. Bloomstein**, ***Verdict: The Jury System*** **(1968)**

107. Justice William H. Rehnquist, *On the Seventh Amendment* (1979). William H. Rehnquist, appointed Associate Justice of the Supreme Court by President Nixon in 1972 and Chief Justice by President Reagan in 1986, was "generally regarded as the Burger Court's most conservative member."[876] Yet he was an ardent defender of the civil jury. In his dissent in *Parklane Hosiery Co. v. Shore*, he wrote of the Court's obligation to enforce the *Seventh Amendment* and said that "the right of trial by jury in civil cases at common law is fundamental to our history and jurisprudence."

> *It is perhaps easy to forget, now more than 200 years removed from the events, that the right of trial by jury was held in such esteem by the colonists that its deprivation at the hands of the English was one of the important grievances leading to the break with England. . . .*
>
> *. . . The founders of our nation considered the right of trial by jury in civil cases an important bulwark against tyranny and corruption, a safeguard too precious to be left to the whim of the sovereign. . . . [Their] concerns for the institution of jury trial . . . led to the passage of the Declaration of Independence and to the Seventh Amendment. . . . Trial by a jury of laymen . . . was important to the founders because juries represented the layman's common sense . . . and thus keep the administration of law in accord with the wishes and feelings of the community.*[877]

When Chief Justice Rehnquist wrote of the right to a civil jury trial as being "a safeguard too precious to be left to the whim of the sovereign," he was referring to our executive and legislative branches of government. In 1786, James Mitchell Varnum of Rhode Island had argued that the notion that the legislature could change the *Constitution* was so dangerous that it "borders upon treason!"[878] Yet, today, in the halls of Congress and in the legislatures of every state, the avowed enemies of trial by jury are at work planning its ultimate destruction.

---

[876] de Gregorio, *The Complete Book of U.S. Presidents*, pp. 599-600 (Dembner Books, 2d ed. 1989).

[877] *Dissenting Opinion* of Justice Rehnquist in *Parklane Hosiery Co. v. Shore*, 439 U.S. 322, 337, 340, 343-344 (1979).

[878] *See* pp. 313-315 above.

108. M.D.A. Freeman, *The Jury on Trial* (1981). In *Current Legal Problems* (London 1981), M.D.A. Freeman wrote that "the jury represents democratic self government" and that attacks upon it were "the predatory ravages of authoritarianism." He maintained that "the jury is a mechanism by which the court's output of justice may be balanced with community sentiment."

> *Juries are part of our inherited political culture. The jury mediates between the Law and the People. The importance of the jury lies in the fact that lawyers and judges know that their arguments must be pitched on a level that the man in the street can understand. The jury rests on a notion of justice "in which law must be made to seem rational and even humane" to laymen. In these terms an attack on the jury is also an attack upon the foundation of our political culture. Without the jury we would not be the society we are now.*

Concerning the method by which the jury determines the credibility of conflicting evidence, Freeman wrote:

> *Trials are about competing pictures of reality. What confronts the court is a multitude of conflicting claims. The tribunal trying the case has the task of making sense of the situation. What the jury does is to compare what it hears with its experiences. It by no means follows that it will pick one side's story. It is quite possible for it to take segments of competing versions put in by different participants and to weld them into a composite picture. It selects using criteria of its own common sense, everyday understanding of situations. In the jury box they function much as they do in the everyday world. They make sense of situations; they construct a reality.*

As to the democratic character of the jury, he said:

> *This is the age of participation. In countless areas of life plans are afoot to allow for participation of ordinary men and women in decisions which affect them. With the jury we actually have an institution where people help to administer themselves.*[879]

---

[879] Freeman, *The Jury on Trial*, pp. 65, 89-90, 96-98 in *Current Legal Problems* (1981) [Ellipsis omitted].

109. Peter W. Culley, *In Defense of Civil Juries* (1983). A former Assistant Attorney General of the State of Maine, Peter W. Culley wrote that "the civil jury is firmly imbedded in our system of justice" and that "the consensus verdict, consisting of liberal doses of common sense and experience, provides the best means of resolving factual disputes of all kinds."

> *The jury system . . . engrafts community values onto our law. No single individual can represent the sense of the community. It is difficult to conceive of a better mechanism than the jury for mirroring community values and establishing standards to which members of the community must conform.*[880]

110. Judge Stephen Reinhardt on the Suspension of Civil Jury Trials for Budgetary Purposes (1986). On June 12, 1986, the Administrative Office of the United States Courts at the direction of the Executive Committee of the Judicial Conference of the United States, ordered that all civil jury trials be suspended for a period of three-and-a-half months "because Congress failed to appropriate sufficient funds for juror payment." Petitioners in California and Alaska filed for a *Writ of Mandamus* and obtained a stay from the Ninth Circuit Court of Appeals. In an opinion by Judge Stephen Reinhardt, the court held that "the availability of constitutional rights does not vary with the rise and fall of account balances in the treasury."

> *. . . Our basic liberties cannot be offered and withdrawn as "budget crunches" come and go. . . . In short, constitutional rights do not turn on the political mood of the moment, the outcome of cost/benefit analyses or the results of economic or fiscal calculations. Rather, our constitutional rights are fixed and immutable, subject to change only in the manner our forefathers established for the making of constitutional amendments. The constitutional mandate that federal courts provide civil litigants with a system of civil jury trials is clear. There is no price tag on the continued existence of that system, or on any other constitutionally-provided right.*[881]

---

[880] Culley, "In Defense of Civil Juries," 35 *Maine L.R.* 17, 19, 28-29 (1983).

[881] *Armster v. United States District Court*, 792 F.2d 1423, 1425, 1429 (9th Cir. 1986).

Our constitutional right to trial by jury does not turn on the political mood of the moment, the outcome of cost/benefit analyses or the results of economic or fiscal calculations. There is no price tag on the continued existence of the civil jury system, or any other constitutionally-provided right.

—Judge Stephen Reinhardt (1986)

111. John V. Singleton, *Jury Trial: History and Preservation* (January 19, 1987). John V. Singleton, Chief U.S. District Judge for the Southern District of Texas, called trial by jury a "cornerstone of our democracy" and said that "the history of the American jury teaches us the importance of trial by jury to the early colonists and founders of our federal and state governments."

> *The jury also permits the average citizen a chance to participate in our democratic society. Most citizens' participation is limited to two activities — voting and jury duty. Serving as a juror is a much more involved exercise of citizenship than pulling a lever in the voting machine. It often permits a group of citizens to express the viewpoint of the community, whether it be on the relative severity of a particular crime, reflected in a verdict, or the magnitude of a civil wrong, reflected in an award of damages.*
>
> *. . . This is participation in our democratic society . . . that our forefathers thought was vital to their new country and that we today should seek to preserve and hold dear as . . . a safeguard to liberty and a palladium of free government.*[882]

112. Judge Morris S. Arnold, *The Civil Jury in Historical Perspective* (1987). U.S. District Judge Morris S. Arnold of the Western District of Arkansas formerly served as Professor of Law and History at the University of Pennsylvania and has written extensively on the history of the jury system. In the Final Report of the 1986 Chief Justice Earl Warren Conference on Advocacy, he wrote that the jury system, "like most of our common-law institutions, is a product of practicality and necessity."

> *It is almost impossible to exaggerate the centrality of the institution of the jury to almost all the important episodes of Anglo-American legal history. Many of the central ideas of the American and English common law owe their origin to the fact that the jury was the chief mechanism for trying factual disputes. It is the single most important institution in the history of Anglo-American law.*[883]

---

[882]Singleton, "Jury Trial: History and Preservation," pp. 273, 280-81 in *1988 Tr. Law. Guide* (Callahan & Co. 1988).

[883]Arnold, "The Civil Jury in Historical Perspective," pp. 9-10 in *The American Civil Jury* (1987).

113. John Guinther, *The Jury in America* (1988). In a research project sponsored by the Roscoe Pound Foundation, John Guinther describes the civil jury's role as guardian of American democracy:

> *The civil jury . . . performs . . . a guardian role against oppression. . . . It helps protect us against those who would threaten our health and safety; it sets standards of responsibility and fair dealing. . . . Were there no other reason for maintaining the civil jury's existence, these would be ample.*
>
> *There is one reason more.*
>
> *We have given much of our democracy away, sometimes willingly and sometimes not. . . . But in one place we still have a direct voice and can be heard, and that is through our juries. Because of them, we are still direct participants in our democracy. . . .*[884]

114. Paul B. Weiss, *Reforming Tort Reform* (1989). In an article in the *Catholic University Law Review*, Paul B. Weiss asked: "*Is there substance to the Seventh Amendment?*" In answer, he noted that the United States Supreme Court has called the *Seventh Amendment* a "fundamental guarantee of the rights and liberties of the people," and said that "any seeming curtailment . . . should be scrutinized with the utmost care." He wrote that "the essential function of the jury in determining the quantum of a plaintiff's damages was deeply entrenched in English common law" and that "absent *Constitutional* amendment, the *Seventh Amendment* cannot alter common law forms of action by the mere imposition of damage caps."

> *. . . The only manner in which the power of legislatures to enact such legislation may be legitimized is by undermining and eroding Seventh Amendment guarantees. If the courts permit this, the implications are grave. . . . This is unacceptable, intolerable, and repugnant to the concept of Constitutional government. . . .*[885]

---

[884]Guinther, *The Jury in America*, pp. 230-231 (Roscoe Pound Foundation 1988).

[885]Weiss, "Reforming Tort Reform: Is There Substance to the Seventh Amendment?" 38 *Catholic Univ. L.R.* 737, 766-767 (1989), quoting *Hodges v. Easton*, 106 U.S. 408, 412 (1882), and *Demick v. Schiedt*, 293 U.S. 474, 486 (1935).

115. Alderman & Kennedy, *In Our Defense: The Bill of Rights in Action* (1991). Ellen Alderman and Caroline Kennedy called the *Bill of Rights* "the most comprehensive protection of individual freedom ever written" and said of the *Seventh Amendment*:

> Historically, the right to a civil jury has been one of the most prized and accepted of all those in the Bill of Rights. It was included in the original Jamestown Charter of 1607, and by 1776 all thirteen colonies protected the right in some form. In fact, the biggest commotion caused by the right to a civil jury occurred when it was left out of the new Constitution. . . .[886]

116. Cynthia J. Cohen, *Whatever Happened to the Seventh Amendment?* (December 15, 1991). On the 200th anniversary of the ratification of the *Bill of Rights*, Cynthia J. Cohen of the Boston Bar wrote that "it is particularly appropriate to reflect upon the *Seventh Amendment* protection of the right of civil jury trial."

> . . . Proponents of the civil jury considered it to be a crucial political institution which would empower ordinary citizens, and act as a populist check on the judicial system. . . .
>
> History teaches us that the civil jury was intended to fulfill a unique and crucial role in our system of government — to serve as a means of political expression for average citizens, to protect disempowered litigants in contests with the wealthy and powerful and, in general, to keep the legal system in touch with the values and beliefs of the people. There is no other political institution and no other method of adjudication that can fulfill this role. The fact of the matter is that as we chip away at the civil jury, we change the constitutional bargain that was made by the founders of our country 200 years ago. Notwithstanding the efforts and desires of those who insisted upon a constitutional provision to preserve the civil jury trial, unless we find new respect for the *Seventh Amendment*, one of the basic elements of our democracy may be lost.[887]

---

[886] Alderman & Kennedy, *In Our Defense: The Bill of Rights in Action*, pp. 14-15, 276 (William Morrow & Co. 1991).

[887] Cohen, "Whatever Happened to the *Seventh Amendment*?" 35 *Boston Bar Journal* 17, 19 (November/December 1991).

Historically, the right to a civil jury has been one of the most prized and accepted of all those in the Bill of Rights. It was included in the original Jamestown Charter of 1607, and by 1776 all thirteen colonies protected the right in some form. In fact, the biggest commotion caused by the right to a civil jury occurred when it was left out of the new Constitution.

—Ellen Alderman & Caroline Kennedy,
In Our Defense: The Bill of Rights in Action (1991)

SUMMARY. For 777 years, trial by jury has been honored and acclaimed by the most eminent minds of England and America as "the cornerstone of our judicial process" for the following reasons:

 (a) *Assurance of Integrity.* Unlike a fixed tribunal, a juror's identity is unknown until the time of trial. With its many safeguards, our American jury system is virtually incorruptible.

 (b) ***Protection of the Fundamental Rights of the American People.*** Jurors are the guardians of public justice and our best protection against the tyranny and oppression of the rich and powerful as well as the unpredictable whims of public opinion.

 (c) *The Voice of the People.* The common sense, sound judgment and collective experience of the jury makes it the most effective method for eliciting the truth, and its reflection of community standards ensures us that "law flows from the people."

 (d) *Reduction of Prejudice.* By bringing together a group of citizens with differing backgrounds and experience, the jury system reduces "the inherent prejudice of the decision-making process."

 (e) ***Reducing the Rigidity of the Rules of Law.*** Injecting the layman into the administration of justice "mitigates the severe logic of the law, and makes its administration tolerable."

 (f) ***Rendering the Rules of Law Understandable to the Public.*** The explanation of legal principles to the jury brings the law down to the level of their own comprehension.

 (g) ***Increasing Respect for the Administration of Justice.*** Greater public confidence in lay jurors increases public respect for the rules of law and the administration of justice.

 (h) *Improvement of the National Character.* As Francis Wellman wrote in 1924, the jury is "a great popular university" which "trains our citizens in the art of self government."

 (i) *The Jury System Has Stood the Test of Time.* As Justice Jeremiah S. Black said in 1866, trial by jury "has borne the test of a longer experience and borne it better than any other legal institution that ever existed among men."

 (j) *It is Our Fundamental Right.* Tampering with our constitutional right of trial by jury "is unacceptable, intolerable and repugnant to the concept of constitutional government."

U. A COMPARISON OF THE BRITISH AND AMERICAN CONSTITUTIONS

1. Three Basic Differences. The decline of the jury system in England was due, in part, to three basic differences in the English and American constitutions. First, our American *Constitution* is a comprehensive, written document, formally adopted by the people, which "sets forth in detail the fundamental rights of the individual which all agencies of government are obliged to respect." The English Constitution, on the other hand, is primarily unwritten. Although it incorporates such fundamental documents as the *Magna Carta* (1215), the *Habeas Corpus Act* (1641), and the *British Bill of Rights* (1689), "there are other elements in the British *Constitution*—notably the rules of the common law, and many well-established customs and conventions."

The second major difference is that of supremacy. "The central concept of the British *Constitution* is the supremacy of Parliament." However, in the United States, the *Constitution* itself is the supreme law of the land.

> *The U.S. concept of constitutions is imbedded in a long tradition that a constitution represents a higher law and is an expression of the permanent will of the people, binding upon all governmental entities. According to this view, the people are the ultimate source of all political power....*[888]

The significance of the distinction based on the supremacy of the United States *Constitution* was discussed by Justice Hugo Black in "The *Bill of Rights* and the Federal Government" in 1963:

> *In England, statutes, Magna Carta, and later declarations of rights had for centuries limited the power of the king, but they did not limit the power of Parliament.... Parliament could change this English "Constitution"; Congress cannot change ours. Ours can only be changed by amendments and ratified by three-fourths of the states. It was one of the great achievements of our Constitution that it ended legislative omnipotence here and placed all departments and agencies of government under one supreme law.*[889]

---

[888] *Guide to American Law, supra* n.867, Vol. 3, pp. 203-209.

[889] Black, "The *Bill of Rights* and the Federal Government," p. 56 in Cahn, *The Great Rights* (Macmillan Co. 1963).

Finally, through the *Doctrine of Separation of Powers* and the creation of an independent judiciary, our Founding Fathers sought to guarantee the preservation of the fundamental principles of individual liberty against encroachment by the legislative and executive branches of government through the *Doctrine of Judicial Review*.

> *. . . In this country the judiciary was made independent because it has . . . the primary responsibility and duty of giving force and effect to constitutional liberties and limitations upon the executive and legislative branches. Judges in England were not always independent and they could not declare Parliamentary acts void. Consequently, English courts could not be counted on to protect the liberties of the people against invasion by Parliament, as many unfortunate Englishmen found out.*[890]

The fundamental principles of individual liberty established in our *Constitution* and *Bill of Rights* are "absolutes."[891] This is the way they were intended by the framers of our *Constitution* and this is the way they must be preserved. Neither the President, nor Congress, nor our state legislatures have the power to tamper with the *Seventh Amendment*. The absolute right of trial by jury in civil cases belongs, not to our representatives in the state and national legislatures, but to the people themselves.

What U.S. Supreme Court Justice John Marshall Harlan wrote in *Maxwell v. Dow* (1900) is equally true today:

> *. . . The privileges and immunities enumerated in these Amendments belong to every citizen of the United States. . . . In order to form a more perfect union, establish justice, ensure domestic tranquility, . . . and secure the blessings of liberty to themselves and their posterity, the . . . people of the United States ordained and established the Constitution of the United States. . . . What they had in view by so doing was to make it certain that the privileges and immunities therein specified — the enjoyment of which, the Fathers believed, were necessary in order to secure the blessings of liberty — could never be impaired or destroyed by the national government.*[892]

---

[890]Black, *supra n.889*, pp. 49-50.
[891]Black, *supra n.889*, p. 45.
[892]*Maxwell v. Dow*, 176 U.S. 581, 605, 608 (1900).

The privileges and immunities enumerated in the Bill of Rights belong to every citizen of the United States. When the people of the United States ordained and established the Constitution, what they had in view was to make certain that those rights could never be impaired by the national government.

—**Justice John Marshall Harlan (1900)**

The provisions of the Bill of Rights that safeguard fair legal procedures came about largely to protect the weak and the oppressed from punishment by the strong and the powerful who wanted to stifle the voices of discontent raised in protest against oppression and injustice in public affairs.

—**Justice Hugo L. Black (1963)**

Justice Hugo Black called these absolute guarantees of individual liberty the "best hope for the aspirations of freedom which men share everywhere" and warned that the evils they guard against "are not only old, they are with us now, they exist today."

The provisions of the Bill of Rights that safeguard fair legal procedures came about largely to protect the weak and the oppressed from punishment by the strong and the powerful who wanted to stifle the voices of discontent raised in protest against oppression and injustice in public affairs. ...[893]

2. Effect Upon Trial by Jury in England and America.

Although the United States "emerged with a jury system comparable to and in direct extension of the English jury,"[894] "in the United States, unlike England, written constitutions have played a part in the adoption and continuation of the right of trial by jury."[895] Not only is the right of trial by jury guaranteed by the *Sixth* and *Seventh Amendments* to our national *Constitution*, but as Justice Joseph Story wrote in 1833, "it is now incorporated into all our state constitutions, as a fundamental right; and the *Constitution of the United States* would have been justly obnoxious to the most conclusive objection, if it had not recognized and confirmed it in the most solemn terms."[896]

In England, Parliament has the power to abridge the right of trial by jury because the latest expression of Parliamentary will is the supreme law of the British realm. However, in the United States, our unique American concepts of constitutional supremacy and judicial review have enabled independent state and federal judiciaries to block repeated attempts by Congress and the state legislatures to deprive the American citizens of their most sacred fundamental right.

In response to the argument that legislative bodies are "the constitutional judges of their own power," Alexander Hamilton wrote in *The Federalist No. 78* (1788) that "it is far more rational to suppose, that the courts were designed to be an intermediate body between the people and their legislature, in order . . . to keep the latter within the limits assigned to their authority."

---

[893]Black, *supra n.889*, pp. 61-62.
[894]Bloomstein, *Verdict: The Jury System*, p. 25 (1968).
[895]Justice Tom C. Clark, *supra n.868*, p. 3.
[896]Story, *supra n.697*, Book III, § 923, pp. 656-657. For state constitutional guarantees of the right of trial by jury, *see* Appendix A on pp. 469-476 below.

3. Judicial Protection of Trial by Jury in the United States. Over the 216 years of the sovereignty and independence of the United States, in the words of Supreme Court Justice Frank Murphy (1942), the right of trial by jury, "a right so fundamental and sacred to the citizen," has been "jealously guarded by the courts" from invasion by our state and federal legislatures. Set forth below are eight typical examples.

(a) *Trevett v. Weeden* **(R.I. 1786).** The Rhode Island *Bank Act* of 1786 was "one of the numerous Legal Tender Acts of the period which compelled people to accept paper money of the state at par value." It also provided that violations of the Act would be tried by a three-judge panel without the benefit of a jury and with no right of appeal. The Supreme Court of Rhode Island declared the *Bank Act* unconstitutional.

> *The Assembly, dismayed by the decision, cited the judges to appear before it and assign the reason that they had "adjudged an Act of the supreme legislature of this state to be unconstitutional and absolutely void.". . . The defense of the Court was made by Justice David Howell, who laid down the principle that the judges were not accountable to the Assembly, and that the right of trial by jury . . . was a fundamental right which the Assembly could not abolish.*[897]

(b) *Bayard v. Singleton* **(N.C. 1787).** The North Carolina *Forfeited Estates Act* of 1785 "would have deprived a litigant of jury trial with respect to real estate which had been confiscated from a British subject."[898] In an opinion by Judge James Iredell, who served as Associate Justice of the United States Supreme Court from 1790-1799, the Superior Court of North Carolina declared the Act to be in violation of "the law of the land, unrepealable by any Act of the General Assembly."

> *That by the Constitution every citizen had undoubtedly a right to a decision of his property by a trial by jury. For if the legislature could take away this right, . . . it might with as much authority require his life to be taken away without a trial by jury.*[899]

---

[897] Chroust, *The Rise of the Legal Profession in America*, Vol. 2, p. 27 n.90 (University of Oklahoma Press 1965).

[898] Dumbauld, *The Constitution of the United States*, p. 16 (University of Oklahoma Press 1964).

[899] *Bayard v. Singleton*, 1 N.C. (1 Mart.) 42, 45 (1787).

> By the Constitution every citizen has a right to a decision of his property by a trial by jury. If the legislature could take away this right, it might with as much authority require his life to be taken away without a trial by jury.
> —Justice James Iredell of North Carolina (1787)

(c) ***State v. Allen*** **(South Carolina 1822).** The South Carolina *Appropriation Act* of 1820 imposed a penalty of $10,000 "on any person who shall sell any lottery tickets within this state" and empowered the tax collector to enforce an execution without the right of trial by jury. The Constitutional Court of South Carolina in an opinion by Justice Abraham Nott, held the statute unconstitutional, stating that "the liability of the party must first be established by a jury of his country, and not by the arbitrary fiat of any individual."

> ... The Constitution intended to impose a restraint upon the legislature as well as upon other departments of government.... The Constitution ... is the form of government delineated by the mighty hand of the people, in which certain first principles of fundamental law are established. It fixes the limits to the exercise of legislative authority, and prescribes the orbit within which it shall move. It says to the legislature, so far shalt thou go and no farther....[900]

(d) ***State Bank v. Cooper*** **(Tennessee 1831).** The Tennessee *Bank Act* of 1829 established a non-jury three-judge panel to hear all cases brought by the Bank of Tennessee against persons who have "become defaulters to said bank," and provided that "no appeal lies from its decision." The Supreme Court of Tennessee held the Act unconstitutional.

> The right of trial by jury has, at all periods in the history of the country and of England, been held in high estimation. ... Legislators are under the same obligation to observe the provisions of the Constitution that is incumbent on the judges and other public officials of the land.... If a legislative Act should be plainly and obviously opposed to the letter and spirit of the Constitution, the Constitution is paramount to any law the legislature can make in opposition to it.... All departments of government are equally bound by the Constitution. It is the ... authority under which all must act. So far as that authority is exceeded the Act is void....[901]

---

[900] *State v. Allen*, 2 McCord (13 S.C.L.) 55, 62 (1822).
[901] *State Bank v. Cooper*, 10 Tenn. (2 Yerg.) 599, 622-623 (1831).

(e) *Hinchly v. Machine* **(New Jersey 1836).** By an Act passed on December 10, 1825, the Courts of Common Pleas in certain counties in New Jersey were authorized to hold special terms for the trial of small causes "in cases where the judgment below had been rendered by a justice of the peace, without the intervention of a jury." Although the right of appeal from the decision of the justice of the peace was preserved, one county "had adopted a rule of practice by which the parties should be considered as waiving their right to such trial, unless they signified their intention of having a jury on or before a certain day in the term in which such appeal should be returned." The New Jersey Supreme Court declared the application of the Act unconstitutional as having deprived the parties of their right to trial by jury "upon a mere implied or constructive waiver of such right."[902]

(f) *State v. Gurney* **and** *Saco v. Wentworth* **(Maine 1853).** Under certain statutes of the State of Maine, appeals were provided from non-jury criminal convictions before a justice of the peace. However, as a condition to obtaining a jury trial on appeal, the defendant was required to post a bond to cover the cost of prosecution and, if later convicted by a jury, his fine was doubled. In companion cases, the Supreme Judicial Court of Maine held the Acts unconstitutional, stating that "the legislature has no power to impair a right given by the *Constitution*" because "it belongs to the citizen untrammeled and unfettered" and "if the legislature can impose penalties upon the exercise of the right, they may be so severe and heavy as practically to destroy it."[903]

> *An Act of the legislature, which takes away this privilege of trial by jury directly, is tyrannical and a palpable violation of the Constitution; one which renders it difficult to obtain, beyond what public necessity requires, impairs individual rights and is inconsistent with this provision for their protection.*[904]

The reasoning of the Supreme Judicial Court of Maine should apply equally to any attempt by our state or federal legislatures to "render it difficult to obtain" a trial by jury by penalizing a litigant for the unfettered exercise of his constitutional rights under our state and federal *Constitutions*.

---

[902] *Hinchly v. Machine*, 15 N.J. Law (3 J.S. Green) 476 (1836).
[903] *State v. Gurney*, 37 Maine 156, 163 (1853).
[904] *Saco v. Wentworth*, 37 Maine 165, 173 (1853).

(g) ***Ex Parte Milligan* (U.S. Supreme Court 1866).**[905] On March 3, 1863, Congress adopted an Act authorizing President Lincoln to suspend the *Writ of Habeas Corpus* throughout the United States during the rebellion. By Proclamation dated September 15, 1863, reciting this statute, President Lincoln suspended the *Writ of Habeas Corpus* and authorized the trial of all "prisoners of war, spies, or *aiders and abettors of the enemy*" before a military tribunal. On October 5, 1864, Lamdin P. Milligan, a civilian resident of the State of Indiana, was arrested and tried before a military tribunal for "affording aid and comfort to rebels against the authority of the United States." Upon his conviction, Milligan appealed the denial of his right to a trial by jury to the United States Supreme Court. Jeremiah S. Black, formerly Chief Justice of the Supreme Court of Pennsylvania, U.S. Attorney General and Secretary of War, argued in his behalf that the American colonists from Britain had regarded the right to trial by jury "as the most precious part of their inheritance" and that "the immigrants from other places, where trial by jury did not exist, became equally attached to it as soon as they understood what it was."

> *There was no subject upon which all the inhabitants of the country were more perfectly unanimous than they were in their determination to maintain this great right unimpaired.*[906]

The United States Supreme Court in an opinion by Justice David Davis held the Act under which Milligan was tried to be an unconstitutional deprivation of "the fundamental principles of American liberty" for depriving Milligan of "the inestimable privilege of a trial by jury" which the Court regarded as "one of the most valuable in a free country" and as a "vital principle, underlying the whole administration of criminal justice."

In a separate concurring opinion, speaking for himself and Associate Justices James M. Wayne of Georgia, Noah H. Swayne of Ohio, and Samuel F. Miller of Iowa, Chief Justice Salmon P. Chase stated:

> *We assent, fully, to all that is said, in the opinion, of the inestimable value of trial by jury, and of the other constitutional safeguards of civil liberty....*[907]

---

[905] *See* ¶¶ 35 & 36 on pp. 341-343 above.
[906] *Ex Parte Milligan*, 71 U.S. (4 Wall.) 2, 109, 123 (1866).
[907] *Ex Parte Milligan, supra,* 71 U.S. at 137 (1866).

> We assent, fully, to all that is said of the inestimable value of trial by jury, and of the other constitutional safeguards of civil liberty.
>
> —**Chief Justice Salmon P. Chase (1866)**

(h) *Arneson v. Olson* **(North Dakota 1978).** In 1977, the General Assembly of North Dakota adopted an Act designed "to encourage physicians to enter the practice of medicine in North Dakota." Among its many provisions, it limited the liability of a health-care provider qualified under the Act to $300,000 for all claims arising from any one occurrence. It also required all health care providers to obtain liability insurance coverage in the amount of $100,000 for each occurrence. If the liability insurer agreed to settle its liability for the policy limit of $100,000, the Act provided for suit in the district court without a jury naming the Patient Insurance Fund as a defendant.

Stating that it seems obvious that the total expense of caring for a seriously injured malpractice victim might well exceed $300,000, the Supreme Court of North Dakota held that the $300,000 limitation on recovery in malpractice cases was a violation of the equal protection provision of the North Dakota *Constitution*. It further held that the Act "constitutes an unconstitutional deprivation of the right to a jury trial."

> *... The right to a jury trial is a basic right in this state. The right to a jury trial remains inviolate. ...* [908]

Notwithstanding these decisions, the legislative appetite for undermining the right to trial by jury has not diminished. It is apparently difficult for Congress and state legislatures to comprehend the principle that the privileges and immunities enumerated in the *Bill of Rights* "belong to every citizen of the United States."

> *... Liberty, it has been well said, depends not so much upon the absence of actual oppression, as on the existence of constitutional checks upon the power to oppress. ... If some guaranties of life, liberty and property which at the time of the adoption of the national Constitution were regarded as fundamental and as absolutely essential to the enjoyment of freedom, have in the judgment of some ceased to be of practical value, it is for the people of the United States so to declare by an amendment of that instrument. ...* [909]

---

[908] *Arneson v. Olson*, 270 N.W.2d 125, 135-137 (N.D. 1978).

[909] *Dissenting Opinion* of Justice John Marshall Harlan in *Maxwell v. Dow*, 176 U.S. 581, 605, 617 (1900).

V. THE RISE AND FALL OF THE JURY SYSTEM IN ENGLAND

As we have seen, after the germ of the modern jury crossed the Channel with William the Conqueror in 1066, it eventually became an exclusively English institution. Cultivated by Henry II, it grew into the bulwark of English liberty that our forefathers were so proud to claim as their birthright when they populated North America. The concept of trial by jury as a fundamental right which came from the *Magna Carta* ultimately became the symbol of American justice.

> *Magna Carta thus became a symbol of the vital principle that there is a definite body of law, superior to all men, including the king and his government.... Long after feudalism had disappeared, Magna Carta still emphasizes that "The Law is no respecter of Persons." The implications of this familiar phrase are vast. The achievement of those desperate barons facing an angry king at Runnymede may be seen reflected in the words emblazoned on the lintel of a white marble building in the capital of a land unknown to those men — "Equal Justice under Law."*[910]

But the pride of Parliament had been stung by an independent English jury in the trial of William Owen in 1752,[911] and its resentment smoldered for many generations. Rebuffed in its attempt to undermine the colonial jury system by the advent of the American Revolution, England turned its anti-democratic ardor inward.

Justice William Blackstone had warned against "secret machinations" that might undermine trial by jury in 1768[912] and Thomas Erskine repeated his warning in 1784.[913] In 1823, Lord John Russell emphasized the danger to the right of trial by jury from "trifling and vexatious enactments."[914] However, the determination of the House of Commons to destroy the effectiveness of the English jury persisted and Parliament finally put the kiss of death on the British civil jury system in the latter half of the nineteenth century.

---

[910]Lovell, *English Constitution and Legal History*, p. 118 (Oxford University Press 1962).
[911]*See* pp. 289-293 above.
[912]*Blackstone's Commentaries*, Vol. 4, p. 343 (1768).
[913]*See* p. 316 above.
[914]*See* pp. 318-319 above.

In 1839, J. Sydney Taylor had attacked the *Metropolitan Police Courts Bill* as a "dangerous innovation on the rights and liberty of the subject" for its proposed restrictions on the right of trial by jury in criminal cases. The freedom of Englishmen, he said, was "threatened with extinction, not by the hands of a foreign conqueror, not by the splendid despotism of a Cromwell or a Napoleon, but by the laborious insignificance and presumptuous incapacity of a committee of Parliament."[915] Notwithstanding these attacks, trial by jury continued its downward path. In 1852, the *Common Law Procedure Act* "introduced for the first time the possibility of trial by judge alone." The *Judicature Acts* of 1873 and 1875 "preserved the right of trial by jury while making it clear that trial by judge alone was equally acceptable, to the legislature at least." The Rules of the Supreme Court in 1883 then decreed that the right to a civil jury trial was limited to actions for slander, libel, false imprisonment, malicious prosecution, seduction and breach of promise of marriage.[916]

Nor was this decline limited to the civil jury. In "The Decline of the English Jury," London law professor James Driscoll wrote that "by the mid-19th century . . . a substantial inroad into the principle of jury trial had emerged with the massive redistribution of criminal cases into magistrates' courts." In 1879, magistrates acquired jurisdiction over certain theft, embezzlement and receiving offenses; and after 1925, criminal damage, serious assaults, forgery and attempted suicide were added to the list. "A further major addition occurred in 1962 when certain burglary offenses became triable summarily."[917]

This "enormous redistribution of work away from the jury" took place despite a general distrust of non-jury tribunals[918] and the continued affection of the English jury among all classes of British society. In 1867, Serjeant Alexander Pulling, a member of the British Law Amendment Society, said:

> *Trial by jury, which was one of the most ancient features of the English Constitution, had the advantage of enlisting the affections of every class, both of those who had to administer and those who had to call on the aid of the law, or submit to its decrees.*[919]

---

[915] *See* Vol. 1, pp. 65-68 above.

[916] Buckley, "Civil Trial by Jury," *Current Legal Problems* 63 (1966).

[917] Driscoll, "The Decline of the English Jury," 17 *Am. Bus. Law J.* 99, 104 (1979).

[918] Driscoll, *supra*, pp. 105, 110.

[919] *The Law Times*, Vol. 48 (1867).

FROM *THE ORDER OF THE COIF* (1884) [A SPECIAL EDITION BY THE LEGAL CLASSICS LIBRARY (1989)]

Trial by jury, which was one of the most ancient features of the English Constitution, had the advantage of enlisting the affections of every class, both of those who had to administer and those who had to call on the aid of the law, or submit to its decrees.

—**Serjeant Alexander Pulling (1867)**

According to Driscoll's "Decline of the English Jury," those who brought about "the demise of the civil jury" in Britain were "commercial interests [who] were particularly influential in the enormous procedural changes that occurred during the 19th century." As a result of their continuing influence, "jury trial in England and Wales has become circumvented in criminal cases . . . and is also virtually extinct in civil litigation."[920]

This situation prompted English author M.D.A. Freeman to write in 1981:

> *It was Thomas Jefferson who wrote that "the execution of the laws is more important than the making of them." He saw the jury as an anchor which would hold government to the principles of its constitution. . . . We are not talking about a perfect institution. But where does a perfect institution exist? With all its faults I believe we should fight to preserve the jury. . . . But make no mistake "the gang of twelve" is on trial in this country today. If we don't come to its defense its chances of survival are indeed slim.*[921]

Theoretically, in the United States, with the right of trial by jury guaranteed by the *Seventh Amendment* and comparable provisions of virtually every state constitution,[922] the American citizen's right to trial by jury should be relatively safe. Yet, history teaches us that this is not the case.

The same "commercial interests" who were "particularly influential" in Great Britain in the 19th century are busily at work in the corridors of Congress and in the halls of our state legislatures. Although their initial attacks have been limited to our civil jury system, the experience of England should teach us that erosion of the criminal jury system will inevitably follow. The salvation of the civil jury in America is dependent upon the support of the American citizen. "If we don't come to its defense, its chances of survival are indeed slim."

---

[920]Driscoll, *supra n.917*, pp. 99, 106-107, 112. According to Guinther, *The Jury in America*, p. 34 (1988), civil jury trials in England today are "less than a fraction of one percent of all civil trials."

[921]M.D.A. Freeman, "The Jury on Trial," *Current Legal Problems*, pp. 65, 97-98 (London 1981).

[922]*See* state constitutional provisions guaranteeing the right of trial by jury in Appendix A on pages 469-476 below.

W. THE RISE AND FALL OF THE JURY SYSTEM IN EUROPE

1. The Jury System in France. Emperor Louis the Pious of France is credited with the creation of the jury of administrative inquest in 829 A.D. However, although it was later carried to England by William the Conqueror,[923] his system did not survive on the continent and there were no recorded jury trials in France prior to the French Revolution of 1789. Following Pope Innocent IV's authorization of the use of torture to obtain confessions in 1252,[924] the *Medieval Inquisition* in France soon became "an engine of grievous injustice and horrible torture" which endured for five centuries.[925]

> *The jury was issued into continental countries as a result of the French revolutionary movement. It had been among the English institutions greatly admired by the French philosophies.... Only a jury of citizens could be left free to judge on the basis of their own intimate conviction. Thus the cahiers of 1789 demanded the introduction of trial by jury in criminal cases, and the Constituent Assembly established it by the law of ... September, 1791.... When its retention was debated in ... 1808, it was curiously Napoleon who was its staunchest defender, for [he] realized that it would be a useful weapon ... against the old aristocracy....*[926]

However, trial by jury in France "soon became a mockery."

> *... Although by law of 1793 it was enacted, that the extraordinary tribunals there established should proceed only upon the verdict of a jury, they soon, during the Reign of Terror, became permanent commissions, which dispensed with even the form of a jury, and committed murder by wholesale, refusing even the aid of advocates to the accused. When this frightful period had passed away, trial by jury again emerged....*[927]

---

[923] *See* Vol. 1, p. 9 nn. 14-15 above.
[924] *Encyclopædia Britannica Micropædia*, Vol. V, p. 366.
[925] Forsythe, *supra* n.714, p. 295.
[926] William Seagle: "Jury: Other Countries," *Encyclopædia of Social Sciences*, Vol. 7, p. 498 (Macmillan Co. 1942).
[927] Forsythe, *supra* n.714, p. 296.

Following Napoleon's death on St. Helena Island on May 5, 1821, Monsieur M. Cottu, General Counsel of the Royal Society of Prisons, undertook an intensive study on "the spirit of the English government," following which he authored a treatise on the administration of criminal justice in England. In it, he observed that the essential character of the institution of trial by jury in England was its dedication to the selection of impartial jurors "on whose integrity, knowledge, and above all, on whose independence, there could not arise the remotest doubt." This independence, he believed, had a most beneficial effect upon the national character:

> I cannot refrain . . . from remarking on the difference in the genius of the English people from ours. It is only under the influence of fear that we in France dare perform our duties as magistrates and citizens; we exercise our political rights in the dark. . . . It is quite the reverse in England, where the courage of the citizen is in nothing inferior to that of the soldier. Everyone there fearlessly takes upon himself the responsibility of all he does, whether a private individual or public functionary: the judges deliberate and give their decision in open court; the jury, obliged to be unanimous in their verdict, necessarily make known their individual opinion in each case. . . . In this manner, the abilities, opinions and intentions of all are ascertained, and estimated at their proper value. . . .

If this "genius of the English people" could be captured, Cottu wrote, "we shall see the French resume for the trial by jury the enthusiasm displayed for it in the early days of its institution; they would regard it as one of their proudest privileges, and perform its duties with the same zeal, the same courage, and the same independence as their neighbors."[928]

Following its institution in 1791, the French criminal jury system persevered for 150 years until it was abolished by the Nazis at the onset of World War II. Unfortunately, "France never restored the jury abolished during the German occupation in the 1940's."[929]

---

[928] Cottu, *On the Administration of Criminal Justice in England*, pp. 114-115, 300, 302-303, 312 (Lincoln's Inn, London, 1822).

[929] *Encyclopædia Britannica Macropædia*, Vol. 10, p. 361 (15th ed. 1979).

Napoleon Bonaparte (1769-1821), Emperor of France
Napoleon was a staunch defender of trial by jury, realizing that it would be "a useful weapon" against the entrenched French aristocracy.

2. The Jury System in Germany.

In his *History of Trial by Jury* published in 1852, William Forsythe described the nature of criminal procedure in Germany at the turn of the 19th century as "a prolonged system of moral torture" which "was, and still is, except where the jury trial has been introduced, resorted to with the professed view of extracting a confession of guilt from the accused." Life and liberty, he wrote, depend on the sentence of judges "appointed by the state, and removable at the pleasure of the sovereign."[930]

The judicial system in Germany in the early 19th century has been described as an "inquisitorial system" which was "cunningly contrived for securing convictions, with little regard to the guilt or innocence of the accused." The secrecy of such proceedings "afforded a ready cloak for oppression and injustice." On the 19th century judicial system of Germany, J. J. Cook wrote:

> The reputation of the philosophic jurists of Germany has long been deservedly high, but until a comparatively recent date the provision made in that country for the application and enforcement of the law fell very far short of the completeness of its theoretical development. The genius of the [German] people has always been speculative and metaphysical rather than political; and, while the scientific jurists were discoursing loftily upon the eternal principles of Law and Justice, or spinning wondrous webs of legal sophistry, the country groaned under many harsh and unequal laws and a judicial system which, while lending itself readily to the powerful and unscrupulous as an instrument of oppression, was of little value as a means for the redress of wrong or the punishment of the really guilty. . . .[931]

By the early nineteenth century, according to Forsythe, the subject of trial by jury had "occupied the minds of profound thinkers and writers in Germany for many years" and "the yearning desire for its adoption . . . has long been felt and expressed by the ablest and most influential of the German jurists."[932] When Napoleon seized the reins of power in France, he introduced trial by jury for major criminal offenses in Bavaria and other conquered German provinces of the Confederation of the Rhine.

---

[930]Forsythe, *supra n.714*, p. 317.

[931]Cook, "The Judicial System of Germany," 1 *The Judicial Rev.* 70-71 (Edinburgh 1889).

[932]Forsythe, *supra n.714*, p. 314.

> *When the French ... made themselves ... masters of the provinces bordering the Rhine, they introduced there trial by jury in criminal cases. ... The institution took vigorous root, and flourished so as to outlive ... the invaders. ...*

Following the defeat of Napoleon at Waterloo in 1815, the inhabitants of the Rhineland clung to trial by jury "with the affection of men who knew by experience the benefits it conferred." The German government then appointed a commission "to investigate the practical working of the system."

> *.... After a long and deliberate inquiry, the commissioners made their report in 1819, and they were unanimous in favor of the continuance of jury trial. ... The other provinces of the Rhine, such as Rhenish Hesse and Bavaria, also retained the same mode of trial, and their attachment increased with time.*

In his *History of Trial by Jury*, Forsythe quotes an unnamed German judge upon the opening of court in Bavaria in 1834:

> *... The first impression certainly amongst us all is a feeling of joy that we are still in possession of an institution which the freest nations of two hemispheres regard as their most precious jewel, and watch over with jealous eyes — an institution which calls on the unprejudiced, independent citizen to be the judge of his equal; — which surrounds the holiest rights of man —the rights of liberty and honor — with the strongest guards which human foresight could devise ... [and which] offer[s] every possible guarantee for a discerning and impartial administration of justice. The people who possess such an institution stand higher than those who are still without it. They are ... more free. The citizen who from time to time is summoned from the round of his usual avocations to the judgment-seat, must feel himself in a high degree honored and elevated by the trust reposed in him. He becomes more conscious of his worth as a man and a citizen. He gains both in experience and intelligence. Rightly, therefore, may a certain degree of pride mingle with the feeling of joy of which I have spoken.*[933]

---

[933] Forsythe, *supra n.*714, pp. 325-326, 378-379.

According to Lesser's *Historical Development of the Jury System* (1894), following the revolutions of central Europe in 1848, trial by jury had become so popular in Germany that "it was constitutionally recognized by Bavaria and Hesse in 1848, by Wurtemberg and Baden in 1849, and by Austria in 1850."[934] Calling trial by jury in Germany "eagerly demanded" and "gladly received," Forsythe concluded in 1852 that:

> ...There can be no doubt that the new system is a valuable boon and an immense improvement upon the former procedure. All friends of constitutional freedom and enemies of judicial oppression must wish well to the great experiment; and we may hope that amongst a people so truthful, so honest, and so enlightened as the Germans, trial by jury will soon become one of their most efficient as well as cherished institutions.[935]

Following the creation of a "unified Fatherland" after the Franco-German War of 1870-71, the right of trial by jury was preserved for major criminal offenses[936] in Germany through the political upheavals accompanying World War I. It was ultimately abolished by the Weimar Republic on grounds of "economic necessity" in 1924, following which the Fascist regime of Adolf Hitler suspended the criminal jury systems in France and other conquered territories at the outset of World War II.

> It is remarkable that a number of Continental countries abolished trial by jury after they had abandoned democratic principles. That was the case with Italy in 1931 after the Fascist Party had formed the government. In Portugal, trial by jury was abolished in 1927 after Gomes da Costa had established a dictatorship. In Spain, trial by jury was given up when General Franco seized power in 1936, and in France the Vichy government of 1941 is responsible for the abolition of the jury....[937]

---

[934]Lesser, *The Historical Development of the Jury System*, p. 159 (Lawyers Cooperative Publishing Co. 1894).

[935]Forsythe, *supra n.714*, p. 330.

[936]*See* Trowbridge, "A German Jury Trial," 2 *Cal. L.R.* 34 (1913).

[937]Knittel & Seiler, "The Merits of Trial by Jury," 30 *Cambridge L. J.* 316, 323-324 (1972).

Adolf Hitler (1889-1945)
The Fascist regime of Adolf Hitler suspended the criminal jury systems in France and other conquered territories at the outset of World War II.

3.　　The Jury System in Other European Countries. In 1809, a member of the Swedish House of Burgesses advocated the introduction of a jury system on the English and French pattern, stating:

> *Should we any longer hesitate to use an institution which is so highly valued by the most enlightened nations of Europe?*[938]

In 1812, the Spanish *Constitution* introduced the right of trial by jury in criminal cases as "an expression of popular sovereignty which would enable the populace to participate in the judicial process."[939] Thereafter, criminal jury systems, similar to those of France and Germany, were introduced in Sweden (1915),[940] Belgium (1831), Portugal (1838), Greece (1844), Austria (1850), Russia (1864), Switzerland and Norway (1887).[941]

The jury systems in these European countries continued to protect the individual rights of those accused of serious criminal offenses until the early 20th century when "the decline of jury trial in some nations [was] linked to the decline of democracy."[942] "Both the Soviet Bloc and the Fascist states abolished it outright."[943]

Throughout the world, a decline in democratic values and the antagonism of increasingly powerful commercial interests have contributed to the demise of the once flourishing jury systems of England and Western Europe. Today, more than 90% of all jury trials in the world are held in the United States,[944] the only nation on earth where "courthouse democracy" plays a significant role in the administration of civil justice.

The same antidemocratic interests that successfully destroyed the civil jury system in England are poised to accomplish the same objective here in the United States. Whether they are successful will depend on the dedication of the defenders of democratic self government to the preservation of the principle that the people themselves should administer the affairs of their own government.

---

[938] Vallinder, "The Swedish Jury System in Press Cases," *J. of Legal His.*, Vol. 8, pp. 190, 194 (1987).

[939] Burros, "The Spanish Jury: 1888-1923," 14 *Cas. W. Res. J. Int'l L.* 177, 178 (1982).

[940] Vallinder, *supra n.938*.

[941] Lesser, *supra n.676*, pp. 156-159.

[942] Lynn, *Jury Trial Law and Practice*, p. 1 (John Wiley & Sons 1986).

[943] *Encyclopædia Britannica Macropædia*, Vol. 6, p. 486 (15th ed. 1979).

[944] *See* Kalven & Zeisel, *The American Jury* (1966).

X. THE TYRANNY OF THE MAJORITY

John Dahlberg Acton (1834-1902), the historian, moralist and philosopher who profoundly influenced British politics as a member of Parliament, founder of the *English Historical Review* and author of the *Cambridge Modern History*,[945] warned that "if democracy could not restrain itself, liberty would be lost." The true test of a country's freedom, he said, was "the amount of security enjoyed by minorities." In *The History of Freedom in Antiquity*, published in 1907, he wrote that "*the one pervading evil of democracy is the tyranny of the majority.*"[946]

Any serious student of history can recall countless occasions where the fickle whims of public opinion have led to disastrous results for individual rights. It was majority rule that crucified Christ, instigated the *Spanish Inquisition* and perpetuated the institution of human slavery in the American South. Victims of the fickle whims of public opinion include Joan of Arc, St. Stephen and six million European Jews. It was the Puritan majority in Massachusetts who burned witches at the stake. Fortunately for the inhabitants of the "Quaker State," William Penn said that there was "no law in Pennsylvania against riding on broomsticks."[947]

Perhaps Penn remembered that an eight-to-four majority had initially voted to convict him of unlawful assembly in 1670. Fortunately, through the inherent safeguards of an impartial jury, he was acquitted. That is why Thomas Jefferson believed that "trial by juries impartially selected" was an essential element of "the bright constellation which has gone before us and guided our steps through an age of revolution and reformation."

> *... The wisdom of our sages and the blood of our heroes has been devoted to their attainment. They should be the creed of our political faith ... ; and should we wander from them in moments of error or alarm, let us hasten to retrace our steps and to regain the road which alone leads to peace, liberty and safety.*[948]

---

[945] *Encyclopædia Britannica Micropædia*, Vol. I, p. 71 (15th ed. 1979).

[946] *Bartlett's Familiar Quotations*, p. 750a (14th ed. 1968).

[947] Flexner, *I Hear America Talking: An Illustrated History of American Words and Phrases*, pp. 312-313 (Simon & Schuster 1976).

[948] First Inaugural Address, March 4, 1801, *Annals of America*, supra n.675, Vol. 4, pp. 143-145.

It was with these "moments of error and alarm" in mind that the Founding Fathers drafted our *Constitution* and *Bill of Rights*. Edmund Randolph of Virginia was concerned about "the indefinite and dangerous power given by the *Constitution* to Congress." Gouverneur Morris of Pennsylvania warned that "we should remember that the people never act from reason alone." George Mason of Virginia was of the same mind.

> He admitted that notwithstanding the superiority of the republican form [of government] over every other, it had its evils. The chief ones, were the danger of the majority oppressing the minority. . . .[949]

If we have proved nothing more in this book, we have shown that our Founding Fathers firmly believed that the guarantee of trial by jury in civil cases was *a vital constitutional right*. In his first inaugural address in 1861, Abraham Lincoln said that if "a majority should deprive a minority of a clearly written constitutional right, it might . . . justify revolution [and] certainly would if such right were a vital one."[950] That is why the founders of free government in the United States identified the right to a civil jury as a vital and clearly written constitutional right by incorporating it into the *Seventh Amendment*.

When the issue of civil juries was first raised at the Constitutional Convention, Roger Sherman of Connecticut said that "the legislature may be safely trusted."[951] James Madison forcefully expressed his opinion to the contrary, stating:

> Wherever the real power in a government lies, there is the danger of oppression. In our government the real power lies in the majority of the community, and the invasion of private rights is chiefly to be apprehended . . . from acts in which the government is the mere instrument of the major number of the constituents. . . . [T]he danger of oppression lies in the interested majorities of the people. . . .[952]

---

[949] Madison, *Records of the Debates of the Federal Convention of 1787*, pp. 321, 529, 736 (Gov. Printing Off. 1927).

[950] *Abraham Lincoln: Speeches and Writings 1859-1865*, pp. 219-220 (Library of America 1989).

[951] Madison, supra n.949, p. 716.

[952] Kammen, *The Origins of the American Constitution: A Documentary History*, pp. 369-370 (1986).

It is rather for us to be here dedicated to the great task remaining before us — that this nation shall have a new birth of freedom — and that government of the people, by the people, for the people, shall not perish from the earth.

—**Abraham Lincoln**, *Gettysburg Address* **(1863)**

To the people of America, the *Seventh Amendment* and the fundamental freedoms of the *Bill of Rights* act as an umbrella which protects us from the three greatest enemies of individual liberty: the inveterate blindness of public authority, the greed and corruption of the rich and powerful and the tyranny of prevailing opinion. As John Stuart Mill wrote in *On Liberty* in 1859:

> *Like other tyrannies, the tyranny of the majority . . . is still . . . held in dread, chiefly as operating through the acts of the public authorities. But reflecting persons perceived that when society is itself the tyrant — society collectively, over the separate individuals who comprise it — its means of tyrannizing are not restricted to the acts which it may do by the hands of its political functionaries. Society can and does execute its own mandates: and if it issues wrong mandates instead of right, or any mandates at all in things with which it ought not to meddle, it practices a social tyranny more formidable than many kinds of political oppression; since, though not usually upheld by such extreme penalties, it leaves fewer means of escape, penetrating much more deeply into the details of life, and enslaving the soul itself. Protection, therefore, against the tyranny of the magistrate is not enough: there needs protection also against the tyranny of the prevailing opinion and feeling; against the tendency of society to impose, by other means than civil penalties, its own ideas and practices as rules of conduct on those who dissent from them; to fetter the development, and, if possible, prevent the formation, of any individuality not in harmony with its ways, and compel all characters to fashion themselves upon the model of its own. There is a limit to the legitimate interference of collective opinion with individual independence: and to find that limit, and maintain it against encroachment, is as indispensable to a good condition of human affairs, as protection against political despotism.*[953]

The individual citizen's only reliable guarantees of individuality and protection against unlawful encroachment by the tyranny of prevailing opinion are those enumerated in our *Bill of Rights*, including our constitutional right to a civil jury trial.

---

[953] John Stuart Mill, *On Liberty*, pp. 13-14 (1859) [The Classics of Liberty Library (1992)].

Y. THE INSIDIOUS SCREW OF JUDICIAL ARISTOCRACY

The underlying principle of American democracy is the equal participation of all citizens in the affairs of government. An aristocracy, on the other hand, contemplates the *exclusion* of certain segments of society based upon their presumed incapacity for intelligent participation in the decision-making process.

The same distinction applies to the administration of justice. Trial by jury as "courthouse democracy"[954] contemplates the equal participation of all of our citizens in the administration of civil justice. It recognizes the principle expressed by Winston Churchill that government should "flow from the people."

The opposing concept advocated by the commercial coalition is a form of "courthouse aristocracy," that is, the administration of civil justice by a select few, *exclusive* of the great mass of the population, on the assumption that the supposedly superior intellect and judgment of those in control will produce more desirable results. This concept naturally assumes that the great majority of our citizens are incapable of governing themselves and thus must be *excluded* from the administration of one of the three branches of their own government.

Those left in complete command of the administration of justice, therefore, would constitute an *exclusive* class of citizens, whether they be judges or arbitration panels. In either case, they are the fortunate few in our society who are more likely to have attended *exclusive* private schools, live in *exclusive* residential subdivisions and belong to *exclusive* private clubs. They are more often found in coats and ties than in overalls, in luxury cars than in pickup trucks, and on golf courses than on rabbit hunts. In essence, they do not represent a true cross-section of the community, nor do they reflect a true cross-section of the community's views.

The fundamental distinction between democratic and aristocratic institutions is citizen participation, and jury service is the only means of citizen participation in our judicial system. When the jury is eliminated, judicial democracy becomes judicial aristocracy and, as Richard Henry Lee wrote in 1788, "the few, the well-born, . . . in judicial decisions as well as in legislation are generally disposed, and very naturally too, to favor those of their own description."[955]

---

[954]Lambert, *supra n.551*, p. 27.
[955]*See* quotation in Vol. 1, p. 206 n.486, above.

Speaking on the dangers of governmental aristocracy at the Constitutional Convention of 1787, George Mason, author of the *Virginia Declaration of Rights*,[956] said that Congress should be the "grand depository of the democratic principles of government" and "ought *to know and sympathize with* every part of the community."

> *We ought to attend to the rights of every class of people. [Mason] had often wondered at the indifference of the superior classes of society to the dictates of humanity and policy; considering that however affluent their circumstances . . . , the course of a few years . . . would distribute their posterity throughout the lowest classes of society. Every selfish motive . . . ought to recommend . . . a system [which] would provide no less carefully for the rights . . . of the lowest than of the highest orders of citizens.*[957]

Mason argued that the members of our national legislature "should sympathize with their constituents; should think as they think, and feel as they feel." He spoke at length upon "the abuses and corruption of the British Parliament" and warned that abuse of legislative power could soon produce *an aristocracy*.

> *His idea of an aristocracy was that it was the government of the few over the many. An aristocratic body, like the screw in mechanics, working its way by slow degrees, and holding fast whatever it gains, should ever be suspected of an encroaching tendency.*[958]

This encroaching tendency of an aspiring aristocracy is no less dangerous in our judicial system. The insidious nature of a judicial aristocracy, "like the screw in mechanics, working its way by slow degrees, and holding fast whatever it gains," will soon render our civil justice system an exclusive aristocratic institution which neither knows nor sympathizes with the interests of the American public.

---

[956] *See* Helen Hill Miller, *George Mason: Gentleman Revolutionary* (Univ. of North Carolina Press 1975). *See also* Davidow, ed., *Natural Rights and Natural Law: The Legacy of George Mason* (George Mason Univ. Press 1986).

[957] Madison, *Records of the Debates in the Federal Convention of 1787*, pp. 125-126 (Government Printing Office 1927) [Legal Classics Library 1989], May 31, 1787.

[958] Madison, *supra*, pp. 161, 263, 336, 449.

An aristocratic body, like the screw in mechanics, works its way by slow degrees, holds fast to whatever it gains, and should ever be suspected of an encroaching tendency.

—George Mason of Virginia (1787)

An aristocracy has been defined as "a combination of many powerful men, for the purpose of advancing their own particular interests." Its hallmarks are its power, its exclusivity and its selfish purposes. By this definition, the commercial coalition currently seeking to sabotage the civil jury is an *exclusive* commercial aristocracy seeking to create an *exclusive* judicial aristocracy sympathetic to its own selfish interests.

Carl Sandburg has said that the term "*exclusive*" is the most *cruel* word in the English language. He could have added that the concept of exclusivity has been the most insidious cancer on the body of American democracy.

In its rush to restructure our civil justice system, the commercial coalition takes great comfort from the fact that Great Britain has dismantled the English civil jury. But as Noel Coward wrote in 1838:

> *The Stately Homes of England*
> *How Beautiful they stand,*
> *To prove the upper classes*
> *Still hold the upper hand.*[959]

In his argument before the United States Supreme Court in 1848 in the *Dorr Rebellion Cases*, Daniel Webster declared:

> *The protection of life and property, habeas corpus, trial by jury, the right of an open trial, these are principles of public liberty existing in the best form in the republican institutions of this country. . . . Our American liberty . . . has an ancestry, a pedigree, a history. Our ancestors brought to this country all that was valuable, in their judgment, in the political institutions of England, and left behind them all that was without value. . . .*[960]

The fact that England has replaced the democratic institution of trial by jury with the aristocratic institution of trial by judge is no justification for our country to blindly follow suit. For once the insidious screw of judicial aristocracy has taken hold, it will be virtually impossible to dislodge and, thereafter, the collective conscience of the community will no longer be reflected in the administration of our civil justice system.

---

[959] *Macmillan Dictionary of Quotations*, p. 29, ¶ 11 (1987).
[960] *The Great Speeches and Orations of Daniel Webster*, p. 536 (1894) [Legal Classics Library 1989].

Z. PRESERVATION OF THE CIVIL JURY

As a fitting summary of all that has been said of trial by jury by the more than 250 authors quoted in this book, we have borrowed the words of the Supreme Judicial Court of New Hampshire in response to a question posed by the state legislature in 1860:

> *Trial by jury has been steadily regarded, from the earliest judicial history in England, as the great safeguard of the lives, liberty, and property of the subject against the abuses of arbitrary power, as well as undue excitements of popular feeling. In our own country, almost from its earliest settlement, trial by jury was claimed by the people as [their] birthright . . . , and as the most valuable of the rights of free men; and in the great struggle which secured our national independence, no right of the colonists was more urgently and strenuously insisted upon. . . .*[961]

To this, we would add the wisdom of Thomas Jefferson, for no better spokesman can be found for the preservation of individual rights. To him, the concept of direct citizen participation in the affairs of government was "the very essence of a Republic."

> *We of the United States . . . think experience has proved it safer for the mass of individuals composing the society to reserve to themselves personally the exercise of all rightful powers to which they are competent. . . .*
>
> *Hence, with us, the people . . . being competent to judge of the facts occurring in ordinary life, . . . have retained the functions of judges of facts under the name of jurors. . . .*
>
> *I believe . . . that action by the citizens in person, in affairs within their reach and competence, and in all others by representatives chosen immediately and removable by themselves, constitutes the essence of a Republic. . . .*[962]

---

[961] *Opinion of the Justices of the Supreme Judicial Court*, 44 N.H. 550-551 (1860).

[962] Jefferson, Letter to Pierre S. DuPont (April 4, 1816). *Annals of America, supra* n.675, Vol. 4, p. 414.

As our birthright and as the very essence of our democratic republic, the right of trial by jury in civil actions arising under the common law is a valuable property right of every American citizen. It does not belong to Congress, to our state legislatures, or to our courts. It belongs to us. To repeat what Justice John Marshall Harlan wrote in his dissenting opinion in *Maxwell v. Dow* in 1882:

> *It seems to me that the privileges and immunities enumerated in [the Bill of Rights] belong to every citizen of the United States.*[963]

It was also Justice Harlan who said that individual liberty "depends not so much upon the absence of actual oppression, as on the existence of constitutional checks on the power to oppress,"[964] a safeguard "*vital* to the protection of individual liberty against the exercise of arbitrary power."

> *It is not difficult to understand why the [founding] fathers entrenched the right of trial by jury in the supreme law of the land. They regarded the recognition and exercise of that right as vital to the protection of liberty against arbitrary power....*[965]

In the words of a leading legal encyclopedia:

> *Trial by jury... was in England first guaranteed as such by the Magna Carta. It was introduced into this country by the English colonists who considered it a right under English law, and has, since the organization of our government, been incorporated in the form of express guarantees in all of the constitutions, both state and federal. It is a substantial right which has always been very highly esteemed and carefully guarded against infringement....*[966]

How does the right to a civil jury trial protect the individual citizen from the exercise of arbitrary power? Four examples are discussed below.

---

[963] *Maxwell v. Dow*, 176 U.S. 581, 608 (1900).
[964] *Maxwell v. Dow, supra*, 176 U.S. at 617.
[965] *Maxwell v. Dow, supra*, 106 U.S. at 609.
[966] 35 *Corpus Juris* § 12 (1924).

It is not difficult to understand why the founding fathers entrenched the right of trial by jury in the supreme law of the land. They regarded the recognition and exercise of that right as vital to the protection of liberty against arbitrary power.
—**Justice John Marshall Harlan (1900)**

(a) *Protection for the small businessman.* Adam Smith said in 1776 that "people of the same trade hardly meet together even for merriment and diversion but the conversation ends in a conspiracy against the public or in some contrivance to raise prices;" and one of the recommendations of Thomas Jefferson which was not incorporated into the *Bill of Rights* was "freedom of commerce against monopolies."[967] What followed was predictable.

By the mid-1870's, the Chicago Lumberman's Exchange had begun to control the price of lumber, combinations at the Chicago Stockyards controlled the price of beef, and Cornelius Vanderbilt controlled the price of coal. In 1878, the New York legislature reported on the plight of private coal producers:

> *To those who will not make such contracts, rates are fixed excluding them from the market, with the result, usually, of forcing them to sell their property to the lords of the pool.*[968]

Following the adoption of the Sherman Act in 1890 outlawing combinations in restraint of trade, it became the duty of federal district attorneys "to institute proceedings in equity to prevent and restrain such violations." However, even that great "trust buster" Theodore Roosevelt called governmental enforcement of the Sherman Act a "miscarriage of justice."[969]

But state and federal antitrust acts provided for private enforcement by "any person who shall be injured in his trade or business." As a result, small businessmen, exercising their right to trial before impartial American juries often succeeded in dampening the predatory appetite of big business. As the United States Supreme Court said in 1959:

> *The right to trial by jury applies to treble damages suits under the anti-trust laws, and is, in fact, an essential part of the congressional plan for making competition rather than monopoly the rule of trade.*[970]

The right of trial by jury also provides similar protection for the small businessman under state unfair trade practices acts and in causes of action arising under the common law.

---

[967]Schwartz, *supra* n.696, Vol. 3, p. 612.
[968]Henry Demarest Lloyd, "Monopoly and Social Control (June 1884)," *Annals of America, supra* n.675, Vol. 11, pp. 7-9.
[969]*Annals of America*, Vol. 12, p. 281; Vol. 13, p. 319.
[970]*Beacon Theatres v. Westover*, 359 U.S. 500, 504 (1959).

(b) *Protection for farm and industrial workers.*
With the advent of the industrial revolution, farm and industrial machinery, often unequipped with the most elemental safety devices, produced a grisly, annual harvest of human hands, arms, legs and lives, "untimely ripped" from the bodies of American workmen by the unguarded jaws of farm and industrial machinery. The constitutional right of the injured victim, or his grieving widow and orphans, to a jury trial in a civil action against the manufacturers and marketers of defective and unreasonably dangerous farm and industrial machinery has had a significant effect on the improvement of the safety of such products.

(c) *Protection for the consumer.* Since Ralph Nader published *Unsafe At Any Speed* in 1966, the economic impact of civil jury verdicts against the automotive industry in motor vehicle crashworthiness litigation has hastened the advent of such basic "second collision" protection measures as improved dashboard and steering column impact cushioning, shoulder harnesses, air bags, improved door locks, more adequate roll cages, safer gasoline tanks and the complete redesign of such unstable vehicles as the Jeep CJ and early versions of the Ford Bronco.

The safety of other consumer products such as toys, lawn mowers, firearms, prescription drugs, children's sleepwear, infant cribs, cosmetics, birth control devices and tampons have been significantly improved as a result of the impact of civil jury verdicts on the economic interests of product manufacturers. So long as American corporations maintain a balance-sheet mentality, it is reasonable to anticipate that their actions will be significantly affected by their prediction of an impartial American jury's reaction to the reasonableness of their conduct. Product manufacturers realize that a typical American jury would frown upon their failure to incorporate reasonable injury-prevention measures into the design of their products and this realization should continue to enhance the safety of consumer products and the welfare of the American public.

(d) *Protection for the isolated individual.* Other areas in which the protection of the right to a civil jury trial provides a meaningful deterrent to improper conduct include instances of reckless or intentional infliction of injury such as environmental contamination, civil conspiracy, securities fraud, false arrest, personal violence, abusive collection practices and insurance industry bad faith. It is a fair generalization that an impartial American jury, as the conscience of the community, will not tolerate reprehensible conduct.

Charles S. May, one of the most brilliant lawyers and eloquent orators in Michigan, was described by the Chicago *Times* as "one of the ablest independent thinkers of the West."[971] In 1875, he told the graduating class of the University of Michigan Law School that trial by jury was an indispensable armament of civil liberty against tyranny and oppression and warned:

> *Rome, Sparta and Carthage fell because they did not know it, let not England and America fall because they threw it away.*[972]

Mr. May's analogy on judicial democracy is supported by historian Edward Gibbon's observations on legislative democracy in his *Decline and Fall of the Roman Empire* (1776):

> *... If such an institution, which gave the people an interest in their own government, had been universally established ..., the seeds of public wisdom and virtue might have been cherished and propagated in the Empire of Rome. ... Under the mild and generous influence of liberty, the Roman Empire might have remained invincible and immortal.*[973]

The United States, the last remaining refuge of the civil jury, stands today as the final hope for the survival of true democracy in a world devoted to economic progress at the expense of personal liberty. The civil jury is our last chance for the preservation of individual independence and the future of American freedom.

> *Do the people of this land ... desire to preserve those [freedoms] so carefully protected by the [Bill of Rights] ...? If so let them withstand all beginnings of encroachment. For the saddest epitaph which can be carved in memory of a vanished liberty is that it was lost because its possessors failed to stretch forth a saving hand while yet there was time.*[974]

---

[971] *See* advertising circular, p. 2; text, p. 4 of *Speeches of Charles S. May* (Review & Harrell Pub. Co. 1899).

[972] May, *supra* n.971, p. 284.

[973] Gibbon, *Decline and Fall of the Roman Empire*, Vol. 40, p. 522, *Great Books of the Western World* (1952).

[974] Justice George Sutherland, dissenting opinion in *Associated Press v. N.L.R.B.*, 301 U.S. 103, 141 (1937).

The saddest epitaph which can be carved in memory of a vanished liberty is that it was lost because its possessors failed to stretch forth a saving hand while yet there was time.

—Justice George Sutherland (1937)

An institution that has so long stood the trying tests of time and experience, that has been guarded with scrupulous care and has commanded the admiration of so many of the wise and good, justly demands our jealous scrutiny against any attempted innovations.
—**Justice Rufus P. Ranney of Ohio (1853)**

The founders of our nation considered the right of trial by jury in civil cases an important bulwark against tyranny and corruption, a safeguard too precious to be left to the whim of the sovereign. Juries represent the layman's common sense and thus keep the administration of law in accord with the wishes and feelings of the community.

—**Chief Justice William H. Rehnquist (1979)**

THE PEOPLE'S PRAYER

When the *Bill of Rights* was written with that great eternal pen
  By the sacred hand of freedom in the manuscripts of men,
It was with the solemn promise so that golden scroll recites
  That this everlasting charter of our fundamental rights,
For which our Founding Fathers fought, for which so many died,
  For which they paid so grand a price, should never be denied.

Two hundred years have come and gone, the ink has long been dry,
  Without one change, no "t" uncrossed, not one undotted "i".
The Mighty Fortress of the Free remains the same today
  In war and peace, thru thick and thin, with skies of blue or gray;
The tide of time has ebbed and flowed, our path has often swerved,
  But we kept our eyes upon that prize —
                      THESE RIGHTS MUST BE PRESERVED!!!

Our government shall never hold the power to impeach
  Our right to worship as we please, the freedom of our speech;
No heavy handed bureaucrat may legally withdraw
  Those *fundamental freedoms* of the due process of law;
A speedy public hearing for all crimes and no denial
  Of that sacred right of the common law to a civil jury trial.

May it ever be in the *Land of the Free,*
                      henceforth for a thousand years,
  Where "alabaster cities gleam, undimmed by human tears";
So long as freedom's flag shall fly above a land so fair,
  Eternal Father of us all, take heed of the *People's Prayer*,
Through the heat of a hundred thousand days —
                    Through the dark of a million nights,
  As long as human life shall last, *God Save our Bill of Rights!*

                                      —J. Kendall Few (1992)

I want my case to be tried before a fair and impartial jury. That's my Constitutional right under the Seventh Amendment. I believe in the Bill of Rights and I have great faith in the integrity of an impartial American jury.

—A Typical Victim of Defective & Unreasonably Dangerous Products

ILLUSTRATION BY AL PHILLIPS

The right to a jury trial is a fundamental right, recognized as such throughout our nation by the constitutions of all our states and our federal government.

—Justice John H. Dimond of Alaska (1969)

APPENDIX A
STATE CONSTITUTIONS

Alabama Constitution (1901): That the right of trial by jury shall remain inviolate. [Article I, § 11].

Alaska Constitution (1956): In civil cases where the amount in controversy exceeds two hundred fifty dollars, the right of trial by a jury of twelve is preserved to the same extent as it existed at common law.

Arizona Declaration of Rights (1910): The right of trial by jury shall remain inviolate. [§ 23].

Arkansas Constitution (1874): The right of trial by jury shall remain inviolate, and shall extend to all cases at law, without regard to the amount in controversy. [Article II, § 7].

California Constitution (1879): Trial by jury is an inviolate right and shall be secured to all. [Article I, § 16].

Colorado Constitution (1876): The right of trial by jury shall remain inviolate. [Article 2, § 23].

Connecticut Laws and Liberties (1682): All cases, where the debt or damage shall exceed forty shillings, shall be tried by a jury of twelve men.

Connecticut Declaration of Rights (1965): The right of trial by jury shall remain inviolate. [Article I, § 19].

Delaware Statute (1727): No free man shall be disseized of his freehold or liberties but by the lawful judgment of his twelve equals.

Delaware Declaration of Rights (1776): Trial by jury of facts where they arise is one of the greatest securities of the lives, liberties, and estates of the people. [§ 13].

Delaware Bill of Rights (1897): Trial by jury shall be as heretofore. [Article I, § 2].

Florida Constitution (1968): The right of trial by jury shall be secured to all and remain inviolate. [Article I, § 22].

Georgia Constitution (1777): Freedom of press and trial by jury [are] to remain inviolate forever. [§ 51].

Georgia Constitution (1976): *The right of trial by jury shall remain inviolate.* [Article I, § 1, ¶ 11].

Hawaii Constitution (1985): *In suits at common law where the value in controversy shall exceed one thousand dollars, the right of trial by jury shall be preserved.* [Article I, § 13].

Idaho Constitution (1890): *The right of trial by jury shall remain inviolate.* [Article I, § 7].

Illinois Constitution (1970): *The right of trial by jury as heretofore enjoyed shall remain inviolate.* [Article I, § 13].

Indiana Constitution (1851): *In all civil cases, the right of trial by jury shall remain inviolate.* [Article I, § 20].

Iowa Bill of Rights (1857): *The right of trial by jury shall remain inviolate.* [Article I, § 9].

Kansas Constitution (1859): *The right of trial by jury shall be inviolate.* [Bill of Rights § 3].

Kentucky Constitution (1891): *The ancient mode of trial by jury shall be held sacred, and the right thereof remain inviolate.* [Bill of Rights § 7].

Maine Constitution (1983): *In all civil suits, and in all controversies concerning property, the parties shall have a right to a trial by jury, except in cases where it has heretofore been otherwise practiced.* [Article I, §20].

Maryland Declaration of Rights (1867): *The inhabitants of Maryland are entitled to the common law of England, and the right of trial by jury, according to the course of that law.* [Article V]. *The right of trial by jury of all issues of fact in civil proceedings in the several courts of law in this state, where the amount in controversy exceeds the sum of five hundred dollars, shall be inviolably preserved.* [Article XXIII].

Massachusetts Body of Liberties (1641): *In all actions at law it shall be the liberty of the plaintiff and defendant by mutual consent to choose whether they will be tried by the bench or by a jury.* [§ 29].

For centuries the system of trial by jury has been carefully preserved and developed as an institution which firmly undergirds the judicatory structure in common law jurisdictions. Having stood the test of long experience as one of the best means of protecting property and human liberty, the system must be jealously guarded against any unauthorized encroachment.

—**Chief Justice Wilfred C. Tsukiyama of Hawaii (1960)**

General Privileges of Massachusetts (1692): *No freeman shall be disseized of his freehold or liberties but by the lawful judgment of his peers.*

Massachusetts Constitution (1780): *In all controversies concerning property, and in all suits between two or more persons, except in cases in which it has heretofore been otherways used and practiced, the parties have a right to a trial by jury; and this method of procedure shall be held sacred.* [Declaration of Rights, Article XV].

Michigan Constitution (1963): *The right of trial by jury shall remain.* [Article I, § 14].

Minnesota Constitution (1857): *The right of trial by jury shall remain inviolate, and shall extend to all cases at law without regard to the amount in controversy.* [Article I, § 4].

Mississippi Constitution (1916): *The right of trial by jury shall remain inviolate.* [Article III, § 31].

Missouri Constitution (1875): *The right of trial by jury as heretofore enjoyed shall remain inviolate.* [Article I, § 22(a)].

Montana Constitution (1972): *The right of trial by jury is secured to all and shall remain inviolate.* [Article II, § 26].

Nebraska Constitutio.n (1920): *The right of trial by jury shall remain inviolate.* [Article I, § 6].

Nevada Constitution (1864): *The right of trial by jury shall be secured to all and remain inviolate forever.* [Article I, § 3].

New Hampshire General Laws and Liberties (1680): *All trials between man and man, both respecting maritime affairs as well as others, shall be tried by a jury of twelve good and lawful men.*

New Hampshire Constitution (1988): *In all controversies concerning property, and in all suits between two or more persons except those in which another practice is or has been customary and except those in which the value in controversy does not exceed fifteen hundred dollars and no title to real estate is involved, the parties have a right to a trial by jury.* [Article I, § 20].

Charter of West New Jersey (1677): *No inhabitants shall be deprived of life, liberty, property, or anyways hurt without a due trial by twelve good and lawful men.*

New Jersey Constitution (1776): *The inestimable right of trial by jury shall remain confirmed as part of the law of this colony, without repeal, forever.* [§ 22].

New Jersey Constitution (1844): *The right of trial by jury shall remain inviolate.* [Article I, § 9].

New Mexico Bill of Rights (1911): *The right of trial by jury as it has heretofore existed shall be secured to all and remain inviolate.* [Article II, § 12].

New York Charter of Liberties (1683): *All trials shall be by verdict of twelve men, and as near as may be peers and equals of the neighborhood.*

New York Constitution (1938): *Trial by jury in all cases in which it has heretofore been guaranteed by constitutional provision shall remain inviolate forever.* [Article I, § 2].

North Carolina Constitution (1946): *In all controversies at law respecting property, the ancient mode of trial by jury is one of the best securities of the rights of the people, and shall remain sacred and inviolable.* [Article I, § 25].

North Dakota Constitution (1899): *The right of trial by jury shall be secured to all, and remain inviolate.* [Article I, § 13].

Ohio Constitution (1838): *Trial by jury shall be as heretofore, and the right thereof remain inviolate.* [Article I, § 6].

Ohio Constitution (1851): *The right of trial by jury shall be inviolate.* [Article I, § 5].

Oklahoma Constitution (1968): *The right of trial by jury shall be and remain inviolate, except in civil cases wherein the amount in controversy does not exceed one hundred dollars.* [Article II, § 19].

Oregon Constitution (1859): *In all civil cases the right of trial by jury shall remain inviolate.* [Article I, § 17].

Pennsylvania Constitution (1776): *In controversies respecting property, and in suits between man and man, the parties have a right to trial by jury, which ought to be held sacred.* [§ 11].

Pennsylvania Constitution (1838): *Trial by jury shall be as heretofore, and the right thereof remain inviolate.* [Article I, § 6].

Rhode Island Code (1647): *No person shall be disseized of his lands or liberties but by the lawful judgment of his peers.*

Rhode Island Constitution (1986): *The right of trial by jury shall remain inviolate.* [Article I, § 15].

Fundamental Constitutions of Carolina (1669): *No cause, whether civil or criminal, of any freeman, shall be tried without a judgment of his peers.*

South Carolina Jury Act (1731): *No subject shall be disseized of his free-hold, liberty or free customs without lawful trial of a jury of his peers.*

South Carolina Constitution (1971): *The right of trial by jury shall be preserved inviolate.* [Article I, § 14].

South Dakota Constitution (1889): *The right of trial by jury shall remain inviolate and shall extend to all cases at law without regard to the amount in controversy.* [Article VI, § 6].

Tennessee Constitution (1834): *The right of trial by jury shall remain inviolate.* [Article I, § 6].

Texas Constitution (1935): *The right of trial by jury shall remain inviolate.* [Article I, § 15].[1]

---

[1] The "Interpretive Commentary" to this section states that "one of most characteristic elements of the American constitutional inheritance from England is that of trial by jury" and that "trial by jury has been considered as a fundamental safeguard of constitutional liberty." It further states that "the Texas *Declaration of Independence*" complained of the Mexican government for denying Texans of their right to trial by jury as "that palladium of civil liberty, and only safe guarantee for the life, liberty, and property of the citizen."

If there is any right to which, more than all others, the people of Pennsylvania have clung with unrelaxing grasp, it is that of trial by jury.
—Justice William Strong of Pennsylvania (1862)

Utah Constitution (1896): *In capital cases the right of trial by jury shall remain inviolate. . . . A jury in civil cases shall be waived unless demanded.* [Article I, § 10].[2]

Virginia Jury Act (1642): *If either plaintiff or defendant shall desire the verdict of a jury for the determining of any suit depending within any of the courts of this colony, they shall so signify.*

Virginia Constitution (1776): *In controversies respecting property, and in suits between man and man, trial by jury is preferable to any other, and ought to be held sacred.* [Article I, § 11].

Vermont Constitution (1777): *That in controversies respecting property, and in suits between man and man, the parties have a right to a trial by jury, which ought to be held sacred.* [Article 13, Ch. 1].

Vermont Constitution (1786): *That when any issue of fact, proper for cognizance of a jury is joined in a court of law, the parties have a right to trial by jury, which ought to be held sacred.* [Chapter I, Article XII].

Washington Constitution (1889): *The right of trial by jury shall remain inviolate.* [Article I, § 21].

West Virginia Constitution (1880): *In suits at common law, where the value in controversy exceeds twenty dollars exclusive of interest and costs, the right of trial by jury, if required by either party, shall be preserved.* [Article III, § 13].

Wisconsin Constitution (1922): *The right of trial by jury shall remain inviolate, and shall extend to all cases at law without regard to the amount in controversy.* [Article I, § 4].

Wyoming Constitution (1980): *The right of trial by jury shall remain inviolate in criminal cases. A jury in civil cases and in criminal cases where the charge is a misdemeanor may consist of less than twelve persons, but not less than six, as may be prescribed by law.* [Article I, § 9].

---

[2] According to the Supreme Court of Utah, this section guarantees the right of jury trial in civil cases. See *International Harvester Credit Corp. v. Pioneer Tractor & Implement, Inc.*, 626 P.2d 418 (Utah 1981).

APPENDIX B
STATE COURT OPINIONS ON THE SANCTITY OF TRIAL BY JURY*

Alabama

Whatever may be the origin or true history of the jury trial, it is certain that, ever since the Magna Carta, the right to it has been esteemed a peculiar and inestimable privilege by the English race.... The English colonists who settled in America brought with them this love for and veneration of this cherished right.

—**Justice James J. Mayfield (1910)**[3]

Alaska

The right to a jury trial is a fundamental right, recognized as such throughout our nation by the constitutions of all our states and our federal government.

—**Justice John H. Dimond (1969)**[4]

Arizona

The right of trial by jury is justly dear to the American people.... As a people we have watched with jealousy and deep concern any tendency to encroach upon or impair any of the essential elements of trial by jury. We know the blood and treasure it has cost to get and keep this birthright of every American, of every free man.

—**Chief Justice Alfred Franklin (1918)**[5]

That the right to a trial by jury is a most substantial right is beyond question. It has been referred to as the birthright of every free man, and a right which is justly dear to the American people.

—**Justice Arthur T. LaPrade (1947)**[6]

Arkansas

Trial by jury is a great constitutional right, ... incorporated, ... into the Constitution of the country, ... [by] reference to the jury trial as known and recognized by the common law.

—**Chief Justice Thomas Johnson (1848)**[7]

---

[3] *Alford v. State*, 170 Ala. 178, 54 So. 213, 214 (1910).
[4] *Green v. State*, 462 P.2d 994, 997 (S. Ct. Alaska 1969).
[5] *Priestly v. Arizona*, 19 Ariz. 371, 171 P. 137, 3 A.L.R. 1201, 1203 (1918).
[6] *USF&G v. State*, 65 Ariz. 212, 177 P.2d 823, 826 (1947).
[7] *Larillian v. Lane & Co.*, 8 Ark. 372 (1848).

*Some of the quotations in this volume have been condensed due to space limitations.

California

The framers of the California constitution regarded the right of trial by jury as too sacred and valuable to be entrusted to the guardianship of the legislature.

—Justice W. W. Cope (1861)[8]

The right to trial by jury is a basic and fundamental part of our state and federal systems of jurisprudence.

—Justice Louis C. Drapeau (1954)[9]

Colorado

The right of trial by jury is universally regarded as an important one.

—Justice Louis W. Cunningham (1913)[10]

Connecticut

The institution of trial by jury is not the product of any one generation or any one age; but it is the growth of centuries, changing and improving with time and experience. . . . The institution was so thoroughly imbedded in the British Constitution that it came to be regarded as the birthright of every Englishman, and as such was carefully watched and preserved unimpaired through all changes and even revolutions.

—Justice Elisha Carpenter (1878)[11]

Delaware

An act of the legislature which denies a litigant the right of trial by jury in the form which existed at the time of the adoption of the Constitution of 1897, is unconstitutional.

—Judge Joseph T. Walsh (1975)[12]

The citizens of Delaware are guaranteed the right to jury trial "as heretofore." This provision of the Delaware Constitution guarantees the right to a jury trial as it existed at common law.

—Judge Vincent A. Bifferato (1981)[13]

---

[8] *Grimm v. Norris*, 19 Cal. 140, 142 (1861).

[9] *Lofy v. Southern Pacific Co.*, 129 Cal. 2d 459, 277 P.2d 423, 425 (Cal . App. 1954).

[10] *W. H. Peeps Fixture Co. v. Gove*, 24 Colo. App. 149, 133 P. 143, 144 (1913).

[11] *State v. Worden*, 46 Conn. 349, 365 (1878).

[12] *Hopkins v. Justice of the Peace*, 342 A.2d 243, 247 (Del. Super. 1975).

[13] *Lacey v. Green*, 428 A.2d 1171, 1175 (Del. Super. 1981).

The institution of trial by jury was so thoroughly imbedded in the British Constitution that it came to be regarded as the birthright of every Englishman, and as such was carefully watched and preserved unimpaired through all changes and even revolutions.
—**Justice Elisha Carpenter of Connecticut (1878)**

Florida

Under our system of jurisprudence, trial by jury is an organic right and should under no circumstances be denied.

—**Justice Glenn Terrell (1937)**[14]

The importance of preserving the jury system, and the concomitant right of a litigant to a jury trial on the merits of his cause, should be zealously protected.

—**Judge Donald K. Carroll (1959)**[15]

The jury system is the foundation stone of our whole judicial concept.

—**Judge William C. Pierce (1967)**[16]

Georgia

The general diffusion of knowledge and education among the people of this country, much better fits them for weighing and comparing the evidence, than in any other nation or age since the institution of trial by jury.

—**Justice Joseph Henry Lumpkin (1849)**[17]

Hawaii

The right of trial by jury is a common law right, of which "the antiquity and excellence of this trial for the settlement of civil property has before been explained at large."

—**Justice Ralph Petty Quarles (1915)**[18]

For centuries the system of trial by jury has been carefully preserved and developed as an institution which firmly undergirds the judicatory structure in common law jurisdictions. Having stood the test of long experience as one of the best means of protecting property and human liberty, the system must be jealously guarded against any unauthorized encroachment.

—**Chief Justice Wilfred C. Tsukiyama (1960)**[19]

---

[14] *Orr v. Avon Florida Citrus Corp.*, 130 Fla. 306, 177 So. 612, 614 (1937).

[15] *Gaymon v. Quinn Menhaden Fisheries*, So.2d 641, 644 (Fla. App. 1959).

[16] *Florida Power Corp. v. Smith*, 202 So.2d 872, 882 (Fla. App. 1967).

[17] *Potts v. House*, 6 Ga. 324, 345 (1849).

[18] *Territory v. Nishimura*, 22 Haw. 614 (1915), quoting from *Blackstone's Commentaries*, Vol. 4, p. 349 (1768).

[19] *Chau v. Nagai*, 44 Haw. 290, 353 P.2d 998, 90 A.L.R.2d 1156, 1160 (1960).

Idaho

Trial by jury is justly esteemed one of the principal excellencies of our Constitution.

—**Chief Justice George H. Stewart (1911)**[20]

Illinois

The hatred of the admiralty courts for their refusal of a jury trial was shared by colonies under British rule. The history of the struggles of the colonists for the right of jury trial naturally found response in the federal Constitution. The background of those provisions of the Constitution was the belief that the right of trial by jury was essential to free government.

—**Chief Justice Clyde E. Stone (1931)**[21]

Courts jealously guard the right of a person to a trial by jury.

—**Justice William J. Fulton (1943)**[22]

The right of trial by jury is recognized in the Magna Carta, our Declaration of Independence and both our state and federal Constitutions. It is a fundamental right in our democratic judicial system.

—**Justice Ralph L. Maxwell (1954)**[23]

Utmost caution should be exercised to uphold the sanctity of trial by jury.

—**Justice Henry C. Burman (1960)**[24]

Indiana

In all civil cases, the right of trial by jury shall remain inviolate and our courts have scrupulously guarded this right against encroachment.

—**Judge Harry J. Curtis (1940)**[25]

---

[20] *Ex Parte Dawson*, 20 Idaho 178, 117 P. 696, 698 (1911).

[21] *People v. Cornavache*, 347 Ill. 403, 179 N.E. 909, 79 A.L.R. 553, 558 (1931).

[22] *Stephens v. Kasten*, 383 Ill. 127, 48 S.E.2d 508, 511 (1943).

[23] *Ney v. Yellow Cab Co.*, 2 Ill.2d 74, 117 N.E.2d 74, 80 (1954).

[24] *Mokrzycki v. Olson Rug Co.*, 28 Ill. App. 2d 117, 170 N.E.2d 635, 638 (1960).

[25] *Kettner v. Jay*, 107 Ind. App. 643, 26 N.E.2d 546, 547 (1940).

Iowa

The Iowa Constitution provides that "the right of trial by jury shall remain inviolate." Misjoinder, camouflage, or subterfuge cannot deprive the plaintiff of this right.
—**Justice James W. Kindig (1927)**[26]

Kansas

The Constitution preserves inviolate the right of trial by jury as it exists at common law. . . . The legislature has not the power, even if it should attempt it, to deprive a party of the right of trial by jury. . . .
—**Justice David J. Brewer (1881)**[27]

The right to a trial by jury has ever been regarded as important, and it may not be abridged or limited beyond the fair import of the constitutional and statutory provisions by which it is guaranteed.
—**Justice Charles B. Graves (1910)**[28]

The right of every individual citizen to a trial by jury is of ancient origin, and as now practiced is the result of a long process of development. . . . It . . . is regarded as a basic and fundamental feature of American jurisprudence, and has . . . been incorporated in the form of expressed guarantees in the constitutions of both state and federal governments. It is a substantial and valuable right and should never be lightly denied. The law favors trial by jury, and the right should be carefully guarded against infringements.
—**Justice William J. Wertz (1965)**[29]

Kentucky

The jury are taken from various walks of life, and their combined knowledge and experience afford the very best opportunity for safe and wise conclusions. Twelve good and lawful men are better judges of disputed facts than twelve learned judges.
—**Chief Justice James H. Hazelrigg (1899)**[30]

---

[26] *Cosman v. Thompson*, 204 Iowa 1254, 215 N.W. 261, 266 (1927).

[27] *Bodwell v. Crawford*, 26 Kan. 292, 40 Am. Rptr. 306, 307-308 (1881).

[28] *Gordon v. Munn*, 83 Kan. 242, 111 P. 177, 178 (1910).

[29] *Gard v. Sherwood Constr. Co.*, 194 Kan. 541, 400 P.2d 995, 1002 (1965).

[30] *Hudson v. Adams Administrator*, 20 Ky.L.R. 1267, 49 S.W. 192 (1899).

The jury are taken from various walks of life, and their combined knowledge and experience afford the very best opportunity for safe and wise conclusions. Twelve good and lawful men are better judges of disputed facts than twelve learned judges.
—**Chief Justice James H. Hazelrigg (1899)**

Louisiana

The regard which we entertain for trial by jury, and the high opinion we hold of its value in ascertaining facts, would induce us to support the citizen who claims its aid, and the investigation of his rights.
—**Justice Alexander Porter, Jr. (1825)**[31]

It is noted that [Louisiana statutes] expressly recognized the right to jury trial [and] . . . its purpose [was] to preserve inviolate a litigant's right to trial by jury. The jurisprudence also establishes that this is fundamental in character and that the courts will indulge every presumption against waiver, loss or forfeiture thereof.
—**Judge Grover L. Covington (1977)**[32]

Maine

An act of the legislature, which takes away the privilege of trial by jury directly, is tyrannical and a palpable violation of the Constitution; one which renders it difficult to obtain, beyond what public necessity requires, impairs individual rights and is inconsistent with this provision for their protection. If an act requires conditions for the purpose of preventing a trial by jury, the spirit of such a provision is at war with the spirit of the Constitution, and so far as it deprived one of this means of protection, it is void.
—**Justice John S. Teeney (1853)**[33]

Maryland

Provisions of the Declaration of Rights which were intended to safeguard the rights of the people to the privilege of trial by jury are that the people are "entitled to the common law of England, and the trial by jury, according to the course of that law." . . . Almost all of the constitutions of the various states of the Union contain similar provisions, and it is everywhere held that the effect of them . . . is to preserve the common law right of trial by jury, with such incidents as are essential elements to that right.
—**Justice Henry Page (1899)**[34]

---

[31] *La Croix v. Menard*, 3 Mart. (N.S.) 339, 15 Am. Dec. 161, 162 (1825).

[32] *Duplantis v. USF&G*, 342 So.2d 1142, 1143 (La. App. 1977).

[33] *Saco v. Wentworth*, 37 Maine 165, 173 (1853).

[34] *Danner v. State*, 42 A. 965, 966-967 (Maryland 1899).

Massachusetts

It is familiar law that the right of trial by jury secured by the Declaration of Rights is sacred and must be sedulously guarded against every encroachment.
—**Chief Justice Arthur P. Rugg (1929)**[35]

The right to trial by jury as set forth in the Constitution must be and has been strictly preserved.
—**Chief Justice Arthur P. Rugg (1935)**[36]

Michigan

Whatever its origin, the right of trial by jury of twelve men became fixed centuries ago in the common law, and . . . wherever the Anglo-Saxon tongue was spoken, and in many other countries, [this right] came to be regarded as the great bulwark of the liberty of the citizen. . . . When separated from the mother country, we regarded it as a birthright, and have ever been jealous of any attempted innovations upon the system.
—**Justice Charles D. Long (1892)**[37]

Minnesota

The Constitution of this state provides that "the right of trial by jury shall remain inviolate, and shall extend to all cases at law, without regard to the amount in controversy.". . . The effect of this clause of the Constitution is, first, to recognize the right of trial by jury as it existed at the time of the adoption of the state constitution; and second, to continue such right unimpaired and inviolate.
—**Justice Charles E. Flandrau (1860)**[38]

The constitutional right to trial by jury [is] a right of which no statute can deprive. . . . The legislature cannot impair the right of trial by jury.
—**Justice Royal A. Stone (1923)**[39]

---

[35] *H. K. Webster v. Mann*, 269 Mass. 381, 169 N.E. 151, 153 (1929).

[36] *Commissioner of Banks v. Harrison*, 291 Mass. 353, 197 N.E. 92, 94 (1935).

[37] *McRae v. Grand Rapids L. & D. R.R. Co.*, 93 Mich. 399, 53 N.W. 561 (1892).

[38] *Whallon v. Bancroft*, 4 Minn. 109 (Gil. 70, 74) (1860).

[39] *Westerlund v. Peterson*, 157 Minn. 379, 197 N.W. 110, 111, 112 (1923).

Mississippi

At the time of the formation of the federal government, . . . the right of trial by jury, being of the highest importance to the citizen, and essential to liberty, was not left to the uncertain fate of legislation, but was secured by the Constitution of this and all the other states as sacred and inviolable.

—**Chief Justice William L. Sharkey (1834)**[40]

Missouri

The right to jury trial is immemorial. It was brought from England by the colonists, and it has become a part of the birthright of every free man. It is a right which is justly dear to the American people, and one which is expressly guaranteed by the federal Constitution and the constitutions of the several states.

—**Judge Edward J. McCullen (1947)**[41]

The right to trial by jury should be jealously guarded by the courts and any curtailment should scrutinized with utmost care.

—**Judge Solbert M. Wasserstrom (1974)**[42]

Montana

The right of trial by jury . . . cannot be taken away by legislative enactment. It cannot become obsolete, for it is perpetuated by the state constitution, and it continues so long as the constitutional provision continues.

—**Justice W. H. Poorman (1905)**[43]

Nebraska

It is a part of our fundamental law that the right of trial by jury shall remain inviolate.

—**Justice Edward F. Carter (1959)**[44]

Nevada

The right of trial by jury is a sacred constitutional right, which no litigant, in a proper case, can be deprived without his consent.

—**Justice Orville R. Leonard (1877)**[45]

---

[40] *Bird v. State*, 1 How. 163, 177 (Miss. 1834).

[41] *Dowell v. City of Hannibal*, 200 S.W.2d 546, 555 (Mo. App. 1947), quoting 31 AM. JUR. *Jury* § 3.

[42] *Attebury v. Attebury*, 507 S.W.2d 87, 93 (Mo. App. 1974).

[43] *Chessman v. Hale*, 31 Mont. 577, 79 P. 254, 256 (1905).

[44] *Fugate v. State*, 169 Neb. 420, 99 N.W.2d 868, 871 (1959).

[45] *Treadway v. Jonas*, 12 Nev. 108, 115 (1877).

At the time of the formation of the federal government, the right of trial by jury, being of the highest importance to the citizen, and essential to liberty, was not left to the uncertain fate of legislation, but was secured by the Constitution of this and all the other states as sacred and inviolable.
    —**Chief Justice William L. Sharkey of Mississippi (1834)**

New Hampshire

In a trial by jury for injury to person or property, the assessment of the plaintiff's damages is as much a part of the verdict for him as the finding of liability. . . . This we regard as an essential part of the trial by jury intended to be secured by the Constitution.

—**Chief Justice Ira Perley (1868)**[46]

Historically and constitutionally, jury trial is a remedial protection of substantive rights. . . . It is trial by the country — by fellow-subjects and peers. It has been steadily regarded, from the earliest judicial history in England, as the great safeguard of the lives, liberty and property of the subject against the abuses of arbitrary power, as well as against undue excitements of popular feeling. In our own country, almost from the earliest settlement, the trial by jury was claimed by the people as the birthright of Englishmen, and as the most valuable of the rights of freemen. . . . [W]e are to look at it as one of the greatest securities of private right, handed down to us among the liberties and privileges which our ancestors enjoyed at the time of their emigration, and claimed to hold and retain as their birthright.

—**Chief Justice Charles Doe (1882)**[47]

New Jersey

The more I see of juries and their verdicts, the more I am satisfied that it is the best mode of determining disputed facts ever devised by the wit of man.

—**Justice Edward W. Whelpley (1860)**[48]

The fundamental right of trial by a fair and impartial jury is jealously guarded by the courts.

—**Justice Henry E. Ackerson, Jr. (1951)**[49]

New Mexico

The New Mexico Constitution guarantees a trial by an impartial jury.

—**Justice Irwin S. Moise (1960)**[50]

---

[46] *East Kingston v. Tole*, 48 N.H. 57, 64 (1868).

[47] *Wooster v. Plymouth*, 62 N.H. 193, 194, 196 (1882). *See also Opinion of the Court*, 41 N.H. 550-551 (1860).

[48] *Black v. Shreve*, 13 N.J.Eq. 455, 469 (1860).

[49] *Panco v. Flintkote Co.*, 7 N.J. 55, 80 A.2d 302, 305 (1951).

[50] *State v. McFall*, 67 N.M. 260, 354 P.2d 547, 548 (1960).

New York
The institution of trial by jury is entitled to all the reverence which a custom deserves that is so historically interwoven with the growth and development of the rights of English people.
—**Justice John C. Gray (1899)**[51]

The sacredness and importance of the right to trial by jury is attested by the arrangement, no less than by the language, of our Constitution. . . . The inevitable implication of this language is that the citizen is . . . entitled to trial by jury in all cases in which it has been heretofore used. . . .
—**Justice William E. Werner (1912)**[52]

North Carolina
In the formal Declaration of Independence the King of Great Britain . . . was arraigned before the world "for depriving us in many cases of trial by jury." . . . This language evinces the purpose of our representatives to risk their lives and fortunes . . . to secure . . . the ancient right of trial by jury.
—**Justice Alphonso C. Avery (1892)**[53]

North Dakota
The right to a trial by jury, in actions at law, with certain limitations, is a basic and fundamental part of our state and federal systems of jurisprudence.
—**Justice Alvin C. Strutz (1966)**[54]

The right to a jury trial is a basic right in this state. The right to a jury trial remains inviolate.
—**Justice Robert Vogel (1978)**[55]

Ohio
An institution that has so long stood the trying tests of time and experience, that has so long been guarded with such scrupulous care, and commanding the admiration of so many of the wise and good, justly demands our jealous scrutiny when innovations are attempted to be made upon it.
—**Justice Rufus P. Ranney (1853)**[56]

---

[51] *People v. Dunn*, 157 N.Y. 528, 52 N.E. 572, 573 (1899).
[52] *People v. Cosmos*, 205 N.Y. 91, 98 N.E. 408, 409 (1912).
[53] *State v. Cutshall*, 110 N.C. 538, 543 (1892).
[54] *C.I.T. Corp. v. Hetland*, 143 N.W.2d 94, 100 (N.D. 1966).
[55] *Arneson v. Olson*, 270 N.W.2d 125, 137 (N.D. 1978).
[56] *Word v. Ohio*, 2 Ohio St. 296, 303 (1853).

Oklahoma

Courts cannot be too strict in compelling a rigid and vigilant observance of the provisions of the statutes designed to preserve inviolate the right of trial by jury and the purity of jury trials.

—**Justice Thomas H. Doyle (1911)**[57]

Oregon

The fathers of free government in Oregon were jealous of any encroachment on the right of jury trial. . . . [T]he right of trial by jury is one so precious, so vital to our liberties. . . . [I]t is a coal from the altar of liberty. . . .

—**Justice James A. McBride (1912)**[58]

Pennsylvania

If there is any right to which, more than all others, the people of Pennsylvania have clung with unrelaxing grasp, it is that of trial by jury.

—**Justice William Strong (1862)**[59]

No power in our government can take from the litigant the right to have his case tried by a jury. . . .

—**Justice George Sharswood (1870)**[60]

Rhode Island

The right to trial by jury is a fundamental right which the legislature cannot abolish.

—**Justice David Howell (1786)**[61]

In this state, trial by jury is inviolate. The state constitution so declares. The right is thus placed absolutely beyond the power of the legislature to alter or abolish it.

—**Chief Justice Francis B. Condon (1964)**[62]

---

[57] *Ridley v. State*, 5 Okla. Crim. 522, 115 P. 628, 630 (1911).

[58] Dissenting Opinion in *Stephens v. Myers*, 62 Ore. 272, 126 P. 29, 37 (1912).

[59] *North Pennsylvania Coal Co. v. Snowden*, 6 Pa. 488, 491 (1862).

[60] *Norris's Appeal*, 64 Pa. (14 P.F. Smith) 275, 281 (1870).

[61] *Trevett v. Weeden* (1786). See Chroust, *The Rise of the Legal Profession in America*, Vol. 2, p. 27 n.90 (University of Oklahoma Press 1965).

[62] *Dyer v. Keefe*, 97 R.I. 418, 198 A.2d 159, 160 (R.I. 1964).

The fathers of free government in Oregon were jealous of any encroachment on the right of jury trial. The right of trial by jury is one so precious, so vital to our liberties. It is a coal from the altar of liberty.

—Justice James A. McBride of Oregon (1912)

South Carolina

The Constitutions adopted by the different States of this Union, as well as the whole current of legislation and adjudication, demonstrate the great jealousy of the American people on the subject of jury trial. So universally regarded as a great palladium in England and America, we may well be cautious of any innovation. . . . The trial by jury has taken the place of other forms once in favor, and the judgment of a panel of twelve men has been incorporated as an indispensable element in the judicial administration of the country. Our notions may well be pronounced inveterate as to this mode of securing rights and redressing wrongs.

—Justice Joseph N. Whitner (1856)[63]

South Dakota

The doctrine declared in states where the right of trial by jury is merely preserved, as it existed when the Constitution was adopted, has no application in this state, because here it is not only to remain inviolate, but is expressly extended to all cases at law, without regard to the amount in controversy.

—Justice Dick Haney (1896)[64]

Tennessee

The right of trial by jury has, at all periods in the history of this country and of England, been held in high estimation. . . .

—Judge William E. Kennedy (1831)[65]

The right of trial by jury as it existed at common law has been declared to be the glory of England, and the common law was no less zealous to provide for the impartiality of the juror than to uphold the right to the jury in civil as well as criminal cases.

—Justice John S. Wilkes (1899)[66]

It is universally held that a litigant's right of trial by jury, whether guaranteed by the Constitution or provided by statute, should be jealousy guarded by the courts.

—Judge Thomas A. Shriver (1960)[67]

---

[63] *McCoy v. Lemmon*, 11 Rich. (45 S.C.L.) 165, 176 (1856).
[64] *Belatti v. Pierce*, 8 S.D. 456, 66 N.W. 1088 (1896).
[65] *State Bank v. Cooper*, 10 Tenn. (2 Yer.) 599, 621 (1831).
[66] *Gribble v. Wilson*, 101 Tenn. 612, 49 S.W. 736 (1899).
[67] *Shook & Fletcher Supply v. City of Nashville*, 47 Tenn. App. 339, 338 S.W. 2d 237, 242 (1960).

Texas

The right of a jury trial is a sacred one. . . .
—**Chief Justice Roy C. Archer (1956)**[68]

The right to trial by jury is a valuable right which will be jealously guarded.
—**Justice Bill J. Cornelius (1975)**[69]

Utah

The right of trial by jury should be scrupulously safeguarded.
—**Justice J. Allen Crockett (1957)**[70]

In our democratic system, the people are the repository of power whence the law is derived; from its initiation and creation to its final application and enforcement, the law is the expression of their will. The functioning of a cross-section of the citizenry as a jury is the method by which the people express this will in the application of law to controversies which arise under it. Both our constitutional and statutory provisions assure trial by jury to citizens of this state.
—**Justice J. Allen Crockett (1957)**[71]

Vermont

The language of our first state constitution, which has ever since been retained, that trial by jury "ought to be held sacred," shows vividly the strong attachment of the people of this state to this mode of trial, and their implicit belief that it is essential to the honest and enlightened administration of justice. At the time of the adoption of the federal and state constitutions, this feeling was very strong with the American people. . . . There has always been a strong inclination both with the bench and bar, as well as with the people, to maintain the integrity of trial by jury.
—**Justice Asa O. Aldis (1860)**[72]

---

[68] *Silver v. Shefman*, 287 S.W.2d 316, 319 (Tex. Civ. App. 1956).

[69] *Rayson v. Johns*, 524 S.W.2d 380, 382 (Tex. Civ. App. 1975).

[70] *Abdulkadir v. Western Pacific RR Co.*, 7 Utah 2d 53, 318 P.2d 339, 341 (1957).

[71] *Stickle v. Union Pacific R. Co.*, 122 Utah 477, 251 P.2d 867, 871 (1952).

[72] *Plimpton v. Town of Somerset*, 33 Vt. 106, 108 (1860).

Virginia

The laws are framed and enacted by the people for the common benefit; and among the fundamental principles of our government we find the trial by jury is guaranteed to the citizens.
—**Justice Benjamin W. Lacey (1883)**[73]

Courts are zealous in protecting one's constitutional right of a trial by an impartial jury.
—**Justice Harold F. Snead (1959)**[74]

Washington

The constitution of this state provides that the right of trial by jury shall remain inviolate. This is a valuable right, jealously guarded by the courts.
—**Justice Walter B. Beals (1941)**[75]

West Virginia

The right to trial by jury is immemorial; . . . it was brought from England to this country by the colonists and it has become a part of the birthright of every free man.
—**Judge Harlan M. Calhoun (1964)**[76]

Wisconsin

Our fathers brought trial by jury with them to this country more than two centuries ago, and, by making it part of the Constitution, they intended to perpetuate it for their posterity, and neither legislatures nor courts have any power to infringe even the least of its privileges.
—**Chief Justice Alexander W. Stowe (1850)**[77]

Wyoming

It is so well settled as to require no reference to authorities that when the Constitution secures to litigants the right of trial by jury the legislature has no power to deny or impair such right.
—**Judge Samuel T. Corn (1900)**[78]

---

[73] *James v. Stokes*, 77 Va. 225, 228 (1883).
[74] *Farrar v. Commonwealth*, 201 Va. 5, 109 S.E.2d 112, 114 (1959).
[75] *Watkins v. Siler Logging Co.*, 9 Wash. 2d 703, 116 P. 2d 315, 321 (1941).
[76] Dissenting in *Pyles v. Boles*, 148 W.Va. 465, 135 S.E.2d 692, 711 (1964).
[77] Dissenting in *State v. Cameron*, 2 Pin. 490, 499 (1850).
[78] *First Nat'l v. Foster*, 9 Wyo. 157, 61 P. 466 (1900).

Chief Justice Roy C. Archer
of Texas

Justice Harold F. Snead
of Virginia

Chief Justice Alexander W. Stowe
of Wisconsin

Justice Samuel T. Corn
of Wyoming

Our fathers brought trial by jury with them to this country more than two centuries ago, and by making it part of the Constitution, they intended to perpetuate it for their posterity, and neither legislatures nor courts have any power to infringe the least of its privileges.
   —**Chief Justice Alexander W. Stowe of Wisconsin (1850)**

Justice Joseph Story

Justice William Johnson

Justice Levi Woodbury

Chief Justice Roger Taney

The right of trial by jury is justly regarded in every state in the union as among the most inestimable privileges of a free man.
—**Justice William Johnson, U.S. Supreme Court (1833)**

APPENDIX C
U.S. SUPREME COURT OPINIONS ON THE SANCTITY OF TRIAL BY JURY

... *One of the most powerful objections urged against [the Constitution] was that in civil cases it did not secure the trial of facts by a jury.* ...
—**Justice Joseph Story (1812)**[79]

Trial by jury is justly dear to the American people. It has always been the object of deep interest and solicitude, and every encroachment upon it has been watched with great jealousy. The right to such a trial is ... incorporated into, and secured by every state constitution in the Union.... One of the strongest objections originally taken against the Constitution of the United States, was the want of an express provision securing the right of trial by jury in civil cases. As soon as the Constitution was adopted, this right was secured by the Seventh Amendment ... which received the assent of the people so general, as to establish its importance as a fundamental guarantee of the rights and liberties of the people....
—**Justice Joseph Story (1830)**[80]

... *The right of trial by jury ... is justly regarded in every state in the Union, as among the most inestimable privileges of a free man.*
—**Justice William Johnson (1833)**[81]

... *Trial by jury and the common law [were] so ardently adhered to by the Anglo-Saxons ... from the highest principles of safety to the common law, English liberties, and the inestimable trial by jury—principles surely no less dear in a republic than a monarchy.*
—**Justice Levi Woodbury (1847)**[82]

... *Among the most cherished and familiar principles of the common law was the trial by jury in civil, and ... criminal cases.... [It] was regarded as a right of inestimable value, and the best and only security for life, liberty and property.*
—**Chief Justice Roger B. Taney (1851)**[83]

---

[79]*U.S. v. Wonson*, 28 Fed. Cas. 745, 750 (1812).
[80]*Parsons v. Bedford*, 3 Pet. 433, 445 (1830).
[81]*Lessees of Livingston v. Moore*, 7 Pet. 469, 552 (1833).
[82]Dissenting in *Waring v. Clark*, 5 How. (46 U.S.) 441, 470-71 (1847).
[83]*U.S. v. Reid*, 13 L.Ed. 1023, 1024 (1851).

The right of trial by jury involves the very framework of the government and the fundamental principles of American liberty. The inestimable privilege of trial by jury is one of the most valuable in a free country.
　　　　　　　　　　　　　　　—Justice David Davis (1866)[84]

Twelve men in a jury box know more about the common affairs of life and can draw wiser and safer conclusions.
　　　　　　　　　　　　　　　—Justice Ward Hunt (1873)[85]

The founding fathers regarded the right of trial by jury as vital to the protection of liberty against arbitrary power.
　　　　　　　　　　　　—Justice John Marshall Harlan (1882)[86]

The right of trial by jury in the courts of the United States is expressly secured by the Seventh Amendment to the Constitution. This Court has guarded this constitutional right with jealousy.
　　　　　　　　　　　　　　—Justice Stanley Matthews (1885)[87]

The Constitution, in the Seventh Amendment, declares that "in suits at common law where the value in controversy shall exceed twenty dollars, the right of trial by jury shall be preserved." In the federal court this right cannot be dispensed with except by the consent of the parties entitled to it; nor can it be impaired by any blending with a claim, properly cognizable at law, of a demand for equitable relief in aid of the legal action, or during its pendency. Such aid in the federal courts must be sought in separate proceedings, to the end that the right to a trial by jury in the legal action may be preserved intact.
　　　　　　　　　　　　　　—Justice Stephen J. Field (1891)[88]

It must therefore be taken as established, by virtue of the Seventh Amendment, that either party to an action at law in a court of the United States where the value in controversy exceeds twenty dollars has the right to a trial by jury.
　　　　　　　　　　　　　　—Justice Horace Gray (1899)[89]

---

[84] *Ex Parte Milligan*, 71 U.S. (4 Wall.) 2, 109, 123, 137 (1866).
[85] *Railroad Co. v. Stout*, 84 U.S. 657, 664 (1873).
[86] *Hodges v. Easton*, 106 U.S. 408, 412 (1882).
[87] *Baylis v. Travelers Ins. Co.*, 113 U.S. 316, 321 (1885).
[88] *Scott v. Neely*, 140 U.S. 106, 109-110 (1891).
[89] *Capital Traction Co. v. Hoff*, 174 U.S. 1, 13 (1899).

Justice Ward Hunt

Justice Stanley Matthews

Justice Stephen Field

Justice Horace Gray

It must therefore be taken as established, by virtue of the Seventh Amendment, that either party to an action at law in a court of the United States where the value in controversy exceeds twenty dollars has the right to a trial by jury.

—**Justice Horace Gray, U.S. Supreme Court (1899)**

It is not difficult to understand why the founding fathers entrenched the right of trial by jury in the supreme law of the land. They regarded the recognition and exercise of that right as vital to the protection of liberty against arbitrary power. . . . The value of that institution was recognized by the patriotic men of the revolutionary period , . . . in the Declaration of Independence. . . .
—Justice John Marshall Harlan (1900)[90]

The absence of any provision respecting the mode of trial in civil actions was so generally regarded as endangering the right of trial by jury and evoked so much criticism on that ground, that the First Congress proposed the Seventh Amendment which was promptly ratified.
—Justice Willis Van Devanter (1913)[91]

When a penalty of triple damages is sought . . . , the [Sherman Antitrust Act] should not be read as attempting to authorize liability to be enforced otherwise than through the verdict of a jury in a court of common law. On the contrary, it plainly provides the latter remedy. . . .
—Justice Oliver Wendell Holmes, Jr. (1916)[92]

The concern of the framers of the Constitution was to make clear that the right of trial by jury should remain inviolable.
—Justice George Sutherland (1930)[93]

Maintenance of the jury as a fact-finding body is of such importance and occupies so firm a place in our history and jurisprudence that any seeming curtailment of the right to a jury trial should be scrutinized with utmost care.
—Justice George Sutherland (1935)[94]

As the right of jury trial is fundamental, courts indulge every reasonable presumption against waiver.
—Justice Pierce Butler (1937)[95]

---

[90] Dissenting in *Maxwell v. Dow*, 176 U.S. 581, 609 (1900).
[91] *Slocum v. New York Life Ins. Co.*, 228 U.S. 364, 377 (1913).
[92] *Fleitmann v. Welsbach Street Lighting Co.*, 240 U.S. 27, 29 (1916).
[93] *Patton v. United States*, 281 U.S. 276, 297 (1930).
[94] *Dimick v. Schiedt*, 293 U.S. 474, 585-586 (1935).
[95] *Aetna Ins. Co. v. Kennedy*, 301 U.S. 389, 393 (1937).

It is essential that the right to trial by jury be scrupulously safeguarded.
—**Justice Hugo Black (1939)**[96]

The right of jury trial in civil cases at common law is a basic and fundamental feature of our system of federal jurisprudence which is protected by the Seventh Amendment. A right so fundamental and sacred to the citizen, whether guaranteed by the Constitution or provided by statute, should be jealously guarded by the courts.
—**Justice Frank Murphy (1942)**[97]

The right to trial by jury is a basic and fundamental feature of our system of federal jurisprudence. . . .
—**Justice William O. Douglas (1943)**[98]

The call for the true application of the Seventh Amendment is not to words, but to the spirit of honest desire to see that constitutional right preserved. . . . Our duty to preserve this one of the Bill of Rights . . . is a matter of high constitutional importance. . . .
—**Justice Hugo Black (1943)**[99]

The broad representative character of the jury should be maintained, partly as assurance of a diffused impartiality and partly because sharing in the administration of justice is a phase of civic responsibility.
—**Justice Felix Frankfurter (1946)**[100]

Trial by jury is a vital and cherished right, integral in our judicial system.
—**Justice Frank Murphy (1949)**[101]

---

[96]*Lyon v. Mutual Benefit Health & Acc. Assn.*, 305 U.S. 484, 492 (1939).
[97]*Jacob v. City of New York*, 315 U.S. 752 (1942).
[98]*Bailey v. Central Vermont Ry.*, 319 U.S. 350, 354 (1943).
[99]Dissenting in *Galloway v. United States*, 319 U.S. 399, 407 (1943).
[100]Dissenting in *Thiel v. Southern Pacific Co.*, 328 U.S. 217, 227 (1946).
[101]*City of Morgantown v. Royal Ins. Co.*, 337 U.S. 254, 258 (1949).

There is a strong federal policy against allowing state rules to disrupt the judge-jury relationship in the federal courts. . . . Perhaps even more clearly in light of the influence of the Seventh Amendment, the function assigned to the jury is an essential factor in the process for which the federal Constitution provides.
    —**Justice William J. Brennan, Jr. (1958)**[102]

The right to trial by jury applies to treble damages suits under the anti-trust laws, and is, in fact, an essential part of the congressional plan for making competition rather than monopoly the rule of trade.
    —**Justice Hugo Black (1959)**[103]

The federal rules did not . . . purport to change the basic holding . . . that the right to trial by jury of legal claims must be preserved. Quite the contrary, Rule 38(a) expressly reaffirms that constitutional principle, declaring: "the right of trial by jury as declared by the Seventh Amendment to the Constitution or as given by a statute of the United States shall be preserved to the parties inviolate."
    —**Justice Hugo Black (1962)**[104]

The federal policy favoring jury trials is of historic and continuing strength.
    —***Per Curiam* Opinion (1963)**[105]

. . . The founders of our nation considered the right of trial by jury in civil cases an important bulwark against tyranny and corruption, a safeguard too precious to be left to the whim of the sovereign. . . . [Their] concerns for the institution of jury trial . . . led to the passage of the Declaration of Independence and to the Seventh Amendment. . . . Trial by a jury of laymen . . . was important to the founders because juries represented the layman's common sense . . . and thus keep the administration of law in accord with the wishes and feelings of the community.
    —**Chief Justice William H. Rehnquist (1979)**[106]

---

[102]*Byrd v. Blue Ridge Electric Co-op.*, 356 U.S. 525, 538-539 (1958).
[103]*Beacon Theatres v. Westover*, 359 U.S. 500, 504 (1959).
[104]*Dairy Queen v. Wood*, 369 U.S. 469, 471-472 (1962).
[105]*Simler v. Conner*, 372 U.S. 221, 222 (1963).
[106]Dissenting in *Parklane Hosiery Co. v. Shore*, 439 U.S. 322, 340, 343-344 (1979).

Justice Willis Van Devanter

Justice Pierce Butler

Justice Felix Frankfurter

Justice William J. Brennen, Jr.

The federal policy favoring jury trials is of historic and continuing strength.
  —**U.S. Supreme Court *Per Curiam* Opinion (1963)**

The right of trial by jury is justly dear to the American people. We have watched with jealousy and deep concern any tendency to encroach upon or impair any of the essential elements of trial by jury. We know the blood and treasure it has cost to get and keep this birthright of every American, of every free man.
—**Chief Justice Alfred Franklin of Arizona (1918)**

APPENDIX D
INDEX OF QUOTATIONS BY STATE

ALABAMA: *Hugo **BLACK** (1939, 1943, 1959, 1962, 1963) 384, 429, 501, 502; H. H. **GROOMS** (1965) 409; James J. **MAYFIELD** (1910) 477*

ALASKA: *John H. **DIMOND** (1969) 477*

ARIZONA: *Alfred **FRANKLIN** (1918) 477, 504; Arthur T. **LaPRADE** (1947) 477; William H. **REHNQUIST** (1979) 416, 502*

ARKANSAS: *Thomas **JOHNSON** (1848) 477; Morris S. **ARNOLD** (1987) 420; Henry Clay **CALDWELL** (1899) 268, 281, 357; Charles T. **COLEMAN** (1919) 370*

CALIFORNIA: *Sigfredo A. **CABRERA** (1988) 285; W. W. **COPE** (1861) 478; Louis C. **DRAPEAU** (1954) 478; Stephen J. **FIELD** (1891) 498; Delphin M. **DELMAS** (1918) 155, 284, 368; Ned **GOOD** (1981) 285-286; William J. **PALMER** (1958) 400; John Norton **POMEROY** (1865) 338; Stephen **REINHARDT** (1986) 418; Earl **WARREN** (1962) 402*

COLORADO: *Louis W. **CUNNINGHAM** (1913) 478*

CONNECTICUT: *Elisha **CARPENTER** (1878) 478, 479; William O. **DOUGLAS** (1943, 1954) 393, 501*

DELAWARE: *Vincent A. **BIFFERATO** (1981) 478; John **DICKINSON** (1788) 106, 228; Joseph T. **WALSH** (1975) 478*

FLORIDA: *Donald K. **CARROLL** (1959) 480; William C. **PIERCE** (1967) 480; Glenn **TERRELL** (1937) 480*

GEORGIA: *Joseph Henry **LUMPKIN** (1849) 280, 480*

HAWAII: *James L. **COKE** (1922) 372; Ralph Petty **QUARLES** (1915) 480; Wilfred C. **TSUKIYAMA** (1960) 480*

IDAHO: *George H. **STEWART** (1911) 481*

ILLINOIS: *Henry C. **BURMAN** (1960) 481; David **DAVIS** (1866) 498; William J. **FULTON** (1943) 481; Harry **KALVEN**, Jr. (1964) 405; Richard S. **KUHLMAN** (1981) 273; Abraham **LINCOLN** (1861) 450; David **DAVIS** (1866) 342; Ralph L. **MAXWELL** (1954) 481; John C. **McKENZIE** (1985) 300; Clyde E. **STONE** (1931) 481; John E. **WALL** (1926) 376; John Henry **WIGMORE** (1924) 85-88*

INDIANA: *Harry J.* **CURTIS** *(1940) 481*

IOWA: *Henry Clay* **CALDWELL** *(1899) 268, 281, 357; James W.* **KINDIG** *(1927) 482*

KANSAS: *David J.* **BREWER** *(1881, 1902) 361, 482; Charles B.* **GRAVES** *(1910) 482; William J.* **WERTZ** *(1965) 482*

KENTUCKY: *John Marshall* **HARLAN** *(1900) 360, 426, 436; James H.* **HAZELRIGG** *(1897, 1899) 281, 482-83; William H.* **HOLT** *(1905) 281, 362; W. J.* **KALLBRIER** *(1916) 268; E. C.* **O'REAR** *(1910) 364*

LOUISIANA: *Grover L.* **COVINGTON** *(1977) 484; Alexander* **PORTER**, *Jr. (1825) 484*

MAINE: *Peter W.* **CULLEY** *(1983) 285, 418; John S.* **TEENEY** *(1853) 484*

MARYLAND: *Alexander* **HANSON** *(1788) 210; Henry* **PAGE** *(1899) 484; Roger B.* **TANEY** *(1851) 497*

MASSACHUSETTS: *John* **ADAMS** *(1765) 189; John Quincy* **ADAMS** *(1839) 180, 332; Samuel* **ADAMS** *(1772) 193;* **ALDERMAN & KENNEDY** *(1991) 422; C. J.* **COHEN** *(1991) 272, 422; John* **DeWITT** *(1788) 210; Felix* **FRANKFURTER** *(1946) 501; Elbridge* **GERRY** *(1787) 236; Horace* **GRAY** *(1899) 498, 499; Oliver Wendell* **HOLMES**, *Jr. (1916, 1921) 6, 500; Thomas* **LAMBERT** *(1963) 265, 453; Roscoe* **POUND** *(1942) 14, 256, 535; Arthur P.* **RUGG** *(1929, 1935) 485, 507; Arthur* **SCHLESINGER** *(1968) 202; Theodore* **SEDGWICK** *(1813) 317; Lysander* **SPOONER** *(1854) 337; Joseph* **STORY** *(1830, 1833) xix, 8, 227, 324, 497; James Bradley* **THAYER** *(1898) 353; Emory* **WASHBURN** *(1871) 344*

MICHIGAN: *Thomas M.* **COOLEY** *(1868) 302; Charles W.* **JOINER** *(1962) 404; Charles D.* **LONG** *(1892) 485, 543; Charles S.* **MAY** *(1875) 89-92, 106, 448; Frank* **MURPHY** *(1942, 1949) 388, 501*

MINNESOTA: *Pierce* **BUTLER** *(1937) 500; William O.* **DOUGLAS** *(1943) 501; Charles E.* **FLANDRAU** *(1860) 485; Royal A.* **STONE** *(1923) 485*

MISSISSIPPI: *William L.* **SHARKEY** *(1834) 486, 487*

MISSOURI: *Edward J.* **McCULLEN** *(1947) 486; Solbert M.* **WASSERSTROM** *(1974) 486*

MONTANA: *W. H.* **POORMAN** *(1905) 486*

NEBRASKA: *Edward F.* **CARTER** *(1959) 486*

It is familiar law that the right of trial by jury secured by the Declaration of Rights is sacred and must be sedulously guarded against every encroachment. This right as set forth in the Constitution must be and has been strictly preserved.
—**Chief Justice Arthur P. Rugg of Massachusetts (1929, 1935)**

NEVADA: *Orville R.* **LEONARD** *(1877) 486*

NEW HAMPSHIRE: *Charles* **DOE** *(1882) 163, 488;* Ira **PERLEY** *(1868) 488;* **Supreme Judicial Court** *(1860) 457;* Levi **WOODBURY** *(1847) 280, 334, 497*

NEW JERSEY: *Henry E.* **ACKERSON**, *Jr. (1951) 488; William J.* **BRENNEN**, *Jr.(1958) 502; Austin Wakeman* **SCOTT** *(1918) 369; Edward W.* **WHELPLEY** *(1860) 280, 488, 539*

NEW MEXICO: *Irwin S.* **MOISE** *(1960) 488*

NEW YORK: *Albert* **AVERBACH** *(1956) 396; Bernard* **BOTEIN** *(1946) 390; Stanley F.* **BREWSTER** *(1934) 270; D. H.* **CHAMBERLAIN** *(1887) 274, 349; Joseph* **CHOATE** *(1898) 354; Harold* **CORBIN** *(1928) 380; Alfred C.* **COXE** *(1901) 361; F. E.* **CRANE** *(1929) 282, 381; David* **EDELSTEIN** *(1956) 397; John C.* **GRAY** *(1899) 489; Alexander* **HAMILTON** *(1788) 224, 429; Howard T.* **HOGAN** *(1964) 282; Ward* **HUNT** *(1873) 280, 344, 498; I. R.* **KAUFMAN** *(1967) 270, 302; James* **KENT** *(1827) 320; Maximus A.* **LESSER** *(1894) 352, 446; James P.* **LEVINE** *(1992) 301; Jefferson* **MEAGHER** *(1964) 272, 406; Harold R.* **MEDINA** *(1951) 282; John* **JAY** *(1774) 194, 226; Elihu* **ROOT** *(1894) 350; Maurice* **ROSENBERG** *(1966) 409; Clinton* **ROSSITER** *(1953) 392; C. R.* **RUNALS** *(1956) 269, 398; Bernard* **SCHWARTZ** *(1980) 220; Melancton* **SMITH** *(1788) 236; Francis L.* **WELLMAN** *(1924) 374; William E.* **WERNER** *(1912) 489; Edward P.* **WILDER** *(1879) 346; René* **WORMSER** *(1949) 390*

NORTH CAROLINA: *Alphonso C.* **AVERY** *(1892) 489; Henry G.* **CONNOR** *(1909) 166; Samuel* **SPENCER** *(1788) 224; James* **IREDELL** *(1787) 430*

NORTH DAKOTA: *Alvin C.* **STRUTZ** *(1966) 489; Robert* **VOGEL** *(1978) 489*

OHIO: *Salmon P.* **CHASE** *(1866) 434; Rudolph* **JANATA** *(1974) 285; Stanley* **MATTHEWS** *(1885) 348, 498; Rufus P.* **RANNEY** *(1853) 464, 489*

OKLAHOMA: *Thomas H.* **DOYLE** *(1911) 490; Truman B.* **RUCKER** *(1961) 272*

OREGON: *James A.* **McBRIDE** *(1912) 365, 490, 491; James L.* **COKE** *(1922) 372*

PENNSYLVANIA: *J. S.* **BLACK** *(1866) 341, 434; Samuel* **BRYAN** *(1788) 237; John* **DICKINSON** *(1788) 106, 228; Benjamin* **FRANKLIN** *(1787) 171; Andrew* **HAMILTON** *(1735) 157; Thomas* **HARTLEY** *(1788) 217; Gouverneur* **MORRIS** *(1787) 98, 186, 450; Thomas* **PAINE** *(1777) 73-76; Eli K.* **PRICE** *(1863) 278, 340; George* **SHARSWOOD** *(1870) 490; William* **STRONG** *(1862) 490; James* **WILSON** *(1788) 217; Robert* **VON MOSCHZISKER** *(1930) 254, 381-383*

RHODE ISLAND: *Francis B.* **CONDON** (1964) *490; David* **HOWELL** (1786) *490; James M.* **VARNUM** (1786) *313*

SOUTH CAROLINA: *William H.* **BRAWLEY** (1897) *281; D. H.* **CHAMBERLAIN** (1887) *274, 349; William* **JOHNSON** (1833) *326, 497; Abraham* **NOTT** (1822) *432; Joseph N.* **WHITNER** (1856) *179, 338, 492; Sam M.* **WOLFE** (1911) *364; Charles* **WOODMASON** (1767) *190*

SOUTH DAKOTA: *Dick* **HANEY** (1896) *492*

TENNESSEE: *William E.* **KENNEDY** (1831) *492; Thomas A.* **SHRIVER** (1960) *492; Robert H.* **WHITE** (1961) *300; John S.* **WILKES** (1899) *492*

TEXAS: *Roy C.* **ARCHER** (1956) *493; Bill J.* **CORNELIUS** (1975) *493; Tom C.* **CLARK** (1966) *410; John V.* **SINGLETON** (1987) *270, 420*

UTAH: *J. Allen* **CROCKETT** (1957) *493; George* **SUTHERLAND** (1930, 1935, 1937) *80-84, 106, 384, 452, 500*

VERMONT: *Asa O.* **ALDIS** (1860) *493*

VIRGINIA: *Richard* **BLAND** (1776) *74, 174, 392; Patrick* **HENRY** (1778) *77-79, 197, 232, 449; Thomas* **JEFFERSON** (1788, 1801) *114, 193, 240, 317, 449; Benjamin W.* **LACEY** (1883) *494; Richard Henry* **LEE** (1787) *233; John* **MARSHALL** (1788) *222-223; George* **MASON** (1787) *232, 454; Stanley E.* **SACKS** (1965) *269, 408; Harold F.* **SNEAD** (1959) *494; James* **MADISON** (1787-88) *226, 450; George* **WASHINGTON** (1789) *114*

WASHINGTON: *Walter B.* **BEALS** (1941) *494; Lester P.* **EDGE** (1925) *300, 376*

WEST VIRGINIA: *Harlan M.* **CALHOUN** (1964) *494; Ashton* **FILE** (1940) *388; Clarence E.* **MARTIN** (1934) *382*

WISCONSIN: *Donald K.* **ROSS** (1965) *408; Alexander W.* **STOWE** (1850) *494, 495; A. C.* **UMBREIT** (1924) *270, 373*

WYOMING: *Samuel T.* **CORN** (1900) *494; Willis* **VAN DEVANTER** (1913) *500, 503*

DISTRICT OF COLUMBIA: *William* **SEAGLE** (1946) *389*

PUERTO RICO: *William H.* **HOLT** (1905) *281, 362*

AUSTRALIA: *B. R. WISE (1948) 277*

CANADA: *Justice E. L. HAINES (1979) 270, 414; W. S. MARTIN (1959) 401*

ENGLAND: *Jeremy BENTHAM (1832) 278, 322; Chancellor Lord BIRKENHEAD (F. E. Smith) (1929) 168, 282, 380; Justice William BLACKSTONE (1765) 69-72, 312; Chancellor Henry Peter BROUGHAM (1828) 280, 321; Chancellor Lord CAMDEN (Charles Pratt) (1792) 278, 280; Henry CARE (1680) 277-278, 308; G. K. CHESTERTON (1909) 278; Sir Winston CHURCHILL (1956) 65-68, 394; Chief Justice Edward COKE (1628) 306; Chief Justice COLERIDGE (John Duke) (1879) 346; Judge Patrick DEVLIN (1956) 398; Chief Justice John DUKE (Lord Coleridge) (1879) 346; Giles DUNCOMBE (1725) 310; Thomas ERSKINE (1784) 316; William FORSYTHE (1852) 336, 441, 445, 446; Chief Justice John FORTESCUE (1468) 305; M.D.A. FREEMAN (1981) 270, 301, 417, 440; Chief Justice Lord GODDARD (1958) 282; Chief Justice Matthew HALE (1676) 308; Henry HALLAM (1827) 320; John HAWLES (1680) 309; W. S. HOLDSWORTH (1927) 377; David HUME (1762) 310; Lt. Colonel John LILBURNE (1649-53) 156-159; John LOCKE (1669) 162-164; Frederic William MAITLAND (1912) 366; Henry MARSH (1971) 413; Sir John MAYNARD (1689) 310; Francis PALGRAVE (1832) 322; William PENN (1644-1718) 449; Prime Minister William PITT (1777, 1783) 112, 114; Theodore PLUCKNETT (1956) 396; Sir Frederick POLLOCK (1899) 356; Chancellor Charles PRATT (Lord Camden) (1792) 278, 280, 316; Serjeant Alexander PULLING (1867) 440; Prime Minister John RUSSELL (1823) 318; Chancellor F. E. SMITH (Lord Birkenhead) (1929) 282, 380; Serjeant Henry John STEPHEN (1844) 333; Justice James Fitzjames STEPHEN (1883) 348; Judge J.E.R. STEPHENS (1896) 353; William STUBBS (1880) 274; J. Sydney TAYLOR (1839) 93-96; Joseph TOWERS (1764) 310; William WALWIN (1651) 306; Thomas WILLIAMS, Speaker of the House of Commons (1557) 305*

FRANCE: *Monsieur M. COTTU (1822) 442; Charles de MONTESQUIEU (1748) 511; Alexis de TOCQUEVILLE (1835) 328; Jean Jacques ROUSSEAU (1712-1788) 114; SIKYES (1894) 352*

GERMANY: *Unnamed Bavarian Judge (1834) 445*

SWEDEN: *Unnamed Member of Swedish House of Burgesses (1909) 448*

The judiciary power ought to be exercised by persons taken from the body of the people.
—**Charles de Montesquieu, *The Spirit of Laws* (1748)**

William Few of Georgia (1748-1828)
One of only 10 delegates to the Constitutional Convention of 1787 who served concurrently in the Continental Congress, as a member of the Continental Congress, he voted to guarantee the right of trial by jury in the Northwest Territory.

BIBLIOGRAPHY

Abraham Lincoln: *Speeches and Writings* (Vantage Books/Library of America, 2 volumes, 1989)

Adams, *Constitutional History of England* (Henry Holt & Co. 1938)

Adams, *The Origin of the English Constitution* (Yale U. Press 1912)

Adams & Stephens, *Selected Documents of English Constitutional History* (Macmillan & Co. 1908)

Alderman & Kennedy, *In Our Defense: The Bill of Rights in Action* (William Morrow & Co. 1991)

American State Papers: *The Federalist*, Vol. 43, *Great Books of the Western World* (Encyclopædia Britannica 1952)

Annals of America (Encyclopædia Britannica 1976)

Arnold, "The Civil Jury in Historical Perspective," in *The American Civil Jury* (Roscoe Pound Foundation 1987)

Ashley, *The Golden Century: Europe 1598-1715* (Frederick A. Praeger, Publishers 1969)

Averbach, "Tampering with the Jury System," *Ins. L.J.* 9 (1956)

Bernstein, *The Making of the Constitution* (1987)

Besant's History of London (The Viking Press 3d ed. 1989)

Bethea, *The Contributions of Charles Pinckney to the Format of the American Union* (Garrett & Massie 1937)

Blackstone, *Commentaries on the Laws of England* (In 4 Volumes 1765-1769) [Legal Classics Library 1983]

Bloomstein, *Verdict: The Jury System* (Dodd Mead & Co. 1968)

Botein, "This Right Was Dearly Won," distributed by New York State Citizens' Council (1946)

Bowen, *Miracle at Philadelphia* (Atlantic-Little, Brown 1966)

Brewer, "The Jury," 1 *Canadian L.R.* 302 (1902)

Brewster, *Twelve Men in a Box* (Callaghan & Co. 1934)

Browning, ed., *English Historical Documents* (Oxford U. Press 1953)

Buckley, "Civil Trial by Jury," *Current Legal Problems* (1966)

Burros, "The Spanish Jury: 1888-1923," 14 *Cas. W. Res.* 177 (1982)

Burt, *A History of Parliament in the Middle Ages* (Constable & Co., London 1989)

Busch, *Law and Tactics in Jury Trials* (Bobbs-Merrill 1950)

Butt, *A History of Parliament* (Constable & Co. 1989)

Cabrera, "Why the Jury System is Important to the Legal System," 101 *L.A. Daily Journal* 4 (January 7, 1988)

Cahn, ed., *The Great Rights* (Macmillan Co. 1963).

Caldwell, "Trial by Judge and Jury," 33 *American L.R.* 321 (1899)

Cannon & Griffiths, *The Oxford Illustrated History of the British Monarchy* (Oxford U. Press 1988)

Care, *English Liberties* (1680)

Catton, *The Bold and Magnificent Dream* (Doubleday & Co. 1978)

Chafee, ed., *Documents on Fundamental Human Rights* (Harvard U. Press 1951)

Chamberlain, *The American System of Trial by Jury* (Boston 1887)

Chroust, *The Rise of the Legal Profession in America* (University of Oklahoma Press, 2 Volumes, 1965)

Churchill, *A History of the English Speaking Peoples* (Dorset Press, 4 Volumes, 1956-1958)

Clark, *The Later Stuarts 1660-1714* (Oxford U. Press, 2d ed. 1956)

Clark, "The American Jury: A Justification," 1 *Val. L.R.* 1 (1966)

Cohen, "Whatever Happened to the *Seventh Amendment?*" 35 *Boston Bar J.* 17 (November/December 1991)

Give us competent jurors, able judges, and honest, fearless and learned advocates, and trial by jury, which, to the people of America, will be the best safeguard of their lives, their liberties, and their property.

—**ABA President Joseph Choate (1898)**

Coke, *The First Part of the Institute of the Laws of England* (Two Volumes, 18th ed. 1823) [Legal Classics Library 1985]

Coke, "On Jury Trial," 1 *Ore. L.R.* 177 (June, 1922)

Coleman, "Origin of Trial by Jury," 6 *Va. L.R.* 77 (1919)

Collier, *Decision in Philadelphia* (Ballentine Books 1986)

Colonial Laws of New York (1896)

Connor, "The Constitutional Right to a Trial by a Jury of the Vicinage," 48 *Univ. of Penn. L.R.* 197 (January, 1909)

Constitution of the United States of America: *Analysis and Interpretation,* (U.S. Government Printing Office 1973)

Cook, "The Judicial System of Germany," 1 *Juridicial R.* 70 (1889)

Cook, *A Treasury of Legal Quotations* (Vantage Press 1961)

Cooley, *A Treatise on Constitutional Limitations* (1868)

Cooper, *The Statutes at Large of South Carolina* (S.C.B.A. 1970)

Corbin, "The Jury on Trial," 14 *ABAJ* 507 (1928)

Correspondence: "The Jury System," 18 *American L.R.* 875 (1884)

Cottu, *Administration of Criminal Justice in England* (1822)

Coxe, "The Trials of Jury Trials," 1 *Columbia L.R.* 286 (1901)

Crane, "Judge and Jury," 15 *ABAJ* 201 (1929)

Culley, "In Defense of Civil Juries," 35 *Maine L.R.* 17 (1983)

Cunningham, *In Pursuit of Reason: The Life of Thomas Jefferson* (Ballentine Books 1987)

Davies, *The Early Stuarts* (1603-1660) (Oxford U. Press 2d ed. 1959)

de Gregorio, *The Complete Book of U.S. Presidents* (2d ed. 1989)

Delmas, "The Democracy of Justice," 6 *Ken. L.J.* 245-246 (1918)

Denton, *England in the 15th Century* (1888)

de Tocqueville, *Democracy in America* (1838) [Legal Classics Library 1988]

Devlin, *Trial by Jury,* The Hamlyn Lectures (Stevens & Sons 1956)

Di Perna, *Juries on Trial: Faces of American Justice* (1984)

Donovan, *Modern Jury Trials and Advocates* (4th ed. 1911)

Donovan, *Skills in Trials* (Williamson Law Book Company 1891)

Douglas, *An Almanac of Liberty* (Doubleday & Co. 1954)

Driscoll, "Decline of the English Jury," 17 *Am. Bus. L.J.* 99 (1979)

Dumbauld, *The Constitution of the United States* (University of Oklahoma Press 1964)

Duncombe, *Trial Per Pais Or, The Law of England Concerning Juries* (1725) [William Hein & Co. 1980]

Edge, "Jury System? Yes," 29 *Law Notes* 151 (November, 1925)

Evory, ed., *Contemporary Authors,* Vol. 1 (1976)

Feder, "J-U-R-Y Spells Justice," *Trial* (July, 1986)

The Federalist *(1787-88) Great Books of the Western World, Vol. 43* (Encyclopædia Britannica 1952)

File, "Right of Trial by Jury in Civil Actions," *Proceedings of the 51st Annual Meeting of the Virginia State Bar Association* (1941)

Final Report, The American Jury System (Roscoe Pound Found. 1977)

Fisher, ed., *The Collected Papers of Frederic William Maitland* (Cambridge University Press 1911)

Forsythe, *History of Trial by Jury* (Lenox Hill, 2d ed. 1878)

Fortescue, *In Praise of the Laws of England (1468-1471)* (Cambridge University Press 1949)

Frank, *Law and the Modern Mind* (1930) [Legal Classics Library 1985]

Freeman, M.D.A.: "The Jury on Trial," in *Current Legal Problems* (Stephens & Son, London 1981)

Friedman, *A History of American Law* (Touchstone Books 2d ed. 1985)

Geeting, "Trial by Jury Must Be Preserved," 69 *Albany L.J.* 134 (1907)

Gibbon, *The Decline and Fall of the Roman Empire*, Great Books of the Western World, Vols. 37 & 38 (Encyclopædia Britannica 1952)

Glanville, *A Treatise on the Laws and Customs of the Realm of England* (Oxford U. Press 1965) [Legal Classics Library 1990]

Good, "In Praise of Jury Trials," 7 *Litigation* 51 (1951)

Great Speeches and Orations of Daniel Webster (1894) [Legal Classics Library 1989]

Green, *History of the English People* (Hovendon Company 1874)

Green, "Jury Trial and Mr. Justice Black," 65 *Yale L.J.* 482 (1956)

Green, "Juries and Justice," *Univ. Ill. L.R.* 152 (1962)

Grooms, "Origin of Trial by Jury," 26 *Ala. Law.* 162 (1965)

Gross, "Modes of Trial in Medieval England," 15 *Harv. L.R.* 691 (1902)

Guide to American Law Encyclopedia (West Publishing Co. 1984)

Guinther, *The Jury in America* (Roscoe Pound Foundation 1988)

Haigh, ed., *The Cambridge Historical Encyclopedia of Great Britain and Ireland* (Cambridge University Press 1985)

Haines, "The Role of the Jury in the Control of the Abuse of Power" (Law Society of Upper Canada 1979)

Hale, *History and Analysis of the Common Law of England* (1713) [Legal Classics Library 1987]

Hall, *The Present-Day Jury: A Defense*, 10 *ABAJ* 111 (1924)

The excellent order of trial by jury has all the helps to investigate the truth. It has the unanimous suffrage and opinion of twelve jurors, which carries in itself a much greater weight and preponderation to discover the truth of a fact than any other trial whatsoever.
	—**Matthew Hale, Chief Justice of the King's Bench (1676)**

Hallam, *The Constitutional History of England from the Accession of Henry VII to the Death of George III* (1827) [Garland Publishing Co. 1978]

Halliday, *A Concise History of England* (Viking Press 1965)

Hart, *Long Live the American Jury* (Case Press 1964)

Harvard Classics: *American Historical Documents* (Grolier 1980)

Hawles, *The English Man's Right* (1680) [In *Justices and Juries in Colonial America*, Arno Press 1972]

Hegel, *A Philosophy of History, Great Books of the Western World,* Vol. 46 (Encyclopædia Britannica 1952)

Helfrich, "Chesterton on Juries," 191 *N.Y.L.J.* 2 (1984)

Henderson, "Background of the Seventh Amendment," 80 *Harv. L.R.* 289 (1966)

Hogan, "Joseph Story on Juries," 37 *Ore. L.R.* 234 (1958)

Hogan, "Blackstone and Story — Their Influence on the Development of Criminal Law in America," 40 *Minn. L.R.* 107 (1956)

Hogan, "Some Thoughts on Juries in Civil Cases," 50 *ABAJ* 752 (August, 1964)

Hogan, "Three Essays on the Law by Joseph Story," 28 *So. Cal. L.R.* 1932 (1954)

Holmes, *The Common Law and Other Writings* (Little, Brown & Co. 1881) [Legal Classics Library 1982]

Holt, "The Jury System," 67 *Albany L.R.* 298 (1905)

Holt, ed., *Domesday Studies* (Boydell Press 1987)

Honnold, ed., *The Life of the Law* (Macmillan Publishing Co. 1964)

Hudson, *A Treatise on the Court of Star Chamber* (1792) [Legal Classics Library 1986]

Hume, *History of England* (1761)

Jacobs, "Trial by Jury—Its Origin and Merits," 21 *Australian L.J.* 462 (1948)

Janata, "Federal Jury Trials Should Not Be Abolished," 60 *ABAJ* 934 (August, 1974)

Jefferson, *Public and Private Papers* (Vantage Books 1990)

Jenks, *A Short History of English Law* (Methuen & Co. 1949)

Joiner, *Civil Justice and the Jury* (Prentice Hall 1962)

Journal of Legal History, Vol. 8 (1987)

Judge Medina Speaks (Matthew Bender & Co. 1954)

"**Jury,**" *Encyclopædia Britannica Macropædia,* Vol. 10, pp. 360-362 (15th ed. 1979)

"**Jury Trial on Trial — A Symposium,**" 28 *N.Y.S.B.J.* 322 (1956)

Justices of the United States Supreme Court 1789-1969: *Their Lives and Major Opinions* (Chelsea House Publishers 1969)

Kallbrier, "Trial by Jury," 4 *Ken. L.J.* 25 (1916)

Kalven, "The Dignity of the Civil Jury," 50 *Va. L.R.* 1055 (1964)

Kammen, *The Origins of the American Constitution* (Penguin 1986)

Karcher, "The Case for the Jury System," 45 *Chic.-Kent L.R.* 157 (1969)

Kaufman, "A Fair Jury — The Essence of Justice," 51 *Judicature* 88 (October, 1967)

Kent, *Commentaries on American Law,* 4 volumes (New York: 1826-1830) [Legal Classics Library 1986]

Ketcham, *The Anti-Federalist Papers* (New American Library 1986)

Kinnane, *First Book on Anglo-American Law* (Bobbs-Merrill Co. 1932)

Kiralfy, *A Source Book of English Law* (Sweet & Maxwell 1957)

Knittel & Seiler, "The Merits of Trial by Jury," 30 *Cambridge L.J.* 316 (1972)

Kuhlman, Pontikes & Stevens, "Jury Trial, Progress and Democracy," 14 *John Marshall L.R.* 679 (1981)

Lambert, *In Defense of the Civil Jury,* 29 *NACCA L.J.* 27 (1963)

Lancaster, *The American Revolution* (American Heritage Lib. 1987)

Langguth, *Patriots: The Men Who Started the American Revolution* (Simon & Schuster 1988)

Lawrence, "Development of Trial by Jury," 14 *Green Bag* 239 (1902)

Laws and Liberties of Massachusetts (1648) [Legal Class. Lib. 1982]

Laws of Maryland (April, 1715)

Laws of the State of Delaware (1797)

Law Times, Vol. 48 (1867)

Lesser, *The Historical Development of the Jury System* (Lawyers Cooperative Publishing Co. 1894)

Levine, *Juries and Politics* (Brooks/Cole Publishing Co. 1982)

Levy, ed., *Encyclopedia of the American Constitution* (Macmillan Publishing Co. 1986)

Lieberman, *Milestones! Two Hundred Years of American Law* (West Publishing Co. 1976)

Locke, *An Essay Concerning Civil Government* (1690) *Great Books of the Western World*, Vol. 35 (Encyclopædia Britannica 1952)

Lovell, *English Constitutional and Legal History*, p. 118 (Oxford University Press 1962)

Lyon, *A Constitutional and Legal History of Medieval England* (Harper & Row 1960)

Lynn, *Jury Trial Law and Practice* (John Wiley & Sons 1986)

Trial by jury is the subject's birthright and inheritance. This way of trial is his fence and protection against all frauds and surprises and against all storms of power.
—**Sir John Maynard, Serjeant at Law (1689)**

Madison, *Records of the Debates in the Federal Convention of 1787* (Government Printing Office 1927) [Legal Classics Library 1989]

March, *British Documents of Liberty* (Fairleigh Dickinson University Press 1971)

Marke, *Vignettes of Legal History* (Rothman & Co. 1965)

May, *Speeches of the Stump, the Bar, and the Platform* (Review & Harrell Publishing Co., Battle Creek, Mich. 1899)

Maynard, *Serjeant at Law* (1689)

McKenzie, "What is Truth? A Defense of the Jury System," 44 *ABAJ* 51 (1958)

Meagher, "Trial by Jury Deserves a Fair Trial," 36 *N.Y.S.B.J.* 303 (August, 1964)

Mill, *On Liberty* (1859) [Classics of Liberty Library 1992]

Miller, *George Mason: Gentleman Revolutionary* (UNC Press 1975)

Milsom, *Historical Foundations of the Common Law* (London: Butterworths 1969)

Moore, *A Treatise on Facts or the Weight and Value of Evidence*, Vol. 1 (Edward Thompson Co. 1908)

Moore, *The Jury: Tool of Kings, Palladium of Liberty* (W. H. Anderson Co. 1973)

Morgan, *Justice William Johnson: The First Dissenter* (USC Press 1954)

Morgan, ed., *The Oxford Illustrated History of Britain* (Oxford University Press 1984)

Morrill, John: "The Stuarts (1603-1688)", Ch. 6, *The Oxford Illustrated History of Britain* (Oxford University Press 1984)

Morris, *The Forging of the Union 1781-1789* (Harper & Row 1987)

Morris, *Witnesses at the Creation: Hamilton, Madison, Jay and the Constitution* (Penguin Books 1985)

Morrison, *Sources and Documents Illustrating the American Revolution 1764-1788* (Oxford University Press, 2d ed. 1929)

Mortimer, *Rumpole à la Carte* (1990)

Muddiman, ed., *Trial of King Charles the First* (William Hodge & Co. 1928) [The Notable Trials Library 1990]

Mullins, *In Quest of Justice* (London 1931)

Niebuhr, *The Children of Light and the Children of Darkness* (1944)

Note: "The Changing Role of the Jury in the 19th Century," 70 *Yale L.J.* 170 (1964)

Note: "The Jury System," 12 *Albany L.J.* 292 (1875)

Novick, *Honorable Justice: The Life of Oliver Wendell Holmes* (Little, Brown & Co. 1989) [Legal Classics Library 1990]

Ogg, *England in the Reign of James II and William III* (Clarendon Press 1955)

O'Rear, "The Jury," 17 *Central L.J.* 65-66 (1910)

Palgrave, *The Rise and Progress of the English Commonwealth* (1832)

Palmer, "On Trial: The Jury Trial," 20 *F.R.D.* 65 (1958)

Parker, *Britain's Kings and Queens* (Pitkin Pictorials 2d. ed. 1990)

Pettingal, *An Inquiry Into the Use of and Protection of Juries Among the Greeks and Romans* (London 1769)

Perry & Cooper, *Sources of Our Liberties* (American Bar Foundation 1952) [Legal Classics Library 1991]

Plucknett, *A Concise History of the Common Law* (Little, Brown & Co. 5th ed. 1956)

Plucknett, *Taswell-Langmead's English Constitutional History: From the Tutonic Conquest to the Present Time* (Sweet & Maxwell 1960)

Pocock, ed., *Three British Revolutions: 1641, 1688, 1776* (Princeton University Press 1980)

Pole, *The American Constitution: For and Against* (Hill & Wang 1987)

Pollock & Maitland, *The History of English Law* (2d ed. 1899) [Legal Classics Library 1982]

Poole, *Domesday Book to Magna Carta* (The Oxford History of England, Vol. 3, 2d ed. 1955)

Potter, *An Historical Introduction to English Law and Its Institutions,* Chapter 11, "The Jury System," (Sweet & Maxwell 1932)

Pound, "Jury: England and the United States," *Encyclopedia of Social Sciences* (Macmillan Co. 1942)

Pound, *The Development of Constitutional Guarantees of Liberty* (Yale University Press 1957)

Powell, *The Regulators of North Carolina* (N.C. Arch. & Hist. 1971)

Presser & Zainalden, *Law and Jurisprudence in American History* (West Publishing Co. 2d ed. 1989)

Price, *A Discourse on the Trial by Jury* (Caxton Press 1863)

Proffatt, *A Treatise on Trial by Jury* (Hurd & Houghston 1877)

Ring, "We the Jury," 6 *Trial Diplomacy J.* 18 (1983)

Robbins, *Law: A Treasury of Art and Literature* (Macmillan Publishing Co. 1990)

Root, *Addresses on Government and Citizenship* (Harv. U. Press 1916)

Rosenberg, "The Trial Judge's Verdict on the Civil Jury," 5 *Trial Judge's J.* 11 (January, 1966)

Ross, *Trial by Jury — Preserve It* (Defense Research Inst. 1965)

Rossiter, *1787 The Grand Convention* (1966)

Rossiter, *Seedtime of the Republic: The Origin of the American Tradition of Political Liberty* (Harcourt, Brace & World, Inc. 1953)

Rousse, "Trial by Jury," *Univ. of Tex. Bull.* #3028 (July 22, 1930)

> The English jury has been so highly prized that the verdict of the jurors was deemed to be the voice of the countryside. It was associated with the protection of the weak against the strong and became a cherished institution which was connected in the minds of the people with all the liberties that they held dear.
> —Sir Frederick Pollock, *The History of English Law* (1899)

Rucker, "Justice and the American Jury," 33 *N.Y.S.B.J.* 133 (1961)

Rudyard Kipling's Verse, Definitive Edition (Doubleday & Co. 1940)

Runals, "Jury Trial on Trial — A Symposium," 28 *N.Y.S.B.J.* 322 (October, 1956)

Russell, *An Essay on the History of the English Government and Constitution* (2d ed. 1865) [Kraus Reprint Co. New York 1971]

Sacks, "Preservation of the Civil Jury System," 22 *Wash. & Lee L.R.* 76 (1965)

Santayana, *Dominions and Powers: Reflections on Liberty, Society and Government* (Charles Scribner's Sons 1951)

Schlesinger, *The Birth of a Nation* (American Heritage Lib. 1968)

Schwartz, *The Great Rights of Mankind: A History of the American Bill of Rights,* (Oxford University Press 1977)

Schwartz, *The Roots of the Bill of Rights: An Illustrated Source Book of American Freedom* (Chelsea House Publishers 1980)

Scott, "Trial by Jury and the Reform of Civil Procedure," 31 *Harvard L.R.* 69 (1918)

Seagle, *The History of the Law* (Tudor Publishing Co. 1946)

Selections from the Writings of the Late J. Sydney Taylor, A.M., Barrister at Law (London 1843)

Singleton, "Jury Trial: History and Preservation," in *1988 Tr. Law. Guide* (Callahan & Co. 1988)

Smith, *Law, Life and Letters* (1927)

Snow, "Joseph Story," 5 *Ore. L.R.* 169-184 (1926)

Speeches of Lord Erskine While at the Bar (Callahan & Co. Four Volumes 1876) [Legal Classics Library, Two Volumes, 1984]

Spooner, *An Essay on the Trial by Jury* (1852) [Legal Classics Library 1989]

Stedman, *Our Ageless Constitution* (Stedman Assoc. 1987)

Stenton, *Anglo-Saxon England, Vol. 2 in The History of England* (Clarendon Press 3d ed. 1971)

Stephen, *History of the Criminal Law,* Vol. 1 (London 1883)

Stephen, *New Commentaries on the Laws of England,* Vol. III (1844) [Garland Publishing Co. 1979]

Stephens, "Growth of Trial by Jury In England," 10 *Harv. L.R.* 150 (1896)

Stephenson & Marcham, *Sources of English Constitutional History* (Harper & Row 1937)

Story, *Commentaries on the Constitution of the United States* (1833)

Stubbs, *Constitutional History of England* (Clarendon Press 1880)

Taylor, *The Origin and Growth of the English Constitution* (Houghton Mifflin & Co. 1889)

Thayer, *A Preliminary Treatise on Evidence at the Common Law* (Little, Brown & Co. 1898)

Thayer, "The Jury and its Development," Parts I, II & III 5 *Harv. L.R.* 249, 296, 357 (1892)

"The Jury in Legal History," 180 *Law Times* 48 (July 30, 1935)

The Solicitor's J. 23:178 (1879)

Thompson, *A Historical Essay on the Magna Charta of King John* (London 1829) [Legal Classics Library 1982]

Thompson, *Writings by Candlelight* (1980)

Tongue, "In Defense of Juries as Exclusive Judges of the Facts," 35 *Ore. L.R.* 143 (April, 1956)

Towers, *Observations on the Rights and Duties of Juries* (1764, 1784) [Garland Publishing Co. 1978]

Trowbridge, "A German Jury Trial," 2 *Cal. L.R.* 34 (1913)

Truman, *Memoirs of President Harry S. Truman,* Vol. 1, p. 19 (1955)

Tuchman, *The First Salute: A View of the American Revolution* (Ballentine Books 1988)

Umbreit, "Is Trial by Jury: An Effective Survival?" 8 *Marquette L.R.* 125 (1924)

Vallinder, "The Swedish Jury System in Press Cases," *J. Legal History,* Vol. 8 (1987).

Van Caenegem, *The Birth of the English Common Law* (Cambridge Univ. Press 1973)

Van Doren, *The Great Rehearsal* (Penguin Books 1986)

Von Moschzisker, *Trial by Jury* (George T. Bisel Co., 2d ed. 1930)

Wall, "Efficacy of Trial by Jury," 30 *Law Notes* 7 (April, 1926)

Wallace, *South Carolina: A Short History 1520-1948* (USC 1966)

Walwin, *Juries Justified* (1651) [Garland Publishing Co. 1978]

Warvelle, "The Jurors and the Judge," 23 *Harvard L.R.* 123 (1909)

Washburn, *Lectures on the Study and Practice of the Law* (1871) [Fred B. Rothman & Co. 1982]

The Great Speeches and Orations of Daniel Webster (Little, Brown & Co. 1894) [Legal Classics Library 1989]

Weiss, "Reforming Tort Reform: Is There Substance to the Seventh Amendment?" 38 *Catholic University L.R.* 737 (1989)

Wellman, *Gentlemen of the Jury: Reminiscences of 30 Years at the Bar* (The Macmillan Company 2d ed. 1936)

Wellman, *The Art of Cross Examination* (Macmillan & Co., 2d ed. 1904) [Legal Classics Library 1983]

White, "Origin and Development of Trial by Jury," 29 *Tenn. L.R.* 8 (1961)

The protection of life and property, habeas corpus, trial by jury, the right of an open trial, these are principles of public liberty existing in the best form in the republican institutions of this country.

—Daniel Webster (1848)

Whitney, *Founders of Freedom in America: Lives of the Men Who Signed the Constitution* (J. G. Ferguson Publishing Co. 1965)

Wigmore, *A Treatise on the System of Evidence in Trials at Common Law* (Little, Brown & Co. 1904)

Wilder, "The Clown of the Law?" 20 *Albany Law J.* 45 (1879)

Wilkinson, *A Constitutional History of England in the 15th Century (1399-1425)* (Barnes & Noble, Inc. 1964)

Williams, *The Excellency and Præheminence of the Laws of England* (1557) [Garland Publishing Co. 1979]

Wirt, *The Life of Patrick Henry* (DeSilver, Thomas & Co. 1836)

Wolfe, "A Defense of the Jury," *Case and Comment* (May, 1911)

Wolfram, "The Constitutional History of the *Seventh Amendment*", 57 *Minn. L.R.* 639 (1973)

Wood, *The Creation of the American Republic* (UNC Press 1969)

Wood, *Battles of the Revolutionary War* (Algonquin Books 1990)

Woodmason, *The Carolina Backcountry on the Eve of the Revolution: The Journal and Other Writings of Charles Woodmason, Anglican Itinerant* (Richard J. Hooker, ed., UNC Press 1953)

Wormser, *The Law* (Simon & Schuster 1949)

York, ed., *Toward a More Perfect Union: Six Essays on the Constitution* (Brigham Young Univ. 1988)

Table of Illustrations
Volume I

*King John ....**Inside Cover**
Rudyard Kipling .... **iii**
Seal on *Magna Carta* .... **vii**
Magna Carta Memorial .... **xi**
Magna Carta .... **xiv-xv**
*Joseph Story .... **ix**
*Frank Murphy .... **xx**
*Horace Rumpole **3**
Oliver Wendell Holmes, Jr. **7**
Henry II **11**
Louis the Pious **15**
Henry III **19**
Edward I **23**
*John Fortescue **27**
Charles II **31**
Stanley Matthews **35**
Magna Carta Memorial **36**
Winston Churchill **39**
*William Blackstone **43**
Thomas Paine **47**
*Patrick Henry **51**
*George Sutherland **55**
John H. Wigmore **56, *59**
Charles S. May **63**
J. Sydney Taylor **67**
Patrick Henry **71**
Alphonso C. Avery **72**
*Alexander Hamilton **75**
*Lamp of Liberty **76**
Thomas Erskine **79**
William Pitt **80**
Henry Hallam **83**
*Epitaph to Civil Jury **87**
Roger B. Taney **88**
John Stuart Mill **91**
James I **95**
Execution of Charles I **98-99**
*Francis Palgrave **103**
Elbridge Gerry **107**
Star Chamber **110-111**
John Pym **115**
*William Prynne **119**
*William O. Douglas **123**

Oliver Cromwell **127**
John Lilburne **131**
John Locke **135**
Newgate Prison **139**
James II **143**
Seven Bishops **147**
William & Mary **151**
Delphin M. Delmas **155**
Gouverneur Morris **159**
Charles S. Doe **163**
*John Jay **167**
J. of 1st Continental Congress **168**
Benjamin Franklin **171**
James Kent **175**
Liberty Bell **176**
*Joseph N. Whitner **179**
John Quincy Adams **180**
Shays' Rebellion **183**
Independence Hall **184**
Lord Camden **187**
W. Van Devanter **188**
Constitutional Convention **190-191**
Charles Pinckney **195**
*James Madison **199**
*John Dickinson **203**
*Richard Henry Lee **207**
Alexander Hanson **211**
Jefferson Memorial **214-215**
George Washington **219**
John Marshall **223**
Joseph Story **227**
Bill of Rights **231**
*Thomas Jefferson **235**
Thomas Williams **236**
*John Adams **239**
*Patrick Henry **243**
Jeremiah S. Black **247**
David J. Brewer **251**
F.E. Smith,
   Lord Birkenhead **255**
David Edelstein **259**
Cynthia J. Cohen **263**

*Commissioned Illustrations

533

Table of Illustrations
Volume II

*William Blackstone	**Inside Cover**	Tom C. Clark	411
*Aristotle	267	*An American Jury	415
Irving R. Kaufman	271	Stephen Reinhardt	419
James B. Thayer	275	Alderman & Kennedy	423
Ward Hunt	276	John Marshall Harlan	427
*G. K. Chesterton	279	Hugo L. Black	428
Harold R. Medina	283	James Iredell	431
Henry P. Brougham	287	Salmon P. Chase	435
William Forsythe	288	Alexander Pulling	439
Spanish Inquisition	290-291	Napoleon Bonaparte	443
*Gideon Henfield	295	Adolf Hitler	447
James Wilson	299	Abraham Lincoln	451
Thomas M. Cooley	303	*George Mason	455
*Theodore Sedgwick	304	*John Marshall Harlan	459
Edward Coke	307	*The Hanged Man	463
*David Hume	311	Rufus P. Ranney	464
*James M. Varnum	315	William H. Rehnquist	465
John Russell	319	*Typical Victim	467
Jeremy Bentham	323	John H. Dimond	468
William Johnson	327	Wilfred Tsukiyama	471
*Alexis de Tocqueville	331	William Strong	475
Levi Woodbury	335	Elisha Carpenter	479
John N. Pomeroy	339	James H. Hazelrigg	483
David Davis	343	William L. Sharkey	487
Lord Coleridge	347	*James A. McBride	491
Elihu Root	351	State Court Justices	495
*Joseph Choate	355	Supreme Court Justices	496, 499, 503
Henry Caldwell	359	Alfred Franklin	504
Samuel Adams	363	Arthur P. Rugg	507
Frederic Maitland	367	*Charles de Montesquieu	511
Statue of Liberty	371	*William Few	512
*Francis Wellman	375	*Joseph Choate	515
*W. S. Holdsworth	379	Matthew Hale	519
Robert Von Moschzisker	383	John Maynard	523
*Hugo Black	387	Frederick Pollock	527
Bernard Botein	391	Daniel Webster	531
*Winston Churchill	395	*Roscoe Pound	535
Patrick Devlin	399	Edward W. Whelpley	539
*Earl Warren	403	Charles D. Long	543
Jefferson F. Meagher	407	*Author's Portrait	546

*Commissioned Illustrations

The jury has grown up as representative of the local community whose representative character appealed to democratic America. It seemed to Americans important to preserve the jury as a bulwark of political liberty.
   —**Roscoe Pound, Former Dean of Harvard Law School (1942)**

COMMISSIONED ARTISTS

ALAN E. COBER

Alan E. Cober has served as Professor of Art at the University of Buffalo and the University of Georgia. His visual essays have appeared in *Time, Newsweek, Rolling Stone* and the *New York Times*. He is the author of *The Forgotten Society* and is the recipient of over 300 awards that include the Artist of the Year, 11 medals from the Society of Illustrators and six gold medals from the New York Art Directors Club. Mr. Cober's portrait of U.S. Supreme Court Justice Frank Murphy faces page 1 and his illustrations of Gideon Henfield, James Mitchell Varnum, "The Hanged Man" and William Few are found in Vol. 2 on pp. 295, 315, 463 & 512.

RAUL COLÓN

Raul Colón is a native of New York who studied commercial art and spent 10 years in an instructional television center in south Florida. He is a freelance illustrator whose work appears regularly in *Business Week, New Yorker* and the *New York Times*. He has received awards for excellence in illustration from the Florida Press Club and *Annual Report Five* and a broadcast designer award for his poster of the "Shaka Zulu" TV mini-series. His contributions to *In Defense of Trial by Jury* include lithographic drawings of Justice George Sutherland on p. 55, Sir Francis Palgrave on p. 103, Justice Joseph Whitner on p. 179, W. S. Holdsworth on p. 379, and Dean Roscoe Pound on p.535.

MARK ENGLISH

Mark English is a resident of Liberty, Missouri. His paintings have appeared in *McCall's, Time, Sports Illustrated, Redbook* and *Atlantic Monthly*. He has designed nine stamps for the U.S. Postal Service and has painted numerous covers for *Time* magazine. He has been chosen Artist of the Year by the New York Artists Guild and has been the most awarded illustrator in the history of the Society of Illustrators of New York. In 1983, he was elected to the New York Illustrators Hall of Fame. His pastel portrait of Francis Wellman, author of *The Art of Cross Examination* (1903) and *Gentlemen of the Jury* (1924), is found in Volume 2 on p. 375.

TERESA FASOLINO

Teresa Fasolino is a native New Yorker who graduated from the School of Visual Arts in New York City. Her work has enhanced the covers of best-selling books, magazines, annual reports and records and has been used widely in advertising. Her paintings have appeared in *Life, New York Magazine* and the *New York Times*. Her murals have graced the walls of famous New York restaurants and she is the recipient of a silver medal from the Society of Illustrators. An outstanding realist, Ms. Fasolino's elegant acrylic paintings of American patriots Alexander Hamilton and John Adams are found in Volume 1 on pp. 75 and 239.

MILTON GLASER
Milton Glaser is a native of the Bronx who studied at New York's High School of Music and Art and the Cooper Union Art School prior to receiving a Fulbright Scholarship for study in Italy. Referred to by *Graphis Magazine* as the "Master of Graphic Art," Milton Glaser was the founder and president of *New York Magazine* and currently serves on the Board of Directors of the School of Visual Arts. His work was featured in a one-man show at the New York City Museum of Modern Art in 1975 and he has a permanent collection at the Smithsonian National Archives in Washington, DC. Mr. Glaser created the distinctive portrait of Aristotle on p. 267 in Vol. 2.

DAVID JOHNSON
David Johnson is a native of Detroit who lives in New Canaan, Connecticut. His classic pen-and-ink drawings appear frequently in national publications. His recent commissions have included a series of illustrations of the Democratic Presidential candidates for the *New York Times*. His portrait of Chief Justice John Fortescue (slipcase cover) in 1468 underscores the theme of "500 Years of Praise for Courthouse Democracy." His other contributions include Patrick Henry on pp. 51 & 243, The Lamp of Liberty on p. 76, John Dickinson on p. 203, Justice Theodore Sedgwick on p. 304, Justice Hugo Black on p. 387, and An American Jury on p. 415.

The more I see of juries and their verdicts, the more I am satisfied that it is the best mode of determining disputed facts ever devised by the wit of man.
—Justice Edward W. Whelpley of New Jersey (1860)

DAVID LEVINE
David Levine was born in Brooklyn and studied painting at the Tyler School of Art in Philadelphia. Noted for his unique pen-and-ink caricatures, he has been called "the best social political literary caricaturist of this century." He was a contributing editor of *Esquire* and his drawings appear regularly in the *New York Review of Books, Time*, and other national publications. His oils & watercolors have been exhibited extensively in galleries and museums throughout the world and his caricatures have appeared on the covers of *Time* and *Newsweek*. His drawings of G. K. Chesterton and Alexis de Tocqueville are found on pp. 279 & 331 of Vol. 2.

DANIEL MAFFIA
Daniel Maffia was born in France, moved to the U.S. in 1948, and lives in Englewood, N.J. He graduated from The Parsons School of Design and received a Master of Fine Arts degree from Pratt Institute. His paintings have appeared in *Time, Newsweek, Esquire* and *New York Magazine* and he has had successful painting shows in New York and Paris. His portrait of Saddam Hussein as the "Bully of Baghdad" appeared on the August 13, 1990, cover of *Newsweek*. His contributions include Justice Joseph Story on p. xx, Dean Wigmore on p. 59, Richard Henry Lee on p. 207, David Hume on p. 311, the author on p. 547 and cover portraits of James Madison and Thomas Jefferson.

AL PHILLIPS

Al Phillips was born in Gary, Indiana, and received a Bachelor of Fine Arts degree in painting from DePauw University and a graduate degree in painting and printmaking from Indiana University. He worked as a commercial artist in Chicago prior to a 16-year newspaper career. Currently with the *Charlotte Observer*, he has won several awards from the Society of Newspaper Design. A versatile artist who loves the variety of newspaper work, his illustrations of Justice William O. Douglas, Joseph Choate, Justice James A. McBride and A Typical Victim of Defective and Unreasonably Dangerous Products are found on pp. 123, 355, 467, 491 and 515.

DANIEL B. SCHWARTZ

Daniel B. Schwartz is a New York native who attended the Art Students League and the Rhode Island School of Design. He has taught at the Parsons School of Design, Syracuse University and the School of Visual Arts. An eleven-time winner of the Society of Illustrators gold medal, his portraits have appeared on the cover of *Time* and his works in oils, water color and sculpture have been recognized with awards from the Art Directors Club of New York, the American Institute of Graphic Art and the National Academy of Design. His portraits of Winston Churchill and Justice John Marshall Harlan appear on pp. 395 and 459 in Volume 2.

DOUGLAS SMITH
Douglas Smith was born in New York City and graduated from Rhode Island School of Design. Moving to Boston, he became involved in the unique art of scratchboard illustration in 1980. His work has appeared in the *Society of Illustrators Annual, CA Illustration Annual, American Illustration and Print's Regional Design Annual.* His illustration of the environmental effects of overpopulation was featured in an August, 1991, essay in *Graphis Magazine* and his contributions to *In Defense of Trial by Jury* include John Jay, p. 167; George Mason, p. 455; Charles de Montesquieu, p. 511; and the cover illustrations of the *Magna Carta* Memorial.

JACK UNRUH
Jack Unruh was born in Kansas and lives in Dallas. He graduated from Washington University and taught at East Texas University. His illustrations have appeared in *Outdoor Life, Field & Stream, Sports Afield, Rolling Stone, Sports Illustrated* and *Newsweek.* He has gold & silver medals from the New York Society of Illustrators and his Iroquois Indian at Prayer appeared on the October, 1991 cover of *National Geographic.* His contributions to *In Defense of Trial by Jury* include King John Sealing the *Magna Carta* on the frontispiece of Volume 1 and a distinctive color portrait of Justice William Blackstone on p. 43 and on the frontispiece of Volume 2.

Whatever its origin, the right of trial by jury became fixed centuries ago in the common law, and wherever the Anglo-Saxon tongue was spoken this right came to be regarded as the great bulwark of the liberty of the citizen. We have regarded it as our birthright and have ever been jealous of any attempted innovations.

—**Justice Charles D. Long of Michigan (1892)**

ROBERT WEAVER

Robert Weaver is a resident of New York City now in his 40th year as a professional illustrator. His work has appeared on the covers of *Time, Life, Sports Illustrated, New York Magazine, Fortune* and the *New York Times Magazine.* He has been inducted into the Halls of Fame of the Society of Illustrators and the Art Directors Club of New York, and has won numerous medals from both organizations. He teaches journalistic illustration at the School of Visual Arts in New York and his illustrations of the famous fictional British Barrister Horace Rumpole and Chief Justice Earl Warren are found on pp. 3 and 403.

RON WOLIN

Ron Wolin is a native New Yorker who studied at the Brooklyn Museum, Pratt Institute, the School of Visual Arts and Cal Arts. His woodcuts and oil paintings have appeared in *Boy's Life, Ecology Today* and the *Los Angeles Magazine.* Currently residing in Encino, California, he has won the Society of Illustrators Award for Excellence, and awards from the New York and Los Angeles Society of Illustrators. His is currently working on an epic series of woodcuts depicting the history of *The Holocaust* from 1936 through 1945. His graphic woodcut of William Prynne appears in Volume 1 on page 119.

AUTHOR AND ART DIRECTOR

J. KENDALL FEW

J. Kendall Few is a native of the Piedmont section of South Carolina who graduated in 1966 from the University of South Carolina School of Law where he served as Editor-in-Chief of the *South Carolina Law Review*. A trial lawyer with 27 years of experience in civil litigation, he has lectured to trial lawyers and bar associations in 28 states and the District of Columbia. He has numerous publications and has testified in opposition to proposed legislation infringing the citizen's right to trial by jury before the Senate Commerce and Judiciary Committees. He is the founder, trustee, editor and publisher of the American Jury Trial Foundation.

DON OWENS

Don Owens is a native of Greenville, S.C. He studied at the Ringling School of Art in Sarasota, Florida, and Art Center College of Design in Los Angeles. He was founding Editor/Art Director of *Picture* and *Photo Show* magazines in Los Angeles and *How* magazine in New York. He has won awards from the Art Directors Clubs of Atlanta, Los Angeles and Dallas, a silver medal from the New York Art Directors Show and was the subject of a retrospective feature in *Art Direction* magazine. As a freelance designer he has completed projects for AT&T, Los Angeles *Times*, *The New York Magazine*, Polaroid Corporation and Warner Bros.

THE AMERICAN JURY TRIAL FOUNDATION

The American Jury Trial Foundation is a non-profit corporation whose sole function is the publication and distribution of educational materials outlining the history and importance of trial by jury. A limited number of additional copies of *In Defense of Trial by Jury* are available for $12.50 plus $3 postage. A box of ten may be obtained for $125 plus $10 postage. Other publications of the Foundation include:

(a) A 64-page pamphlet entitled, *A Tribute to Trial by Jury* featuring "The Legacy of the Magna Carta," "The Origin of Trial by Jury," 37 illustrations and 175 quotations. These pamphlets are available in orders of 10 or more for $2 per pamphlet, plus $3 postage.

(b) A series of ten 18"x25" posters, suitable for framing, featuring illustrated quotations on trial by jury, including individual posters of **King John Sealing the *Magna Carta* (1215), Alexander Hamilton (1787), Thomas Jefferson (1788), James Madison (1789)** and **Winston Churchill (1956)** and composite posters featuring nine Justices of the United States Supreme Court, nine famous American patriots, nine distinguished state court justices, nine notable historical figures and nine illustrated quotations on trial by jury as the voice of the people. The cost of these posters is $20 per set, plus $3 postage.

To obtain copies of these publications, please write or call: Barbara G. Jimerson
Executive Secretary
American Jury Trial Foundation
Post Office Box 10085
Greenville, South Carolina 29603
(803) 232-6456

J. Kendall Few (1993)

ILLUSTRATION BY DANIEL MAFFIA

ART DIRECTION AND DESIGN: DON OWENS
TYPOGRAPHY: GARAMOND AND HELVETICA
PRINTER: DYNAGRAPHICS
PAPER STOCK: BENEFIT NATURAL (RECYCLED)

ISBN 0-9636658-0-4

COPYRIGHT ©1993 AMERCIAN JURY TRIAL FOUNDATION